Artificial Intelligence and Fashion

Artificial intelligence (AI) now infiltrates our culture. After a couple of difficult winters, *AI* today is a word on everybody's lips, and it attracts everyone's attention regardless of whether they are experts or not. From Apple's Siri to Amazon's Alexa, Tesla's auto-driving cars to facial recognition systems in CCTV cameras, Netflix's film offering services to Google's search engine, we live in a world of AI goods.

The advent of AI-powered technologies increasingly affects people's lives across the globe. As a tool for productivity and cost-efficiency, AI also shapes our economy and welfare.

AI-generated designs and works are becoming more popular. Today, AI technologies can generate several intellectual creations. Fashion is one of the industries that AI can profoundly impact. AI tools and devices are currently being used in the fashion industry to create fashion models, fabric and jewellery designs, and clothing.

When we talk about AI-generated designs, we instead focus on the fruits of innovation –more best-selling apparels, more fashionable designs and more fulfilment of customer expectations – without paying heed to who the designer is. Designers invest a lot of talent, time and finances into designing and creating each article of clothing and accessory before they release their work to the public. Pattern drafting is the first and most important step in dressmaking. Designers typically start with a general sketch on paper; add styles, elements and colours; revise and refine everything; and finally deliver their design to dressmakers. AI accelerates this time-consuming and labour-intensive process.

Yet the full legal consequences of AI in fashion industry are often forgotten. An AI device's ability to generate fashion designs raises the question of who will own intellectual property rights over the fashion designs. Will it be the fashion designer who hires or contracts with the AI programmer? Will it be the programmer? Will it be the AI itself? Or will it be a joint work of humans and computers? And who will be liable for infringement deriving from use of third-party material in AI-generated fashion designs?

This book explores answers to these questions within the framework of EU design and copyright laws. It also crafts a solution proposal based on a three-step test and model norms, which could be used to unleash the authors, rights holders and infringers around AI-generated fashion designs.

Hasan Kadir Yılmaztekin is the Head of the Department of Foreign Relations (Judge) at the Justice Academy of Türkiye and an associate professor in intellectual property law.

Routledge Research in Fashion Law

Protecting Creativity in Fashion Design
US Laws, EU Design Rights, and Other Dimensions of Protection
Susanna Monseau

Artificial Intelligence, Design Law and Fashion
Hasan Kadir Yılmaztekin

For more information about this series, please visit www.routledge.com/Routledge-Research-in-Fashion-Law/book-series/FASHLAW

Artificial Intelligence, Design Law and Fashion

Hasan Kadir Yılmaztekin

LONDON AND NEW YORK

First published 2023
by Routledge
4 Park Square, Milton Park, Abingdon, Oxon OX14 4RN

and by Routledge
605 Third Avenue, New York, NY 10158

Routledge is an imprint of the Taylor & Francis Group, an informa business

© 2023 Hasan Kadir Yılmaztekin

The right of Hasan Kadir Yılmaztekin to be identified as author of this work has been asserted in accordance with sections 77 and 78 of the Copyright, Designs and Patents Act 1988.

All rights reserved. No part of this book may be reprinted or reproduced or utilised in any form or by any electronic, mechanical, or other means, now known or hereafter invented, including photocopying and recording, or in any information storage or retrieval system, without permission in writing from the publishers.

Trademark notice: Product or corporate names may be trademarks or registered trademarks, and are used only for identification and explanation without intent to infringe.

British Library Cataloguing-in-Publication Data
A catalogue record for this book is available from the British Library

ISBN: 978-1-032-10117-0 (hbk)
ISBN: 978-1-032-41036-4 (pbk)
ISBN: 978-1-003-35592-2 (ebk)

DOI: 10.4324/9781003355922

Typeset in Times New Roman
by Apex CoVantage, LLC

Contents

Preface vi
Acknowledgements ix

Introduction: AI effect 1

1 Artificial intelligence and fashion 18

2 Artificial intelligence and EU design protection 38

3 Artificial intelligence and EU copyright protection 73

4 Authorship of artificial intelligence: global solutions and disjunctions 127

5 A post-modern approach to AI-generated fashion design 160

Index 185

Preface

Just like Mary Shelley's *Frankenstein*, human beings have long imagined the idea of creating an artificial life form. Do human beings wish to clone themselves as they have cloned the sheep? Or do they want to see their intelligence in a robot? Isaac Asimov in his 1950 novel *I, Robot* answers these questions by discussing the concept of artificial intelligence in nine robot stories with interesting aphorisms. In his cult classic, Asimov unfolds how extreme the artificial intelligence form invented by human beings can go. These futuristic and science fiction stories portray and critique the past, present and future dilemmas and circumstances of human beings. In the book, the question of whether technologies and artificial intelligence can be harmful to humanity – one of the most discussed topics of our times – is also explored. To prevent the harm that technology might cause and integrate robots into the human social life, Asimov exhorts the following three laws of robotics that are weaved into the plot of each story in the book:

First Law
A robot may not injure a human being or, through inaction, allow a human being to come to harm.
Second Law
A robot must obey the orders given it by human beings except where such orders would conflict with the First Law.
Third Law
A robot must protect its own existence as long as such protection does not conflict with the First or Second Law.

Artificial Intelligence, Design Law and Fashion is premised on a basis that is different from Asimov's stories: artificial intelligence that creates fashion designs. Thus, it is built on a limited area at the nexus of law, technology and fashion. It does not argue for an immense project of integrating robots into every corner of human social order. Contributions that artificial intelligence makes in creativity, the realm of fashion and in legal relations revolving around them are the main themes of this book.

Fashion is particularly selected as a cultural site to test the impact of artificial intelligence on intellectual property. Fashion might be one of the most important cultural inventions of Western civilisation. It is remarkable evidence of consumer culture's attitude toward the fast-moving trivial. It is often creative to the degree of being artistic, enabling individuals and cultures to express their inner thoughts and personalities. But it is also exploitative to the point of being socially catastrophic, urging people to buy more than is healthy for them or society and the environment. While fashion designs surround our bodies and cultures, the legacy of artificial intelligence begins to reign over the industry. For selling more fashion items, artificial intelligence is more and more incorporated into the designing process to give new wonders to this alluring world of the beautiful and the unreal. This book enters this discussion at the point where the law, creativity, fashion and technology converge and diverge.

Is artificial intelligence creative? Can it create a fashion design? The questions do not end here. What happens when fashion designs of artificial intelligence infringe on those of human beings?

The law, philosophy and technology gurus Annemarie Bridy, Margaret Boden, Ryan Abbott and Arthur Miller adopt a positive attitude toward the authorship of artificial intelligence. For them, we need to get used to creativity of artificial intelligence, embrace this phenomenon and – just like Asimov – adopt comprehensive rules for their creativity.

The US Copyright Office is cold to this idea. Under this understanding, authorship is a legally and socially constructed institution. Designs or works generated by artificial intelligence entities cannot be 'intellectual' property of this legal reality.

As can be seen in every legal and philosophical debate, there are always advocates of the third or middle way between two extremes. For the supporters of the middle way, artificial intelligence machines are sophisticated devices that can automatically carry out some creative acts independent of human beings. Their limited autonomy in creating designs is a functionality that serves the creative urge of human beings. Under this approach, the owner of the creative process and a design should be human beings, namely the first-class citizens and right owners of the republic of creativity.

This book is a modest attempt to discuss the questions of authorship and liability over artificial intelligence-generated fashion designs. It is premised on the 'broken embraces' of the thought landscapes concerning creative agency of artificial intelligence. Its central thesis is quite straightforward: the law should take the stage upon the factual aspects of creating with artificial intelligence, and the legal analysis should determine the *auteurs* and infringers on these creative relational currents. It is hoped that this book can serve to this end.

There is a universal law that always applies to both human and artificial beings when they begin to live together in this world: love. Few poets in Türkiye or elsewhere have ever excelled in the poetry of love at the same level as the 13th-century

Sufi mystic Yunus Emre, who recognises love as the celebration of life and living together:

> *Come let us be friends*
> *And make life easy on ourselves,*
> *Let us love and let us be loved,*
> *No one shall inherit the earth.*

Acknowledgements

This book has been a fantastic journey for me. I wish to thank everyone who took part in this adventure and made this book come to life.

In acknowledging the support I have received from others in this journey, I must begin by giving the greatest thanks to Professor Charlotte Waelde for her invaluable insights and valid and constructive criticism. Her advice on the general organisation of the book has also been enhancing. In fact, she has been genuinely supporting me since my PhD as my supervisor. She has always encouraged me to think outside the box and believed in my ideas, even the ones that might sound absurd to others. For me, she is not only a great law professor in intellectual property but also an inspirational life teacher and a special person.

I am also grateful to Dr Enrico Bonadio for his suggestions and comments. He is a great academic and friend. His advice enabled me to repair some weaknesses of my book.

I must also express my sincere gratitude to Professor Arzu Oğuz for providing insightful comments that really helped me in shaping some of my arguments in the Turkish version of this book, which are reflected here as well.

Despite their great academic contributions and comments, all errors and omissions in this book, of course, remain mine.

I extend my acknowledgement and heartfelt love to my beautiful wife, Emine. I would like to thank her a million times for her loving support and companionship throughout this journey. Without her support, this book would not be written.

I always feel happy to be a member of my family, whose faith in me has been unwavering. I am very grateful to my parents, sisters and brother, who have always supported me in everything I do in life in every possible way.

I want to further thank our sweet cat, Ada – the meaning, love and sunshine of our life. When I felt overwhelmed by long hours of reading and writing, his playfulness and beautiful blue eyes gave me pure joy and more energy than anything.

Some material in this book is translated (but revised and updated) from my Turkish book entitled *Yapay Zekânın Eser Sahipliği* ('Authorship of Artificial Intelligence'), which covers only the question of authorship of artificial intelligence in EU and Turkish copyright laws from a comparative perspective. When I translated these parts, Ayşegül Nihan Çakır, Furkan Bolatkale and Bora

Tütüncü provided great assistance. I owe special thanks to them for their fabulous contributions.

It is impossible for me to express adequately my gratitude to the editor of this work, Siobhán Poole of Routledge, who encouraged me to write a book on artificial intelligence, fashion and design law upon my presentation at the Society of Legal Scholars Conference in 2020. Before her offer, the idea of writing a book was millions of light years away from my mind. I took up the challenge and began to give life to one. With her marvellous editorial touch through this journey, she always supported me with patience and swiftly arranged printing formalities of this book. Consequently, here we have it. I am greatly thankful to her.

The production and copyediting at Routledge have been carried through excellently by the swift and tireless work of not only Siobhán Poole but also Sanjo Joseph Puthumana (assistant editor). I also thank him very much. And thank you, Sanjo, also for the stunning cover design and for arranging the layout of this book. It looks really cool!

In Ankara, on a balmy morning in July 2022 –

Hasan Kadir Yılmaztekin

Introduction
AI effect

Artificial intelligence (AI) now infiltrates our culture. After a couple of difficult winters,[1] *AI* today is a word on everybody's lips, and it attracts everyone's attention regardless of whether they are experts or not.

When we think of the notion of AI, we generally tend to associate it with futuristic themes. Science fiction depictions such as killer robots or human-friendly androids come to our minds. However, if we see AI as 'the study of agents that exist in an environment and perceive and act,'[2] it is possible to consider it as a much broader field of science and technology and to talk about many applications that have an impact on our daily lives. From Apple's Siri to Amazon's Alexa, Tesla's auto-driving cars to facial recognition systems in CCTV cameras, Netflix's film offering services to Google's search engine, we live in a world of AI goods.

The advent of AI-powered technologies increasingly affects people's lives across the globe. As a tool for productivity and cost-efficiency, AI also shapes our economy and welfare. AI-assisted commercial industries are becoming more and more common. It is possible to see that AI increasingly plays an important role in diagnostic medicine, transportation, investment, therapy, intelligence, alternative dispute resolution, contracts, national defence, banking and many other similar fields.[3] Substantial economic investments have been channelled into the development of these technologies.[4]

There are various reasons that have paved the way for another spring for AI. Remarkable innovations have recently been made in the field of machine learning.[5]

---

1 In the literature, 'AI winters' refers to the stagnation periods where the progress in research on AI technologies comes near to halting and the interest and investment in this field are reduced. See; Andrew Burgess, *The Executive Guide to Artificial Intelligence* (1st edn, Palgrave Macmillan, 2018) 11–13.
2 Stuart J Russell and Peter Norvig, *Artificial Intelligence: A Modern Approach* (4th edn, Pearson, 2020) 1.
3 Burgess (n 1) 73–89; Shlomit Yanisky-Ravid and Luis A Velez-Hernandez, 'Copyrightability of Artworks Produced by Creative Robots and Originality: The Formality-Objective Model' (2018) 19(1) *Minnesota Journal of Law, Science & Technology* 4–6.
4 Natasha Bernal, 'AI Investment Reaches Record Levels in the UK' (*The Telegraph*, 9 September 2019) www.telegraph.co.uk/technology/2019/09/09/ai-investment-reaches-record-levels-uk/.
5 Burgess (n 1) 13.

DOI: 10.4324/9781003355922-1

2   *Introduction*

The availability and the enormous volume of big data has facilitated the training of AI systems.[6] The speed of computer processors has exponentially increased.[7] Cloud storage systems offer huge areas to manage this data. Internet access is now much easier and faster.[8]

However, AI does not come without any problems. The upsurge of these novel technologies is at the centre of public debate and policy considerations. Some segments of the society have vocally raised their concern that 'robots are taking over.'[9]

AI-generated designs and works are becoming more popular.[10] Today, AI technologies can generate several intellectual creations. To name a few, they can write fables[11], novels[12] and poetry.[13] They can draft news texts.[14] They can compose

---

6   Ibid 13–15.
7   Ibid 16–17.
8   Ibid 17–19.
9   For discussions on the concept of singularity in reference to the replacement of human intelligence by an advanced AI or a cognitively enhanced biological intelligence, see; Murray Shanahan, *The Technological Singularity* (MIT Press, 2015); Jerry Kaplan, *Artificial Intelligence: What Everyone Needs to Know* (OUP, 2016) 138–141; Margaret A Boden, *Artificial Intelligence: A Very Short Introduction* (OUP, 2018) 130–150.
10 Ryan Abbott states that computer-generated works will become the main economic resource for creative industries as AI becomes more powerful and sophisticated. See; Ryan Abbott, 'Artificial Intelligence, Big Data and Intellectual Property: Protecting Computer Generated Works in the United Kingdom' in Tanya Aplin (ed), *Research Handbook on Intellectual Property and Digital Technologies* (Edward Elgar Publishing, 2020) 322.
11 Alison Flood, 'Computer Programmed to Write Its Own Fables' (*Guardian*, 6 August 2014) www.theguardian.com/books/2014/aug/06/computer-programmed-to-write-fables-moral-storytelling-system.
12 The AI developed by the Future University Hakodate wrote the novel 'The Day a Computer Wrote a Novel' and this work passed the first round of evaluation of the 'Hoshi Shinichi Literary Award'. See; Emiko Jozuka, 'A Japanese AI Almost Won a Literary Prize' (*Vice*, 24 March 2016) www.vice.com/en_us/article/wnxnjn/a-japanese-ai-almost-won-a-literary-prize.
13 Samuel Gibbs, 'Google AI Project Writes Poetry Which Could Make a Vogon Proud' (*Guardian*, 17 May 2016) www.theguardian.com/technology/2016/may/17/googles-ai-write-poetry-stark-dramatic-vogons. For Ray Kurzweil's 'Cybernetic Poet', an AI program based on neural networks and writing poetry see; Ray Kurzweil, *The Age of Spiritual Machines: How We Will Live, Work and Think in the New Age of Intelligent Machines* (Texere Publishing, 2001) 117. Also see; Jukka Toivanen, Oskar Gross and Hannu Toivonen, 'The Officer Is Taller Than You, Who Race Yourself! Using Document Specific Word Associations in Poetry Generation' in Simon Colton, Dan Ventura, Nada Lavrač and Michael Cook (eds), *Proceedings of the Fifth International Conference on Computational Creativity* (Jožef Stefan Institute, 2014) 355–362.
14 Lin Weeks, 'Media Law and Copyright Implications of Automated Journalism' (2014) 4(1) *New York University Journal of Intellectual Property and Entertainment Law* 67–94; Gary Rogers, 'Reporters and Data and Robot: Why 2018 will be the Year of Automation in News' (*Medium*, 31 December 2017) https://medium.com/@urbsmedia/reporters-and-data-and-robots-ee352220c5f1; GPT-3, 'A Robot Wrote This Entire Article. Are You Scared Yet, Human?' (*Guardian*, 8 September 2020) www.theguardian.com/commentisfree/2020/sep/08/robot-wrote-this-article-gpt-3.

music.¹⁵ They can write new parts for a computer game¹⁶ or generate the computer program itself.¹⁷ They can produce films.¹⁸ They can paint.¹⁹ They can even compose musicals along with lyrics, music and storylines.²⁰ It is possible to give a myriad of other examples.²¹

Fashion is one of the industries that AI can profoundly impact. AI tools and devices are currently being used in the fashion industry to create fashion models, fabric and jewellery designs, and clothing.

When we talk about AI-generated designs, we instead focus on the fruits of innovation –more best-selling apparels, more fashionable designs and more fulfilment of customer expectations – without paying heed to who the designer is. Designers invest a lot of talent, time and finances in designing and creating each article of clothing and accessory before they release their work to the public. Pattern drafting is the first and most important step in dressmaking. Designers typically start with a general sketch on paper; add styles, elements and colours; revise and refine everything; and finally deliver their design to dressmakers. AI accelerates this time-consuming and labour-intensive process.

Yet the full legal consequences of AI in fashion industry are often forgotten. An AI device's ability to generate fashion designs raises the question of who will own intellectual property rights over the fashion designs. Will it be the fashion designer who hires or contracts with the AI programmer? Will it be the programmer? Will it be the AI itself? Or will it be a joint work of humans and computers? And who will be liable for infringement deriving from use of third-party material in AI-generated fashion designs?

New era, new perspectives

With the rise of AI, it is obvious that artists, writers, composers, designers, intellectual property professionals, producers and curators are confronted with a new challenge. The phenomenon of the authorship of AI opens all established

---

15 William T Ralston, 'Copyright in Computer-Composed Music: HAL Meets Handel' (2004–2005) 52 *Journal of Copyright Society USA* 281–306.
16 Raffi Khatchadourian, 'World Without End: Creating A Full-Scale Digital Cosmos' (*The New Yorker*, 11 May 2015) www.newyorker.com/magazine/2015/05/18/world-without-end-raffi-khatchadourian.
17 Kim Martineau, 'Toward Artificial Intelligence that Learns to Write Code' (14 June 2019) https://news.mit.edu/2019/toward-artificial-intelligence-that-learns-to-write-code-0614.
18 Annalee Newitz, 'Movie Written by AI Algorithm Turns Out to be Hilarious and Intense' (16 June 2016) https://arstechnica.com/gaming/2016/06/an-ai-wrote-this-movie-and-its-strangely-moving/.
19 For 'The Next Rembrandt' see; www.nextrembrandt.com/.
20 Bob STURM and Oded Ben-Tal, "Machine Folk' Music Composed by AI Shows Technology's Creative Side' (31 March 2017) https://theconversation.com/machine-folk-music-composed-by-ai-shows-technologys-creative-side-74708#:~:text=This%20is%20not%20entirely%20unprecedented,broad%20opportunities%20for%20creative%20research.
21 For other examples of creative works produced by AI, see: Arthur I Miller, *The Artist in the Machine: The World of AI-Powered Creativity* (The MIT Press, 2019) 55–258.

assumptions and acceptances about creativity to discussion. Annemarie Bridy suggests seizing this opportunity and taking action to reconstruct the overall framework of global copyright law for the 21st century rather than waiting for the probable, apparently late and even fragmented intervention of all legislators internationally. The relatively slow development of AI so far could offer a chance for changing the reactive, crisis-driven model of policymaking that has dominated copyright law in the digital era.[22]

Even though it is still hard to make an accurate prediction, it is possible to imagine the impact of AI on creative industries to a certain extent. According to Sam Gaskin, 'AI art will transform the entire art market.'[23] When it first emerged, photography was seen as a method of producing a chemical and mechanical product transposing objects, people and nature as they are, and was not regarded as an art form. Karthik Kalyanaraman contends that AI would create a sort of 'photography moment' in art and initiate the transformation. Kalyanaraman's thoughts can be conveyed as follows:

> [AI] has the potential to radically change non-AI art, as the discovery of photography embodied impressionism, expressionism, and other schools which are more concerned with pure human perception and emotion; ... Human artists can easily create new forms of art in painting, and even the surprising and challenging conceptual art, in a way which is a direct simulation of a description, by using AI. In the age of photography, not only the realistic pictures were no longer attractive, but the artists, whose work looked novel at a simple glance or was more descriptive than felt, saw a decline of interest in their work, and collectors of such works saw these works lose their value.[24]

The World Intellectual Property Organisation (WIPO) has been one of the first organisations to give a timely response to the photography moment impact of AI. WIPO has carried out important studies in the intersection of intellectual property and AI.[25] WIPO has published a report on technology trends in AI.[26] In addition, the Organisation cooperates with national intellectual property offices on the subject.[27] WIPO also called for comments on the 'Impact of Artificial Intelligence on IP Policy' in December 2019 and received more than 250 responses. Later, the

---

22 Annemarie Bridy, 'Coding Creativity: Copyright and the Artificially Intelligent Author' (2012) 5 *Stanford Technology Law Review* 27.
23 Sam Gaskin, 'When Art Created by Artificial Intelligence Sells, Who Gets Paid?' (*Art Market*, 17 September 2018).
24 Karthik Kalyanaraman, 'AI Art: A New Photography Moment' (*Medium*, 17 September 2018) https://medium.com/@info_12534/ai-art-a-new-photography moment-8d7009bfb696.
25 WIPO, *Artificial Intelligence and Intellectual Property* (WIPO, 2019).
26 WIPO, *WIPO Technology Trends 2019*. Also see, WIPO, *WIPO Technology Trends – Artificial Intelligence*. www.wipo.int/tech_trends/en/artificial_intelligence/.
27 WIPO, *WIPO Conversation on Intellectual Property and Artificial Intelligence* (WIPO, 2019).

first edition[28] and second edition[29] of the 'Draft Issues Paper on Intellectual Property Policy and Artificial Intelligence' were published. In the second edition of this document, WIPO pointed out that a balance should be struck between human and machine creativity in terms of protecting AI-generated works.[30]

Similar to WIPO, the European Patent Office (EPO) has also conducted studies in this field.[31] In 2019, IP5 (a forum of the five largest intellectual property offices around the world) created a special task force (coordination unit) on AI and emerging technologies.[32] EPO has also conducted research and surveys on the subjects at the intersection of patent law and AI.[33] Perhaps most importantly, EPO rejected two European patent applications in which an AI system was designated as the inventor.[34] The applications in question were filed by Dr Stephen Thaler in 2018. Dr Thaler applied for patents on the inventions resulting from the collaboration performed by him and his colleagues in 'The Artificial Inventor Project.'[35] Several applications were also submitted to intellectual property offices all around the world – including the USA, Australia, the United Kingdom – for inventions on food containers (fractal containers) and search and rescue lights.[36] The patent applications were filed in the name of Dr Thaler, but it was claimed that the AI called DABUS should be mentioned as the inventor. EPO applied Article 81 of the European Patent Convention (and Article 19E of the European Patent Convention Implementing Regulation) on the designation of the inventor and did not accept the request.

The High Court of England and Wales took up the reasoning of EPO in the case brought before it regarding the same inventions credited to DABUS. The Court dismissed the case, stating that AI could not be designated as an inventor in the patent application document because it is not a person.[37] Later, the Court

---

28 WIPO, *WIPO Conversation on IP and AI'*, *Draft Issues Paper on Intellectual Property Policy and Artificial Intelligence* (WIPO, WIPO/IP/AI/2/GE/20/1, 13 December 2019).
29 WIPO, *Revised Issues Paper on Intellectual Property Policy and Artificial Intelligence* (WIPO, WIPO/IP/AI/2/GE/20/1 REV, 21 May 2020).
30 Ibid 23.
31 EPO, *Artificial Intelligence*. www.epo.org/news-events/in-focus/ict/artificial-intelligence.html.
32 EPO, *World's Five Largest Patent Office's Agree on Joint Task Force for Emerging Technologies and AI* (EPO News, 2019).
33 Eg, see, Noam Shemtov, 'A Study on Inventorship in Inventions Involving AI Activity' http://documents.epo.org/projects/babylon/eponet.nsf/0/3918F57B010A3540C125841900280653/$File/Concept_of_Inventorship_in_Inventions_involving_AI_Activity_en.pdf.
34 For news coverage on the refusal of the patent application, see; www.epo.org/news-events/news/2020/20200128.html. Application numbers: EP3564144 (FOOD CONTAINER) https://register.epo.org/application?number=EP18275163#_blank; and EP3563896 (DEVICES AND METHODS FOR ATTRACTING ENHANCED ATTENTION) https://register.epo.org/application?number=EP18275174#_blank.
35 http://artificialinventor.com.
36 For these applications see; https://artificialinventor.com/patent-applications/.
37 *Thaler v. The Comptroller-General of Patents, Designs and Trade Marks* (2020) EWHC 2412 (Pat). For an academic commentary on the judgment, see; Laura Adde and Joel Smith, 'Patent Pending: The Law on AI Inventorship' (2021) 16(2) *Journal of Intellectual Property Law & Practice* 97–98.

of Appeal of England and Wales upheld the judgment.[38] By contrast, in 2021, the Federal Court of Australia developed an innovative interpretation of patent law. The Federal Court stated that the concept of inventor was not defined by the law. The Court then went on to note that the concept of inventor could be broadly interpreted to include AI. Thus, it was held that the AI (DABUS) can be credited as the inventor.[39]

The Federal Court of Australia was not alone in embracing this innovative perspective. Around the same time when the judgment was delivered in Australia, DABUS and Dr Thaler received heralding news in South Africa. The South African Intellectual Property Office has become the first IP office in the world to grant a patent that shows an AI as the inventor of a product.[40]

The Federal Court of Australia was not the first judicial authority to recognise AI creativity. Courts in China two years ago devised a more friendly solution for the protection of AI and human collaborations in the copyright realm. One of these judicial exegeses came into being in 2019, when the Beijing Internet Court heard the case of *Feilin v. Baidu*.[41] The case concerned a data report summarising judicial judgments on the film and TV industry in Beijing. The report included texts and graphics that were put together by the aid of an AI software. An internet user later published some parts of Feilin's (a Beijing-based law firm) report on a platform managed by Baidu. In the case, Feilin claimed that Baidu had infringed its right of communication of information on networks. In response, Baidu argued that the report could not be protected by copyright at all because it was completely produced by AI software. Thus, the court had to address two issues: whether the report was original; and if it was original, who the author was and whether its copyright was infringed.[42]

The court assessed the originality of the graphic and text parts of the report by separating them. While the graphics were not considered as original expressions and could not be protected by copyright, the texts in the report was found to have originality to a certain extent. However, the court also pointed out that the originality was not a sufficient condition for copyright protection; the work must also be a *human creation*.[43] The court then distinguished the purely AI-generated texts from the texts generated by humans with the aid of AI. For the former, it was concluded that even though they were original, they could not be treated as

---

38 *Thaler v. The Comptroller-General of Patents, Designs and Trade Marks* [2021] EWCA Civ 1374.
39 *Thaler v. Commissioner of Patents* [2021] FCA 879.
40 Tom Knowles, 'Patently Brilliant . . . AI Listed as Inventor for First Time' (*The Times*, 28 July 2021) www.thetimes.co.uk/article/patently-brilliant-ai-listed-as-inventor-for-first-time-mqj3s38mr.
41 *Beijing Feilin Law Firm v. Beijing Baidu Netcom Science Technology Co., Ltd.*, No 239 Minchu (Beijing Internet Ct 2018).
42 Andres Guadamuz, 'Do Androids Dream of Electric Copyright?' in Jyh-An Lee, Reto M Hilty, and Kung-Chung Liu (eds), *Artificial Intelligence and Intellectual Property* (OUP, 2021) 171; Ming Chen, 'Beijing Internet Court Denies Copyright to Works Created Solely by Artificial Intelligence' (2019) 14(8) *Journal of Intellectual Property Law & Practice* 593–594.
43 Chen (n 42) 594.

a protectable literary work. However, the court added, the fact that they did not constitute copyright works did not mean that they were in the public domain, and certain rights and interests related to such reports should be granted to the software user, not the software developer (who had already gained revenue from developing the software).[44] The investment that went into the creation of that part of the report was deemed worthy of protection, albeit without precise explanation of the possible protection modes.

The Feilin report included the expressions added individually by humans as well (the text generated partly by human and partly by AI) and thus was recognised as an original literary work created by a human being, not as a purely AI-generated work.[45] This case suggests that in China copyright will only be considered to subsist in a work if it conveys an original expression of an idea or feeling made by a natural person; and in contrast, purely AI-generated works should not be considered in the public domain.

Can AI write *dreams*? It is not clear whether AI can express its imagination world just like humans, but a court in Shenzhen apparently said that AI can write financial reports, and this would benefit from copyright protection, though under human supervision. In essence, this case, *Tencent v. Yinxun*,[46] was related to the article written by Tencent's AI software called Dreamwriter. The AI software, the codes of which were written by this Chinese technology giant, produced more than a million articles on topics such as weather, finance, sports and real estate since 2015. The company Shanghai Yingxun Technology copied and published a financial article written by Dreamwriter. In response, Tencent filed a lawsuit on grounds of copyright infringement. The court accepted the case and ordered Shanghai Yingxun to pay 1,500 Yuan in damages.[47]

The court held that the 'form of expression of the article at issue in the dispute satisfies the requirements of a literary work and shows that the information and data included in the article on capital markets have been selected, evaluated and judged.' Furthermore, 'The structure of the article was found meaningful and clear in its judgements,' and it was concluded that the article was original. According to the court,

> Dreamwriter's automatic text drafting was not the result of an autonomous or unconscious process. Instead, the automation of the software reflects the choices of the plaintiff. . . . The form of expression of the article was shaped by the personal arrangements and choices of the employees of the plaintiff.

---

44 Ju Yoen Lee, 'Artificial Intelligence Cases in China: *Feilin v. Baidu* and *Tencent Shenzhen v. Shanghai Yingxin*' (2021) 7(1) *China & WTO Review* 214.
45 Guadamuz (n 42) 171.
46 *Shenzhen Tencent Computer System Co Ltd v. Shanghai Yingxun Technology Co, Ltd* No 14010 Minchu (Shenzhen Nanshan District Ct 2019).
47 For English translation of the judgment, see; Xiaoshuai Ren, 'Protection of Works Generated by Machine Learning Software' (2020) 69(7) *GRUR International* 763–767.

In *Tencent*, the court held that the article satisfied the requirements for copyright protection, as it was the human creative contribution that led to an original work in copyright sense.[48] It seems that while Feilin invented a more objective and less human-centred approach, Tencent took a more subjective direction and combined human creation condition and originality. However, both cases show that courts in China have conjured up novel solutions under the rising influence of AI on intellectual property law.

Contours of fashion

Fashion is kaleidoscopic. It has a visceral relationship to the artistic, legal, physical, psychological, sociological, political and technological, and it is so interconnected that making a 'complete' case to demarcate its content and meaning is impossible. This is what makes fashion so interesting – and difficult – to study.

Thinkers in a range of fields have pondered on what fashion is and what accounts for it. The 20th century witnessed prominent fashion theorists such as Thorstein Veblen, John Flügel, Georg Simmel, Herbert Blumer, Walter Benjamin, Roland Barthes and Elizabeth Wilson. They all make a distinction between clothes and fashion. Flügel focuses on the accentuation of various *body* parts through fashion.[49] Benjamin views fashion (*die Mode*) as the epitome of modernity; like modernity, it is ephemeral and confined to the *new*. Talking about the dynamic relationship between dress, body and culture, Barthes observes that fashion links the body to society.[50] For Barthes, fashion creates an entire industry based on codes that signal meaning in everyday life. In that respect, fashion is a social text to be read, and the fashioned body has its signs in certain rhetoric.

The sociologist Georg Simmel formulates the dynamics of social imitation and distinction through clothing. According to Simmel, fashion derives from tension between 'the tendency towards social equalization with the desire for individual differentiation and change.'[51] Fashion is created by social elites for the purpose of distinguishing themselves as a group from the lower classes. The lower classes inevitably admire and imitate the upper classes. Then, the upper classes escape to a new fashion to situate themselves differently. Thus, Simmel describes an unwritten top-down system of emulation where new fashions move down through the *status hierarchy*.[52]

The term *collective selection*, associated with the sociologist Herbert Blumer, is sometimes used to define fashion.[53] Under this theory, fashion is written as a

---

48 Ren (n 47) 765–766. Also see; Guadamuz (n 42) 172.
49 John C Flügel, *The Psychology of Clothes* (Hogarth Press, 1950) 160–166.
50 Roland Barthes, *The Language of Fashion* (Bloomsbury, 2013).
51 Georg Simmel, 'Fashion' (1904) 10(1) *International Quarterly* 133.
52 Ibid 130–155. See also; Thorstein Veblen, *The Theory of The Leisure Class* (Dover Publishing, 1994).
53 Herbert Blumer, 'Fashion: From Class Differentiation to Collective Selection' (1969) 10(3) *The Sociological Quarterly* 275–291.

collective process where many people, through their individual choices among many competing styles, form collective tastes that are manifested in fashion trends. The process of trend formation begins vaguely and then becomes visible when a particular fashion is established. The driver of fashion is not necessarily emulation of high-status people *per se*. Rather, people follow fashion because they desire to be in *fashion*. As Elizabeth Wilson claims, clothes represent the mood of each succeeding age, and what we do with our bodies expresses the *Zeitgeist*.[54]

Beyond and within these theoretical frameworks, fashion emerges in our cultural history in its own unique way. It is a truism that fashion is manifested in the production of clothes, accessories and appearances. But fashion goes beyond the industry of making and selling clothing and plays a complex role in our society.[55] Fashion enables individuals to change their style and look by providing an instrument of self-expression.[56] Fashion is always unpredictable. It is a continuous system of change. A new fashion emerges with a rejection of the old. From the beginning of the 20th century to the present day, fashion has become a mixture of styles, looks, peoples and technological advances.[57] It has seen an exponential expansion of markets and ways of manufacturing that continue centuries-old craft traditions while pushing new boundaries.

In the 20th century, the old hierarchical class system disappeared. There is now a fascinating diversity of possible fashions available due to the new incredible volumes of clothes and wide range of prices. The dissemination of fashion in the modern times is both top-down and bottom-up. For that reason, fashion has become inclusive of the entire society. It transcends the white, Western, heterosexual, upper-middle-class, female consumerist engagements.[58] Fashion can foster social solidarity and impose group norms, while diversification in dress can be experienced as odd and disturbing. The value of fashion derives from social recognition of the fashion, whether it is the logo, textile or cut. Readily identifiable identities define fashion, and status is constructed in many ways including by style, brand affiliation and profession. There are countless ways to define group identity, and fashion plays a central role in this sense. Thus, fashion is a fundamentally *cultural* phenomenon.[59]

Fashion embodies an important proportion of the world of commerce. In commercial terms, *fashion industry* refers to a global supply chain that begins with the production of raw materials, includes commercial design, manufacture, marketing

---

54 Elizabeth Wilson, *Adorned in Dreams* (Rutgers UP, 2003) 47.
55 Jennifer Craik, 'Globalization' in Adam Geczy and Vicki Karaminas (eds), *The End of Fashion* (Bloomsbury Visual Arts, 2019) 133.
56 Heidi Härkönen, *Fashion and Copyright: Protection as a Tool to Foster Sustainable Development* (Unpublished PhD Thesis, 2021) 18.
57 Alexandra Palmer, 'Introduction' in Alexandra Palmer (ed), *A Cultural History of Dress and Fashion in the Modern Age, Volume 6* (Bloomsbury Academic, 2017) 1.
58 Härkönen (n 56) 18.
59 Malcolm Barnard, 'Introduction' in Malcom Barnard (ed), *Fashion Theory: A Reader* (2nd edn, Routledge, 2020) 4.

and sales, and ends with the consumption of garments and accessories. The global fashion market is valued at US$1,500 billion.[60] A few cities in the world, such as Paris, London, New York, Tokyo and Milan, hold high status in terms of the influence they have over what people wear in other countries and regions. Europe is a significant player in fashion industry. Indeed, five million people in the EU are directly employed in the fashion value chain. Europe is also well known for its design houses. It is an important centre for manufacturing, particularly countries in Southern and Eastern Europe such as Portugal, Spain, Italy, Romania and Türkiye. In Europe, higher-quality and more niche items – e.g., sports protection clothing and footwear – are manufactured.[61]

Along with this global fashion market came unprecedented access to fashion and choices. These range from couture-inspired to fast fashion, second-hand, vintage and ethical fashion. Consumption has never been so easy and available due to modern systems of industrial transportation and now post-industrial internet. TikTok and Instagram have further fuels this buying passion. *Fast fashion* is a result of this new consumption model.

Fashion-forward but low-priced retailers like H&M, Zara, Primark, Topshop and Forever 21 have flourished, thanks to their ability to take designs from Paris, Milan, London to the mass market. Almost as soon as new designs appear on the runway, their photographs and sketches are sent to Chinese, Bangladeshi or Indian factories that can produce affordable copies at minimal costs. Rapidly changing trends are made available to consumers quickly after being disclosed to the public. More importantly, prices of fast fashion products are so accessible that the average consumer can renew their wardrobe easily. Fast fashion leads to the rapid circulation of trends. In fast fashion stores, originality is secondary. Speed, imitation, disposability and trendiness lie at the core of fast fashion, whereas fashion prioritises creativity and cultural significance.

A key feature of fashion is constantly evolving trends. *Trend* means a certain style that is popular and considered 'fashionable' at a certain point in time. For example, a silhouette of a dress or a suit, the length of a skirt, the softness of eyeliner, the positioning of a waistline or colour choices can be considered trends. Trends generally spread through imitation and references, and this create possibilities for intellectual property infringements. Products that are part of the same trend are not necessarily close copies or substitutes. Rather, they may be efforts to meet the need of consumers for individual differentiation.[62] Staying in a trend does not, however, support the permissibility of close copying in fashion design.

---

60 P Smith, 'Global Apparel Market – Statistics and Facts' (*Statista*, 3 March 2022) www.statista.com/topics/5091/apparel-market-worldwide/#dossierKeyfigures.
61 Rosie Burbidge, *European Fashion Law: A Practical Guide from Start-up to Global Success* (Edward Elgar, 2019) 2.
62 C Scott Hemphill and Jeannie Suk, 'The Law, Culture, and Economics of Fashion' (2009) 61(5) *Stanford Law Review* 107.

As a marker of social status,[63] fashion also breeds consumer demand for cheaper copies or knockoffs of popular fashion designs.[64] *Knockoffs*, *counterfeits* and *duplicates* are often used interchangeably, but they have slightly different meanings. Knockoffs are closely inspired by the original product but tend to copy the product design without attaching the branding. Removing a brand name or logo does not mean that it has not infringed on any intellectual property rights. A counterfeit is the most serious form of copying. It is an exact copy of the original, including the branding, product labels and swing tags. Counterfeit products are purposely designed to make consumers believe that they are the original product. A duplicate can be either a counterfeit or a knockoff. Thus, it is a copy of the original, but it could fall anywhere on the copying scale from a perfect imitation to an inspired similar product.[65] Imitation that comes too close to the source of its inspiration can harm the original design and its desirability among consumers.

Piracy paradox

Design copying is ubiquitous in the fashion industry. It must be distinguished from other forms of 'borrowing' such as inspiration, adaptation, homage, referencing or remixing. While line-by-line imitations are the most harmful type of copying, borrowing can remain in the legitimate domain.

Fashion designs are embodiments of fashion. Designers lament design copying because they feel their embodied ideas are stolen. Their frustration at seeing their design emulated is understandable. Are knockoffs damaging the fashion business? Fashion sales have remained rather economically stable for years. The high-end fashion companies whose designs are frequently copied have in a way maintained their business. In the legal realm, the legal and social dynamics of creativity and continuity of fashion are most directly dealt with by intellectual property laws. The question of legal protection for fashion design concerns the optimal balance between two dimensions. The law should provide an incentive to create new designs. At the same time, it should promote making existing designs available to consumers and making material available for use by subsequent designers.

Rather interestingly, the US law professors Kal Raustiala and Christopher Sprigman suggest that weak intellectual property norms have instead been intrinsic to fashion's success in maintaining incessant creativity. Raustiala and Sprigman call this effect 'the piracy paradox.'[66]

The paradox derives from the basic dilemma concerning the economics of fashion. For the fashion industry to keep growing, two paradoxical things must happen. Customers must like this season's designs. After a short while, they must

---

63 Jane Tynan, 'Status' in Alexandra Palmer (ed), *A Cultural History of Dress and Fashion in the Modern Age, Volume 6* (Bloomsbury Academic, 2017) 131.
64 Härkönen (n 56) 19.
65 Burbidge (n 61) 371.
66 Kal Raustiala and Christopher Jon Sprigman, 'The Piracy Paradox: Innovation and Intellectual Property in Fashion Design' (2006) 92(8) *Virginia Law Review* 1687–1777.

also become dissatisfied with them so that they feel like buying next season's. A similar problem arises in many other consumer businesses. Fashion cannot rely on functions of clothing to make old products obsolete – unlike, e.g., the technology industry. Raustiala and Sprigman argue that copying fulfils this function in fashion, giving rise to what they call 'induced obsolescence.'[67] Due to copying, designs and styles pass quickly from early adopters to the masses. Then, since no one wants to continue wearing clothes just like everybody else, the copying of designs helps trigger a constant demand for something new.

Designers do not generally agree with this idea, as they must keep coming up with new ideas rather than joining a trend for years. However, it means that in the fashion industry there is more creativity, more competition and probably more sales than there otherwise would be. In the absence of strong intellectual property rights, a more fertile ground provides new opportunities for designers to create, since designers can take other people's ideas in new directions. If the designers were to prevent others from using their creations, there would have been less creativity in fashion. Thus, Raustiala and Sprigman claim that copying is the driving force behind fashion creativity, and it is a bad idea to protect designers from design piracy.

Differentiation and sustainability

Does this classic case 'where the cure may be worse than the disease' represent the correct dynamics of the fashion industry? Some commentators call for 'stopping glorifying fashion piracy.'[68] A proponent for strong intellectual property protection in the fashion industry, the fashion law professor Susan Scafidi describes the contemporary US fashion industry (which lacks strong legal protection) as a system of 'legalised piracy.' Scafidi argues that the possibility of making copies of a fashion design, which is costless, unjustly allows copyists to get a free ride on the designer's concept. Customers frequently buy pirated designs instead of the original design. Thus, the copied substitutes lead to the loss of sales. Scafidi expresses that Raustiala and Sprigman's idea that copying drives the fashion cycle is an outdated argument because it does not acknowledge the impact of new technologies in fashion.[69]

The law professors Scott Hemphill and Jeannie Suk argue that copying is not necessarily integral to a trend to become popular and 'anchor consumers' expectations about what is in style at a given moment.'[70] The success behind new trends

---

67 Ibid 1718.
68 Keyon Lo, 'Stop Glorifying Fashion Piracy: It is Time to Enact the Innovative Design Protection Act' (2022) 21(1) *Chicago-Kent Journal of Intellectual Property* 159.
69 Felix Salmon, 'Susan Scafidi on Copyrighting Fashion' (*UpStart*, 2007) http://upstart.biz journals.com/views/blogs/market-movers/2007/09/19/susan-scafidi-on-copyrighting-fashion.html?page=6.
70 Kal Raustiala and Christopher Sprigman, *The Knockoff Economy: How Imitation Sparks Innovation* (OUP, 2012) 47.

stems from the fact that there are enough stores offering products within the same trend. To satisfy customer demand for differentiation according to their personal style, vendors have to offer trendy products with differentiation in their details.[71] Individuals tend to differentiate themselves through fashion choices. At the same time, they want to remain 'in fashion' to be in line with society. Hemphill and Suk call this attitude 'flocking.' They note that fashion creates a dynamic relationship between 'flocking' and 'differentiation,' because people want to be a part of trend but without necessarily imitating others.[72] For that reason Hemphill and Suk critique Raustiala and Sprigman for not distinguishing 'close copying' from 'trend-joining activities,'[73] which combine differentiation and flocking. According to Hemphill and Suk, in contrast to interpretation or adaptation of a trend style, close copying is more literal and a directly imitative practice in which one emulates the original. They suggest that intellectual property protection should only prevent this practice.[74]

Heidi Härkönen also questions 'the piracy paradox' introduced by Raustiala and Sprigman from the perspective of sustainable development. Härkönen argues that the contemporary fashion industry operates in a low-intellectual property regime, and this brings some problems. A broad space for copying might very well push fashion designers to be more creative, but at the same time it fosters fast fashion, and, as Härkönen warns, this is quite detrimental for sustainability. It seems that there is no reason to advocate for the piracy paradox, as Raustiala and Sprigman draw a one-sided picture of the whole fashion creativity. They have only looked at the incentivising effect of intellectual property rights and disregarded the medium- and long-term environmental and labour-centred costs of fast fashion. Voicing a more robust approach to fashion copying, Härkönen argues that stronger intellectual property rights (particularly copyright) might after all have positive economic effects to foster culturally, environmentally and socially sustainable development.[75]

After 15 years since the piracy paradox paradigm was put forward, Raustiala and Sprigman still believe that copying has been the democratic enabler for flourishing of fashion industry in the USA.[76] Scholars such as Susan Scafidi, however, have criticised the US intellectual property scheme for lagging behind other countries in the protection of fashion design. The protection granted by the European Union (EU) is often cited. It is undeniable that there is a regional normative and judicial consensus on the protection of fashion designs both, though with different

---

71 Hemphill and Suk (n 62) 120–121.
72 Ibid 118–119.
73 Ibid 135.
74 See also; Dagmar Strukelj, 'Comparison of the Intellectual Property Protections Available for Fashion Designs in the US and the EU (2020)' Stanford-Vienna TTLF Working Paper No. 58, https://www-cdn.law.stanford.edu/wp-content/uploads/2020/06/strukelj_wp58.pdf.
75 Härkönen (n 56).
76 Kal Raustiala and Christopher Jon Sprigman, 'Faster Fashion: The Piracy Paradox and its Perils' (2021) 39(2) *Cardozo Arts & Entertainment Law Journal* 535–556.

standards, under design and copyright laws in Europe. And this book will just focus on this consensus instead of discussing whether they are normatively correct ways of sustaining fashion creativity.

Outline of the book

The objective of this book is to seek answers to a couple of questions that surround AI-generated fashion designs. The first question that will be dealt with in this book is whether AI-generated fashion designs would be protected under EU design and copyright laws. If the answer is affirmative, then this inquiry inevitably entails exploring who would be assigned as the author and the owner of intellectual property rights over these designs under these two regimes. The flip side of creating an intellectual creation (and bearing a right holdership) is the infringement. Another question that we confront here is to whom infringement liability can be attributed if a third-party material is used in AI-generated fashion designs. This will be examined by looking at three possible acts that may cause design and copyright infringement.

The first chapter of this book will dwell on the history, definition, types and operational capabilities of AI. The second chapter will discuss the concepts of design authorship and infringement in the context of AI-generated fashion designs under EU design law. The third chapter will deal with the reflections of these concepts under EU copyright law. In the fourth chapter, a systematic analysis will be presented in relation to the legal solutions proposed by academics and some jurisdictions across the globe, which could be pursued in the protection of AI-generated fashion designs. We can list the questions we will seek answers to in the fifth chapter as follows: what does creativity mean in the context of AI? Is AI creative? What does the architecture of AI technologies tell us about their creative capacities? How can human codes around AI technologies be traced? What sort of a legislative arrangement could be enacted in the EU in relation to AI-generated fashion designs?

This book has been drafted with a view to producing a set of policy recommendations within the framework of EU design and copyright laws. At the end of the book, a solution based on a three-step test and model norms are proposed, which could be used to unleash the authors, right holders and infringers around AI-generated fashion designs.

This book takes 'fashion designs' as a testing ground for identifying how the law should treat an AI-generated subject matter. Fashion designs are preferred for two reasons. Fashion designs can be both functional and artistic. They are accordingly addressed in the two fields of intellectual property law: namely, design and copyright laws. For that reason, although the book places AI-generated fashion designs at the centre of its discussion, its proposals and coverage also echo on the broader spheres of EU design and copyright law as 'AI-generated subject matter.'

In several academic studies, the terms *AI-generated*, *AI-aided* and *AI-assisted subject matter* are used. The first of these concepts refers to the subject matter autonomously generated by AI. The last two refer to subject matter created using AI only as a tool (such as camera or a video recorder). The conceptual distinction amongst these terms seems to be correct in theory. In practice, however, none of the AI systems known today can generate a product solely on its own. Therefore, for the purposes of this book, the term *AI-generated (fashion) designs* (or *AI-generated work* where relevant) will be preferred to cover these three and will be understood to refer to subject matter created by using AI systems.

Limitations of the book

The US-based technology company Boston Dynamics posted an interesting video on its YouTube channel on 29 December 2020 to celebrate the new year. In the video, robots called Atlas, Spot and Handle, which were developed by the company for industrial use, dance to the Contours' song 'Do You Love Me.'[77] In a parallel universe, the dancing robots can be imagined as the fashion models walking on the runaway. Just like human models, some day in the future they can display fashion designs in fashion shows in Paris, Milan or London.

Likewise, it is possible to see videos on social media, the internet and even in some advertisements, in which an artist's image is realistically animated by using artificial neural networks. These animations are done by mimicking the artist's voice and acts or impersonating her image in an indistinguishable manner. Known as 'deep fakes,' such digital media products containing simulations of the original performer have been a means of entertainment for many consumers.

In such cases, a series of legal problems arise. Is it possible to consider the dance moves and catwalk of the robots as a performance under copyright law? If they are acknowledged as performance, who will be the performer? Do these 'deep fakes' constitute an infringement of the rights of the artist whose performance is imitated in such videos? If such videos cause infringement, who should be held legally accountable and on what grounds? Therefore, all the issues concerning performers' and personal rights will be left out of this book. Future works can be devoted to these matters.

In the context of AI-generated designs, two further questions arise in addition to the assignment of authorship and liability under design and copyright laws: (i) how can AI technologies themselves be protected under intellectual property laws (including copyright, patents, designs, trademarks, trade secrets and unfair competition)? and (ii) is it possible to protect AI-generated outputs under the related rights schemes? These issues will be excluded from the scope of the book as well.

Based on the example of DABUS, issues arising in relation to AI-generated inventions will not discussed in this book. Brief explanations are given by cross-referencing if they are relevant.

---

77 See; www.youtube.com/watch?v=fn3KWM1kuAw&ab_channel=BostonDynamics.

EU policies on AI and IP

From 2016 until 2020, in the EU, substantial and comprehensive policy documents on the regulation of AI have been created at the institutional level, especially by the European Parliament and the European Commission.[78] In the meantime, the EU institutions have also organised stakeholder forums and launched public consultations devoted to AI. These activities have started important conversations and defined the EU goals for the development and use of a human-centric AI. In April 2021, the Commission published its proposal for AI regulation.[79] An important defining feature of the EU approach to AI is learning from other regions and cooperating globally.[80] The EU has embraced ethical, human-centric and value-based approach to developing an AI strategy for the future, positioning itself as a norm-setting power as well as market regulator.[81]

Most of the EU documents do not directly refer to the intellectual property protection of AI-generated subject matter. However, in the 'Resolution with recommendations to the Commission on Civil Law Rules on Robotics' issued on 16 February 2017, the European Parliament has called the European Commission to support a horizontal and technologically neutral approach to intellectual property applicable to the various sectors in which robotics could be employed.[82] Following this document, the Explanatory Statement on 'Civil Law Rules on Robotics' prepared by the European Parliament Committee on Legal Affairs was issued. The statement proposes 'the elaboration of criteria for "own intellectual creation" for copyrightable works produced by computers or robots.'[83]

On 12 February 2019 a resolution on 'A Comprehensive European Industrial Policy on Artificial Intelligence and Robotics' was adopted by the European Parliament. This decision reiterated the earlier call for 'a horizontal and technologically neutral approach to intellectual property applicable to the various sectors in which robotics could be employed' and underlined the need to monitor the relevance and efficiency of rules on intellectual property rights to govern the development of AI.[84]

---

78 For overviews of these documents, see; Jędrzej Niklas and Lina Dencik, 'European Artificial Intelligence Policy: Mapping the Institutional Landscape' Working Paper DATAJUSTICE project (DATAJUSTICE, 2020); Inga Ulnicane, 'Artificial intelligence in the European Union: Policy, Ethics and Regulation' in Thomas Hoerber, Gabriel Weber and Ignazio Cabras (eds), *The Routledge Handbook of European Integrations* (Routledge, 2022) 254–269.
79 https://eur-lex.europa.eu/legal-content/EN/TXT/?uri=CELEX%3A52021PC0206.
80 Ulnicane (n 78) 265.
81 Ibid 265–266.
82 European Parliament Resolution with Recommendations to the Commission on Civil Law Rules on Robotics (2015/2103(INL)) (European Parliament, 16 February 2017) paras 136–137.
83 European Parliament JURI, Explanatory Statement (European Parliament 2017).
84 European Parliament, Resolution on a comprehensive European industrial policy on artificial intelligence and robotics, (2018/2088 (INI)) (12 February 2019).

Introduction 17

On 20 October 2020, the European Parliament adopted another resolution on 'Intellectual Property Rights for the Development of Artificial Intelligence Technologies.'[85] Regarding AI-generated subject matter, the European Parliament:

> Takes the view that technical creations generated by AI technology must be protected under the IPR legal framework in order to encourage investment in this form of creation and improve legal certainty for citizens, businesses and, since they are among the main users of AI technologies for the time being, inventors; considers that works autonomously produced by artificial agents and robots might not be eligible for copyright protection, in order to observe the principle of originality, which is linked to a natural person, and since the concept of 'intellectual creation' addresses the author's personality; calls on the Commission to support a horizontal, evidence-based and technologically neutral approach to common, uniform copyright provisions applicable to AI-generated works in the Union, if it is considered that such works could be eligible for copyright protection; recommends that ownership of rights, if any, should only be assigned to natural or legal persons that created the work lawfully and only if authorisation has been granted by the copyright holder if copyright-protected material is being used, unless copyright exceptions or limitations apply; stresses the importance of facilitating access to data and data sharing, open standards and open source technology, while encouraging investment and boosting innovation.

Eventually, the European Commission published a report entitled 'Trends and Developments in Artificial Intelligence – Challenges to the Intellectual Property Rights Framework.' It is stated in the report that AI-generated outputs must pass a four-step test to qualify as works that are protected under EU copyright law.[86] Explanations regarding this report will be made where appropriate (particularly in Chapters 3 and 4).

---

85 European Parliament resolution of 20 October 2020 on intellectual property rights for the development of artificial intelligence technologies (2020/2015(INI)), P9_TA-PROV(2020)0277.
86 European Commission, Directorate-General for Communications Networks, Content and Technology, C Hartmann, J Allan, P Hugenholtz *et al*, *Trends and Developments in Artificial Intelligence: Challenges to the Intellectual Property Rights Framework: Final Report* (Publications Office, 2020) 116–117 https://data.europa.eu/doi/10.2759/683128.

1 Artificial intelligence and fashion

1.1 First steps: searching for artificial lives

People have long been contemplating on artificial beings endowed with human-like intelligence.[1] In the *Iliad*, the Greek poet Homer wrote about chairs called 'tripods' that can go by themselves and the golden 'attendants' made by Hephaestus, the lame blacksmith god, to take him around.[2] According to the story, Hephaestus also constructed an autonomous weapons system called 'Talos' that patrolled the coasts of Crete and autonomous vehicles that could go to and from the home of the gods. The ancient Greek philosopher Aristotle in his book *Politics* also dreamed of automation in daily activities.[3] The English philosopher Thomas Hobbes, on the other hand, speaks of an 'artificial animal' in the introduction to his work *Leviathan*, in which he deals with the social contract and the ideal state.[4] Mary Shelley's novel *Frankenstein*, published in 1818, was about a scientist who devoted his life to forming an artificial life. The monster created by the scientist tragically tortures and takes the life of the person who gave him a body (the scientist himself). Stories of artificial life forms have pervaded countless histories and cultures.

The entire history of AI does not consist only of myth or fiction. The word *computer* was originally used for people making manual math calculations. Human computers played a vital role in navigation, science and engineering. However, they were slow and prone to making mistakes.[5] At the beginning of the 19th century, the British scientist Charles Babbage wanted to automate this process. Deciding to build a mechanical computer, Babbage began designing the automatic

---

1 Nils J Nilsson, *The Quest for Artificial Intelligence: A History of Ideas and Achievements* (CUP, 2010) 3.
2 *The Iliad of Homer*, translated by Richmond Lattimore (The University of Chicago Press, 1961) 386.
3 Aristotle, *The Politics*, translated by T A Sinclair (Penguin Books, 1981) 65.
4 Thomas Hobbes, *The Leviathan* (Kessinger Publishing, 2004).
5 Simson L Garfinkel and Rachel H Grunspan, *The Computer Book: From the Abacus to Artificial Intelligence, 250 Milestones in the History of Computer Science* (Sterling Publishing, 2018) 28–30 and 34–36.

DOI: 10.4324/9781003355922-2

calculator he called the 'difference engine.' The machine could create tables for values. Thus, it would be able to compile mathematical tables and simple price lists for traders. Although Babbage completed many designs, the machine itself had never been put into practice. Building the machine was quite difficult. It was contemplated to weigh 15 tons and contain 25,000 parts.[6] Although the construction of the first full-capacity computer, the 'Electronic Numerical Integrator and Calculator,' was completed in 1946, Babbage is sometimes referred as the 'the father of computing' today.[7]

While the difference machine may have been the first modern automatic calculator, its most important contribution was inspiring another invention: the 'analytical engine,' which may have been the first general-purpose computer. What distinguishes this machine from its predecessors was being capable of general-purpose operations and programmable with punch cards.[8] The British mathematician Ada Lovelace, one of Babbage's sponsors, wrote about computer programming in 1843.[9] Lady Lovelace, the daughter of the famous poet Lord Byron, had developed an algorithm that allowed this machine to produce sequences of Bernoulli numbers. Computers were a century away when Lady Lovelace wrote the algorithms. She also claimed that computers could display creativity by processing not only numbers but also symbols.[10] These ideas of Lovelace would earn her the title of the first computer programmer.

The adventure of humanity with robots started centuries ago as well. In 1206, the Muslim scientist Ibn al-Razzaz al-Jazari in his book *The Book of Knowledge of Ingenious Mechanical Devices* depicted a waiter robot that could serve drinks.[11] Leonardo Da Vinci similarly drew designs of humanoid robots in the form of a medieval knight around 1495.[12] Al-Jazari and Leonardo created their mechanical beings before the concept of the robot even emerged. The Czech playwright Karel Capek first used the word *robot*. Capek based the term *robot* on the Czech word for 'forced labour' in a play called *R.U.R.* (an acronym for Rossum's Universal Robots), which he penned in 1920.[13] The first general-purpose robot 'Shakey,' however, was produced in 1969.[14]

The idea of AI in the modern sense relies on the 'Turing test' put forward by the British mathematician Alan Turing.[15] Among the things that Alan Turing thought computers could do was imitating human intelligence. He proposed a test to

6 Ibid 42–44; Ryan Abbott, *The Reasonable Robot* (CUP, 2020) 19.
7 Abbott (n 6) 20.
8 Ibid.
9 Nilsson (n 1) 33.
10 Margaret A Boden, *Artificial Intelligence: A Very Short Introduction* (OUP, 2018) 6–7.
11 For Al Jazari's depiction of the robot see; Salim T S Al-Hassani, *1001 Inventions: The Enduring Legacy of Muslim Civilization* (3rd edn, National Geographic, 2012) 7.
12 See https://en.wikipedia.org/wiki/Leonardo%27s_robot.
13 Abbott (n 6) 20.
14 Blagoj Delipetrev, Chrisa Tsinarakii and Uroš Kostić, *Historical Evolution of Artificial Intelligence*, EUR 30221EN (Publications Office of the European Union, 2020) 7.
15 Alan Turing, 'Computing Machinery and Intelligence' (1950) 59 *Mind* 433.

evaluate whether a machine could show intelligence or not. The Turing test relies on the 'imitation game.' The game was built on the assumption that a machine would be considered intelligent if it had the ability to behave and communicate like humans do.[16] In the game, an evaluator would have a typed conversation with a computer and a human, both hidden behind screens. The computer would pass the test if the evaluator could not distinguish which of the conversations was with a computer or which was with a human.[17]

However, it was John McCarthy and Marvin Lee Minsky who popularised the concept of AI. In 1956, the two scientists (who were leading researchers in this field) defined the concept in their grant application for a workshop entitled 'Artificial Intelligence Summer Research Project,' which they wished to organise at Dartmouth College in the USA. This was a turning point that transformed AI into an independent research discipline.[18]

The road to development of AI as a research discipline and a field of technology has not always been flat and smooth since the conference in 1956. With an upward trend in 1950s and 1960s, this optimistic atmosphere yielded its first results when Frank Rosenbalt invented 'perceptrons' inspired by a human brain. Perceptrons laid the foundation for neural networks and deep learning.[19] Later, a program called *MENACE* (Matchbox Educable Noughts and Crosses Engine) followed this, designed by Donald Michie. Launched in 1961 to play XOX (tic-tac-toe), *MENACE* was the first program that learned how to play a game.[20] In 1966, Joseph Weizenbaum created Eliza, a chat bot that came closest to passing the Turing test. Users were told that Eliza was a psychotherapist who communicated through words typed into a computer. In fact, Eliza was using a simple list-processing language. In response to user statements such as 'I'm depressed,' it asked, 'Why do you say that you are depressed?' etc.[21] Although some of its technical deficiencies pointed to the fact that Eliza was not intelligent, the program managed to make a lot of people believe that it was human.[22]

In the 1970s, the optimism faded, and unfulfilled commitments and expectations led to a decline in interest and investment in the field of AI.[23] This downward trend is called 'the first winter' of AI.

The 1980s witnessed a rebound owing to the development of expert systems. *Expert systems* refers to systems that solve problems using logical rules inferred from the knowledge of human experts. These systems have two features. First,

---

16 Ibid.
17 Andrew Burgess, *The Executive Guide to Artificial Intelligence* (1st edn, Palgrave Macmillan, 2018) 38–39.
18 Nilsson (n 1) 52–56.
19 Delipetrev, Tsinarakii and Kostić (n 14) 7.
20 Ibid 7.
21 Simon Chesterman, 'Artificial Intelligence and the Limits of Legal Personality' (2020) 69(4) *International and Comparative Law Quarterly* 820.
22 Nilsson (n 1) 62.
23 Delipetrev, Tsinarakii and Kostić (n 14) 8.

these systems have a knowledge base consisting of a compilation of cases, rules or relationships regarding a particular field. Second, these are machines that can make inferences by processing symbols.[24] However, in the 1990s, a pessimistic atmosphere loomed for the second time regarding the capacity of AI, and again investments were withdrawn. This period known as the 'second winter' of AI.[25] During these times, researchers called their work 'machine intelligence,' 'informatics' or 'knowledge-based systems' to avoid negative connotations.[26]

Today, a new spring has begun for AI. The deep learning technique has led to this new era. Deep learning has brought technologies that could justify Turing's argument that machines can think like humans do. However, for some scholars, having intelligence requires the ability to understand. Unlike Turing's thesis, supporters of this view suggest that machines cannot be intelligent because they do not have the ability to comprehend what they are doing. Acting without understanding is just a simulation of intelligence.

An advocate of this argument, the American philosopher John Searle distinguishes between acting and understanding in terms of strong (understanding) and weak (unconscious) AI. He explains this through his thought experiment called 'Chinese room.' Imagine a person who cannot speak any Chinese standing in a room. A native Chinese speaker utters some Chinese phrases to this person through a window in the wall. The person in the room does not know the meaning of the words at all; however, he has a book that contains meanings of any combinations of Chinese phrases and answers that can be given to certain questions. The person in the room looks at the book and writes the correct answers on a piece of paper corresponding to the phrases presented to him by imitating the Chinese letters identically. He passes this paper on to the native Chinese speaker who initially messaged him. Thus, the person gets the correct answer. Though functionally slow, the person in the room pretends to communicate like a native Chinese speaker. While this person does not understand the meaning of his correspondence, he can act as though he communicates.

This Chinese room experiment shows why Saerle describes machines that can do something requiring intelligence without understanding it as weak AI. For example, Google Translate can pass Turing's test, but it is a weak AI for Saerle.[27]

1.2 Defining AI

As an independent research field today, what does AI really mean? The definition of AI is still a controversial topic.[28] Defining AI means untangling its two linguistic components: 'artificial' and 'intelligence.' For almost everybody,

---

24 Ibid 9.
25 Ibid 10.
26 Abbott (n 6) 21. Also see Burgess (n 17) 11–13.
27 Abbott (n 6) 25–26.
28 Jani Ihalainen, 'Computer Creativity: Artificial Intelligence and Copyright' (2018) 13(9) *Journal of Intellectual Property Law & Practice* 724.

making sense of *artificial* is easier: things made not by nature, but by humans; i.e. unnatural things.

Defining *intelligence* poses some challenges. Shane Legg and Marcus Hutter probed into many prominent definitions of intelligence and proposed that the concept was mostly defined as the 'ability to achieve goals in a wide range of environments.'[29] Intelligence is generally associated with human beings, sometimes even regarded as their defining characteristic.[30]

Intellectual capacity of human beings has been also a matter of philosophical debate. The philosopher Aristotle, some thousand years ago, considered human intelligence as the ability to make rational decisions and contended that it distinguishes humans from animals. The French philosopher Rene Descartes argued that humans are guided by an immaterial, spiritual mind, while the rest of nature, including animals, is a series of unintelligent objects driven by the laws of physics. Machines, as Descartes argued, are incapable of expressing their thoughts like humans and engaging in meaningful conversations even as much as a dull person.[31]

The characterisation of intelligence as a spectrum grants a special status to the human intelligence. To date, human intelligence has no substitute in the biological and artificial worlds to make such evaluation. This renders human intelligence a natural choice for benchmarking. From this angle, intelligence can be defined, although not precisely, as the abilities to 'reason, achieve goals, use and process language, perceive and respond to sensory input, prove mathematical theorems, play challenging games, synthesize and summarize information, produce works of art and music and keep chronicles.'[32]

More than 60 years after the term was introduced, *AI* still has no universally accepted definition.[33] The lack of a precise, universally accepted definition of AI probably has helped the field to flourish. Still, a definition remains important, and Nils J Nilsson has given a useful one: 'Artificial intelligence is that activity devoted to making machines intelligent, and intelligence is that quality that enables an entity to function appropriately and with foresight in its environment.'[34]

---

29 Shane Legg and Marcus Hutter, 'Universal Intelligence: A Definition of Machine Intelligence' (2007) 17 *Minds and Machines* 444.
30 Abbott (n 6) 23.
31 René Descartes, 'Discourse on Method' in John Cottingham, Robert Stoothoff and Dugald Murdoch (trans), *The Philosophical Writings of Descartes Volume 1* (CUP, 1985) 140.
32 Nilsson (n 1) 13. See also; Peter Stone *et al*, 'Artificial Intelligence and Life in 2030' *One Hundred Year Study on Artificial Intelligence: Report of the 2015–2016 Study Panel* (Stanford University, 2016) 13, http://ai100.stanford.edu/2016-report.
33 Ryan Calo, 'Artificial Intelligence Policy: A Primer and Roadmap' (2017) 51 *University of California Law Review* 404. See also; WIPO, 'WIPO Technology Trends 2019: Artificial Intelligence' (2019) https://public.ebookcentral.proquest.com/choice/publicfullrecord.aspx?p=5982426. As a reference book in this field, see; Stuart J Russell and Peter Norvig, *Artificial Intelligence: A Modern Approach* (4th edn, Pearson, 2020).
34 Nilsson (n 1) 13.

Artificial intelligence and fashion 23

Nilsson's definition characterises AI from its two visible facades: ability of synthesised software and hardware for functioning 'appropriately' and with 'foresight.' By taking human intelligence as a reference, AI is described as 'computer-based systems which are developed to mimic human behaviour.'[35] AI can also be defined by what AI researchers do: AI is 'a discipline of computer science that is aimed at developing machines and systems that can carry out tasks considered to require human intelligence.'[36]

AI, also referred to as *synthesised intelligence*,[37] consists of algorithms to understand, model and replicate intelligence and cognitive processes.[38] A broader definition blends all these features of AI: AI is 'a cross-disciplinary approach to understanding, modelling, and replicating intelligence and cognitive processes by invoking various computational, mathematical, logical, mechanical, and even biological principles and devices.'[39]

In addition to these, there are numerous definitions of AI. The differences between these definitions are due to the development of technology over time. The diversity in definitions is caused by the different approaches and perspectives adopted to define AI in many research and policy areas as well.

AI can be defined by four different approaches:[40]

- Thinking humanly: the proximity to human thinking processes is measured.
- Thinking rationally: the process of thinking as per ideal rationality is measured.
- Acting humanly: adherence to human behaviour processes is measured.
- Acting rationally: the system is considered rational when it does what is right.

Since there is no universal definition of AI, it would be appropriate to rely on the official definitions provided by the EU institutions. One can begin with the definition the European Commission used in the statement 'Artificial Intelligence for Europe'[41] in 2018:

> Artificial intelligence (AI) refers to systems that display intelligent behaviour by analysing their environment and taking actions – with some degree

---

35 Josef Drexl *et al*, 'Technical Aspects of Artificial Intelligence: An Understanding from an Intellectual Property Law Perspective' Max Planck Institute for Innovation & Competition Research Paper No. 19–13 (8 October 2019), available at SSRN: https://ssrn.com/abstract=3465577.
36 WIPO, 'Revised Issues Paper on Intellectual Property Policy and Artificial Intelligence' (*WIPO*, 21 May 2020) 3, www.wipo.int/meetings/en/doc_details.jsp?doc_id=499504.
37 Stone *et al* (n 32) 12.
38 Keith Frankish and William M Ramsey, *The Cambridge Handbook of Artificial Intelligence* (CUP, 2014) 1.
39 Ibid 1.
40 Russell and Norvig (n 33) 1–2.
41 Communication from the Commission to the European Parliament, the European Council, the Council, the European Economic and Social Committee and the Committee of the Regions: Artificial Intelligence for Europe. Brussels, 25.4.2018, COM (2018) 237 final, 1, https://ec.europa.eu/transparency/regdoc/rep/1/2018/EN/COM-2018-237-F1-EN-MAIN-PART-1.PDF.

of autonomy – to achieve specific goals. AI-based systems can be purely software-based, acting in the virtual world (voice assistants, image analysis software, search engines, speech and face recognition systems) or AI can be embedded in hardware devices (advanced robots, autonomous cars, drones or Internet of Things applications).

The Artificial Intelligence High Level Expert Group[42] (AI-HLEG), established after the statement in 2018, recommended an update to the Commission's definition as follows:[43]

> Artificial intelligence (AI) refers to systems designed by humans that, given a complex goal, act in the physical or digital world by perceiving their environment, interpreting the collected structured or unstructured data, reasoning on the knowledge derived from this data and deciding the best action(s) to take (according to pre-defined parameters) to achieve the given goal. AI systems can also be designed to learn to adapt their behaviour by analysing how the environment is affected by their previous actions.
>
> As a scientific discipline, AI includes several approaches and techniques, such as machine learning (of which deep learning and reinforcement learning are specific examples), machine reasoning (which includes planning, scheduling, knowledge representation and reasoning, search, and optimization), and robotics (which includes control, perception, sensors and actuators, as well as the integration of all other techniques into cyber-physical systems).

The AI-HLEG points to two aspects of AI: *AI as a system* and *AI as a scientific discipline*.

An EC White Paper in Artificial Intelligence[44] issued in 2020 introduces a general definition of AI as 'a collection of technologies that combine data, algorithms and computing power.'[45] The White Paper highlights human intervention in AI systems as well:

> In case of machine learning techniques, which constitute a subset of AI, algorithms are trained to infer certain patterns based on dataset in order to achieve a certain goal and determine the actions needed. Algorithms can continue to learn when in use. While AI-based products can act autonomously by perceiving their environment and without following a pre-determined set of

---

42 'High-Level Expert Group on Artificial Intelligence' (*European Commission*, 27 September 2021) https://web.archive.org/web/20211002104453/https://digital-strategy.ec.europa.eu/en/policies/expertgroup-ai.
43 AI-HLEG, 'A Definition of AI: Main Capabilities and Disciplines' (2019) 6, https://ec.europa.eu/futurium/en/system/files/ged/ai_hleg_definition_of_ai_18_december_1.pdf.
44 European Commission, *White Paper on Artificial Intelligence – A European Approach to Excellence and Trust* COM (2020) 65 final (19 February 2020).
45 Ibid 2.

instructions, their behaviour is largely defined and constrained by its developers. Humans determine and programme the goals, which an AI system should optimise for.[46]

A final definition of AI can be found in Article 3 of the 'Proposal for a Regulation Laying Down Harmonised Rules on Artificial Intelligence (Artificial Intelligence Act) and Amending Certain Union Legislative Acts' (AI Act):

> 'Artificial intelligence system' (AI system) means software that is developed with one or more of the techniques and approaches listed in Annex I and can, for a given set of human-defined objectives, generate outputs such as content, predictions, recommendations, or decisions influencing the environments they interact with.[47]

Annex I of the AI Act then lists various techniques and approaches, including: (i) different types of machine learning (supervised, unsupervised and reinforcement) using a variety of different methods (e.g., deep learning); (ii) logic- and knowledge-based approaches; (iii) statistical approaches, Bayesian estimation, search and optimisation methods.

The following section will provide brief explanations on AI-related terminology. These explanations will guide the legal analysis of intellectual property protection on AI-generated subject matter.

1.3 Specific terms

1.3.1 Symbolic and statistical AI

AI as a system usually is composed of software. These systems can in some cases be embedded in or combined with hardware.[48] An AI system consists of inputs, operating logic (with a model or models) and outputs. AI systems in today's technology are goal-driven.[49] *Goal-driven* means that people identify the goal and determine techniques for the goal to be achieved. Various techniques have various levels of autonomy in determining the ways to achieve their goals.[50]

---

46 Ibid 16.
47 European Commission, Proposal for a Regulation of the European Parliament and the Council: Laying Down Harmonised Rules on Artificial Intelligence (Artificial Intelligence Act) and Amending Certain Union Legislative Acts (2021) https://eur-lex.europa.eu/legal-content/EN/TXT/HTML/?uri=CELEX:52021PC0206&from=EN.
48 See; OECD, *Artificial Intelligence in Society* (OECD, 2019), Chapter 1, www.oecd.org/publications/artificial-intelligence-in-society-eedfee77-en.htm.
49 European Commission, Directorate-General for Communications Networks, Content and Technology, C Hartmann, J Allan, P Hugenholtz *et al*, *Trends and Developments in Artificial Intelligence: Challenges to the Intellectual Property Rights Framework: Final Report* (Publications Office, 2020) 23, https://data.europa.eu/doi/10.2759/683128.
50 Hartmann, Allan, Hugenholtz *et al* (n 49) 23.

An AI system can be in different types or follow different approaches.[51] There are two widely accepted approaches: *symbolic* AI (expert systems) and *statistical or sub-symbolic* AI.[52]

Symbolic AI is generally known as 'old-fashioned AI.' It covers systems based on 'the organization of abstract symbols using logical rules' to 'build detailed and human-understandable decision structures to translate real-world complexity and help machines arrive at human-like decisions.'[53] Most of the techniques in the symbolic AI category are denoted as 'reasoning' techniques.[54] Searle's Chinese Room is an example of symbolic AI.

Statistical AI encompasses the techniques for drawing conclusions from a set of data patterns.[55] These techniques are also called 'learning.' Statistical AI includes machine learning, neural networks, deep learning, decision trees and many other learning techniques.[56] The advantage of these techniques over symbolic ones is that they can handle tasks that are particularly difficult to describe and interpret unstructured data more easily.[57]

1.3.2 Machine learning and deep learning

While the concepts of AI and machine learning can sometimes be used interchangeably, they differ. AI covers different sub-areas such as natural language processing, robotics, machine learning, expert systems, speech and voice recognition, intelligent automation, computer vision.[58] Machine learning is one type of the techniques under the heading of AI. Machine learning is an AI model built on programming a computer to be intelligent and maximising its performance over time by learning from data.[59] Machine learning algorithms are technologies that can produce solutions by learning from examples rather than explicitly saying how to solve a problem.

There are three types of machine learning: supervised, unsupervised and reinforcement learning. In *supervised learning*, 'learning' is the ability of an AI system to reproduce data patterns. Scientists use data or events learned through the laws of nature or expertise to train the system. Upon being 'fed,' a learning algorithm tries to find a hypothesis that makes correct predictions; a hypothesis is a number that assigns a default output value to each input value. Therefore, the method is

---

51 Ibid 24.
52 OECD (n 48) Chapter 1.
53 Calo (n 33) 404–405; Hartmann, Allan, Hugenholtz *et al* (n 49) 25.
54 Hartmann, Allan, Hugenholtz *et al* (n 49) 25.
55 OECD (n 48).
56 Hartmann, Allan, Hugenholtz *et al* (n 49) 25.
57 Ibid.
58 For information on subcategories of AI, see; Jerry Kaplan, *Artificial Intelligence: What Everyone Needs to Know* (OUP, 2016) 49–66; Sunila Gollapudi, *Learn Computer Vision Using OpenCV: With Deep Learning CNNs and RNNs* (Apress Media LLC, 2019) 7–29.
59 For more information on machine learning, see; Ethem Alpaydın, *Machine Learning: The New AI* (The MIT Press, 2016).

based on learning the pre-determined outputs; the results that can be obtained through the learning process is unknown. Results of the learning process can be compared to known and correct results, which means they can be supervised.[60]

Unsupervised learning is the machine learning performed with an unlabelled dataset (learning object). The learning machine tries to perceive the patterns within the input data. Here, the artificial neural network guides it based on the similarities among the data input values and adapts the learning-focused evaluation accordingly.[61]

Reinforcement learning is a type of machine learning method in which a machine learns independently and on a reward. Here, the machine is not shown which action is the best in which situation, but rather the machine is rewarded at certain points. This can also be a negative reward. By using these rewards, the machine acts on the axis of a benefit function that defines the value of a situation or an action.[62] The machine determines whether it has reached the right learning through the reward mechanism.

To sum up, there are basically three methods of machine learning. In the first method, feedback is provided to the machine as correct and incorrect. This is called supervised learning. In the second method, the machine itself is expected to find the correct result or pattern. This is called unsupervised learning. In the third method, the machine is rewarded or punished for right or wrong moves. This is called reinforcement learning.

Machine learning is currently the most used subset or branch of AI. Most of the AI-assisted subject matter stems from machine learning systems or a subset of machine learning such as neural networks, deep neural networks and deep learning techniques.[63]

Deep learning is a machine learning technique relying on using artificial neural networks. Artificial neural networks are algorithm models inspired by biological neural networks in the human brain and the hardware they are embodied in.[64] There networks artificially imitate nerve cells in the human brain, though very basically. They also 'modify their own code to find and optimise links between inputs and outputs.'[65]

Thus, machine learning is a subset of AI, and deep learning is a subset of machine learning.

Deep learning does not generate the functional form of the solutions. Instead, it proceeds from the input towards the output, and it learns through many training examples in this process. It has a structure flexible enough to realise this. More recently, deep learning has enabled human-level performance such as in gaming

---

60 https://machinelearningmastery.com/supervised-and-unsupervised-machine-learning-algorithms/.
61 Hartmann, Allan, Hugenholtz *et al* (n 49) 26.
62 Ibid.
63 Ibid.
64 For more information on deep learning, see; Terrence J Sejnowski, *The Deep Learning Revolution* (The MIT Press, 2018).
65 OECD (n 48) Chapter 1.

and computer vision. Deep learning owes its success to the availability of large amounts of data and the existence of computers with high performance.

1.4 Types of AI

There are two most common ways of categorising of AI systems. The first category includes reactive AI, limited memory AI, theory of mind AI and self-aware AI.[66]

Reactive AI systems do not have memory. This type of AI specialises in only one area. It does not have the ability to have social interaction like humans; however, in these systems, the current context is directly perceived as it is and acted upon.[67] IBM's chess-playing AI named *Deep Blue* and Google's GO-playing AI *AlphaGo* belong to this category.

Limited memory AI has a limited memory to make decisions. These machines investigate the past, use it as a pre-programmed representation of the world and then apply it to the current data set.[68] Self-driving vehicles, Amazon's personal digital assistant *Alexa* and Apple's chatbot *Siri* are examples of this kind of AI.

Theory of mind AI machines are intelligent machines that use advanced technologies to understand thoughts and emotions influencing human behaviour.[69] They can learn actively. There is no real-life example, but the robot called *R2-D2* in *Star Wars* represents this kind of AI.

Self-aware AI machines are an extension of theory of mind AI. They include machines that are aware of their existence and their environment. AI systems of this type are a sophisticated form of theory of mind AI, and they have intuition and consciousness. They know their inner world, make predictions on the emotions of people surrounding them, make abstractions and deductions.[70] No prototypes have been developed in this category yet; but it is expected future machines will be like these ones. *Ava*, one of the protagonists in the film *Ex-Machina*, is an example of this category.

The alternate system of classification of AI includes three types: artificial narrow intelligence, artificial general intelligence and artificial super intelligence.[71]

Artificial narrow intelligence (ANI) is a model with a narrow range of abilities and can solve a problem against a given request and performing operations that are planned, based on certain rules. It is also known as weak AI. *Siri* and the robot called *Pillo* (which can diagnose diseases and prescribe drugs) are examples of this type. *Artificial general intelligence* (AGI) literally imitates the human brain. This model refers to a technology that is capable of thinking like humans do. It is

---

66 Gollapudi (n 58) 4.
67 Ibid.
68 Ibid 4–5.
69 Ibid 5.
70 Ibid.
71 Ibid 6.

also known as strong AI. *Artificial super intelligence* (ASI) is the model that can perform tasks beyond what humans are capable of.[72]

Most of the current machines are ANI technologies. AGI and ASI are still being developed.[73] Although still debated, a survey revealed that experts think AGI can be developed within the next 25 years.[74] Ray Kurzweil, one of Google's Directors of Engineering, has a more optimistic prediction: computers will catch human levels of intelligence in about a decade.[75]

1.5 AI in fashion industry

AI technologies create tremendous opportunities in the fashion industry. Researchers and the industry have explored many possibilities of AI in assisting the work of fashion designers.[76] AI can be applied to designing, manufacturing, supply chain management and retailing.[77] Most of the potential has not even been used yet. So far, most of the fashion industry has rather remained circumspect in adapting the latest technology that could benefit the design and sale of garments. The main reason for the slow integration of AI in the fashion industry is the concern that digital technologies would replace craft techniques.[78]

Although not widespread yet, AI has been integrated into almost every segment of the fashion value chain, from product discovery to robotic manufacturing.[79] It is mostly used in retail or designing processes of fashion. The following section only focuses on uses of AI in fashion designing. The possibilities are almost limitless. This makes it difficult to draw a complete list of all the possible ways in which AI can be used in fashion design. However, as Heidi Härkönen describes, it is possible to identify three categories. First, AI can provide guidance to fashion companies on predicting trends to create garments that are popular. Second, AI

---

72 Ibid.
73 Ibid.
74 Vincent C Müller and Nick Bostrom, 'Future Progress in Artificial Intelligence: A Survey of Expert Opinion' in Vincent C Müller (ed), *Fundamental Issues of Artificial Intelligence* (Springer International Publishing, 2016) 555.
75 Peter Rejcek, 'Singularity Hub' (31 March 2017) https://singularityhub.com/2017/03/31/can-futurists-predict-the-year-of-the-singularity.
76 Natalia Särmäkari and Annamari Vänskä, ' "Just Hit a Button!" – Fashion 4.0 Designers as Cyborgs, Experimenting and Designing with Generative Algorithms' (2021) *International Journal of Fashion Design, Technology and Education* 2.
77 Ibid 2; Leanne Luce, *Artificial Intelligence for Fashion* (Apress Media LLC, 2019); Tomruk Üstünkaya, 'Artificial Intelligence: Friend or Foe to Fashion in Consideration of the Functionality Doctrine?' (2020) 42(1) *European Intellectual Property Review* 13–14, 18.
78 Sandy Black, 'Sustainability and Digitalization' in Adam Geczy and Vicki Karaminas (eds), *The End of Fashion* (Bloomsbury Visual Arts, 2019) 123 (noting that the fashion industry is a bit conservative and instead of replacing craft methodologies, digital technology could be integrated to improve designer's practice).
79 Leanne Luce, *Artificial Intelligence for Fashion: How AI is Revolutionizing the Fashion Industry* (Apress, 2018) xxv.

can assist human designers in styling and creating clothes. Third, AI can be an independent fashion designer.[80]

1.5.1 Trend forecasting

Among the famous quotations by Coco Chanel, one stands out: 'Fashion is made to become unfashionable.'[81] Coco Chanel refers to volatile and transient aspects of clothes, hats, shoes and accessories as 'fashion' expressions. AI-based trend forecasting as a novel approach may contribute to the cycle of creating unfashionable from fashionable (or vice versa).

AI-based trend forecasting is done to predict what kind of colours, silhouettes, materials and styles will be popular in the future.[82] Data mining is critical to AI-based trend forecasting. In copyright terms, the Digital Single Market Directive defines text and data mining as 'any automated analytical technique aimed at analysing text and data in digital form in order to generate information which includes but is not limited to patterns, trends and correlations.'[83]

Through data mining AI uncovers patterns from large amounts of data. Data mining generates building blocks for predictive analysis in trend forecasting. Social media platforms such as Instagram, Twitter and Pinterest can unleash how customers think about fashion products and trends.[84] For that reason, they are particularly important for data mining.[85] Data-mining-based trend forecasting is thus 'the step of discovering raw materials for a project.'[86]

AI can deal with significantly larger amounts of data than a human brain. Here emerges AI's benefit of trend forecasting. Fashion companies such as Burberry, Guess, H&M, Tommy Hilfiger, Zalando, Amazon and Levi's are already using AI to predict future trends.[87] It should be noted, however, that trend forecasting indirectly contributes to fashion designing. It can influence a human designer's work by steering it to more fashionable directions. AI in trend-forecasting is used for

---

80 Heidi Härkönen, 'Fashion Piracy and Artificial Intelligence – Does the New Creative Environment Come with New Copyright Issues?' (2020) 15(3) *Journal of Intellectual Property Law & Practice* 164–166.
81 *Life Magazine* (19 August 1957).
82 Luce (n 79) 141.
83 Directive 2019/790 of the European Parliament and of the Council of 17 April 2019 on copyright and related rights in the Digital Single Market and amending -Directives 96/9/EC and 2001/29/EC Art 2(2) (Digital Single Market Directive).
84 Among 10 million creators on Instagram with more than 1,000 followers, fashion is the most engaged topic. see; Aron Levin, *Influencer Marketing for Brands: What YouTube and Instagram Can Teach You About the Future of Digital Advertising* (Apress Media LLC, 2020) 34.
85 Luce (n 79) 144.
86 Ibid.
87 Emma Thomasson and Anna Ringstrom, 'Back on-Trend? H&M Makes AI, Loyalty Drive to Ride Fashion Cycle' (*Reuters*, 17 April 2019) www.reuters.com/article/us-h-m-strategy-ai/back-on-trend-hm-makes-ai-loyalty-drive-to-ride-fashion-cycle-idUSKCN1RT1U7; Nitish Varshney, 'Here's How AI and Data Analytics Changing the Apparel Retail Game' (5 February 2019) https://apparelresources.com/technology-news/retail-tech/heres-how-ai-and-data-analytics-changing-the-apparel-retail-game/.

Artificial intelligence and fashion 31

directing the style of designing. It can in other words portray consumers' attitudes toward what they find alluring.

1.5.2 AI as designer assistant

AI provides further helpful tools for fashion designers in their creative work. It acts as a design assistant in different ways. It can for example be used to customise a garment by relying on a consumer's choices. Imagine that by analysing the consumer's online browsing and purchase history, AI can discover that a particular consumer likes to buy red dresses. This consumer then comes across a dress that is offered in white, blue and purple. In this case, AI can customise the design and display it in red as well. It does so because it can predict that this consumer would find it tempting. The process here is more about submitting a variation of already existing creative works to the consumer's attention and making the garment at issue more appealing to them.[88]

The Japanese designer Yuima Nakazato is another designer bringing AI to the front lines in customisation. Nakazato uses 3D technology and personalised machines to make his designs. He first takes the client's measurements using a 3D scanner. Then the measurement data is transferred to a machine. This machine directly cuts the different parts of the fabric to produce the full garment. In this way, no material is wasted, and the customer receives exactly what they desire in the perfect size. He has even showcased his bio-couture collection at Haute Couture Fashion Week in Paris. This way of designing can bring major changes, particularly for sustainable fashion.[89]

In another intersection between fashion and AI, the fashion designer Kazuya Kawasaki, the designer Kotaro Sano and the machine learning engineer Yusuke Fujihira came together in collaboration called Synflux. Together, they set up the project entitled *Algorithmic Couture*. Using machine learning, Synflux generated optimised modular fashion patterns that were then modelled using computer-aided design software. Synflux also allowed the customisation of form, colour and material. The goal of this approach is to produce patterns that are zero waste as well as comfortable.[90]

AI can also help a designer turn sketches into colour images. This is called image-to-image translation. It uses conditional generative adversarial networks (cGANs).[91] It converts a simple black-and-white drawing into a colour image.[92]

---

88 Härkönen (n 80) 165–166.
89 Mélanie Mollard, 'Bridging the Gap between Artificial Intelligence and Creativity in Fashion' (*Heuritech*, 2 June 2020) www.heuritech.com/articles/fashion-solutions/artificial-intelligence-fashion-creativity/.
90 Ibid.
91 These networks are conditional because instead of starting the generator network (G) from nothing, they are conditioned by using an actual image. The discriminator network (D) is not fed by high numbers of images. Rather, pairs of images, such as a black- and- white image of an object and the same object in colour, is used. Then, a new black- and- white object is put into the generator network. Initially D rejects the new object, so G colours it.
92 For example, the pix2pix software is used to generate designs of handbags and shoes. See; Phillip Isola *et al*, 'Image-to-Image Translation with Conditional Adversarial Networks' in *Proceedings*

This technique turns drawings of garments or accessories to more real-life versions before they are manufactured. It enables a designer to rely on a lot less hand engineering. Designing in this way becomes more accessible to a wider audience.[93] Image-to-image translation is a designer assistant. These AI solutions provide helpful tools for fashion designers in their creative work.

AI can create several design elements as well. The collaboration of Tommy Hilfiger, International Business Machines Corporation (IBM) and New York's Fashion Institute of Technology (FIT) on the project called 'Reimagine Retail' in 2018 is one example. In this project, fashion students created designs for the Tommy Hilfiger brand using IBM's AI tools.[94] These tools were programmed with a library of 15,000 designs from past Tommy Hilfiger collections. The AI designed fabric patterns, colours and silhouettes, which were used by the students in creating their final clothing design. AI acted as a smart design assistant. However, the students still were responsible for conducting colour trend analysis, looking out for social media trends and monitoring product supply.[95]

Heidi Härkönen thinks that the AI-based customisation and image-to-image translation can hardly yield a creative work in the copyright sense. For her, these techniques are not actual designing: and therefore, it is highly unlikely for these techniques to generate original works and obtain copyright protection.[96] It is true that customisation would not be enough to create original works in copyright law. However, image-to-image translation can, in appropriate circumstances, be so if the final design meets the requirements of both design (appearance of a product, novelty and individual character) and copyright (originality and being expressed) protection. Besides, different colourings can in some circumstances give individual character to fashion designs. The proper drafting of representation of a fashion in terms of its colouring can give rise to registration under design law.[97]

1.5.3 AI as a designer

In 2019, the 'AI fashion designer' DeepVogue, created in China by DeepBlue Technology, won a prize at an international fashion competition in Shanghai.[98] The non-human AI designer was applauded as a proper fashion designer. This

---

  of the IEEE Conference on Computer Vision and Pattern Recognition (2017) 1125–1134, https://ieeexplore.ieee.org/document/8100115.
93 Luce (n 79) 129.
94 Jeffrey Greene and Anne Marie Longobucco, 'Is Artificial Intelligence the Newest Trend in Fashion?' (25 August 2018) www.onlyinfotech.com/2018/08/25/is-artificial-intelligence-the-newest-trend-in-fashion-artificial-intelligence/. For project website see; https://dtech.fitnyc.edu/webflow/projects/ibm-tommy-hilfiger.html#2.
95 Greene and Longobucco (n 94).
96 Härkönen (n 80) 166.
97 See Chapter 2.
98 Mayura Jain, 'An AI 'Designer' Just Won Runner-Up in A Major Fashion Design Competition' (22 April 2019) https://radiichina.com/an-ai-designer-just-won-runner-up-in-a-major-fashion-design-competition.

shows that AI can be incorporated into the designing process as well, and AI, perhaps with the help of a human designer, can design. Robbie Barrat is an artist who is pioneering the future of AI fashion.[99] In 2018, Barrat created an entire new collection with AI based on past collections of the luxury brand Balenciaga. Barrat trained the AI (pix2pix neural net) with Balenciaga's lookbooks, advertisements, runway shows and its online catalogue spanning the previous two months. AI generated designs on limbless models. These designs lacked human perception. However, Barrat embraced the inspiration provided by the program and the unique quality of the asymmetrical items of clothing it produced.[100]

In 2017, Amazon announced that it trained 'generative adversarial networks' (GANs) to design garments.[101] Designing by GANs is 'a process of taking a dataset of images, and outputting images that are visually similar but generated by the model.'[102] The images forming the input data set could be images of garments trending on social media. The images in open-access fashion photography websites, such as Deepfashion, can also be used for training. Again, data mining might be a key process to select images to train AI. This type of use of real-time data and GANs for fashion design can enable a fashion company to single out the demand and fashion trends for garments before producing them.[103]

Pınar Yanardağ and Emily Salvador are two computer scientists exploring creative applications of deep learning in art and fashion. One day, they were inspired by the 1920s little black dress concept. They wondered how AI could reimagine this essential item for any woman's wardrobe. Then they began to train GANs on thousands of dress designs. The AI algorithm learned how to generate new designs that do not exist in the dataset. They picked one of the designs AI generated. The final design was surprising: it was a little black dress featuring a normal sleeve accompanied by a bell sleeve and asymmetric details.[104]

As the experiment of the little black dress illustrates, AI can have the capacity to learn styles from large data sets of content. By using this content, it can imitate style of human designers.[105] Deep-learning-based AI is not limited to imitating the styles of already existing fashion designers. It can also be used to mix and combine multiple sources from a variety of styles and generate rather original productions.[106] In this sense, the collaboration Synflux is a successful example

---

99 Katharine Schwab, 'This AI Designs Balenciaga Better than Balenciaga' (*FASTCO*, 22 August 2018) www.fastcompany.com/90223486/this-ai-designs-balenciaga-better-than-balenciaga.
100 Ibid.
101 Will Knight, 'Amazon Has Developed an AI Fashion Designer' (*MIT Technology Review*, 24 August 2017) www.technologyreview.com/2017/08/24/149518/amazon-has-developed-an-ai-fashion-designer/.
102 Luce (n 79) 125.
103 Ibid 125–126.
104 For the little black dress, see; https://lbd-ai.com/.
105 Andreas Guadamuz, 'Artificial Intelligence and Copyright' (*WIPO Magazine*, May 2017) 19.
106 Jean-Marc Deltorn and Franck Macrez, 'Authorship in the Age of Machine Learning and Artificial Intelligence' in Sean M. O'Connor (ed), *The Oxford Handbook of Music Law and Policy* (OUP, 2020).

of combining nature and fashion. It trained GANs with the numerous images of animals existing in cyberspace. The 'imaginary animal patterns' generated by the AI were used on clothes as visual designs.[107]

AI can also design fashion interactively. A notable example of fashion designing in an interactive dialogue between consumers and AI is American fashion brand Marchesa. In 2016, Marchesa and IBM Watson co-created a 'thinking dress.' The dress was exhibited in the annual Met Gala. The AI program IBM Watson scanned vast volumes of fan social data to enable the dress to change colour in response to fan tweets and to showcase them in real time. The dress understood and responded to its fans by changing its colour.[108]

Consumer-driven AI fashion design can also be seen in Project Muze. In this project, Google partnered with Germany-based fashion platform Zalando in 2016. Google's Fashion Trends Report as well as design and trend data sourced by Zalando (50,000 data sets based on the style preferences of more than 600 fashionistas) were used to train a neural network to understand colours, textures, style preferences and other aesthetic parameters. From there, Project Muze used this AI to create designs based on users' interests.[109]

Stitch Fix further exemplifies human and AI interaction in fashion design. This time, the interaction is between human designer (not consumer) and AI. Stitch Fix is an online personal styling service that uses AI algorithms and human stylists working in combination to make recommendations to clients of items of clothing, shoes or accessories. It employs algorithms to design its clothes. Yet, the company also includes human designers in the process. The two sources of intelligence are combined to provide clients personalised clothes choices that are a close fit to their style, size and price preferences.[110]

Metaverse has been the buzzword of recent times. It does not only offer limitless possibilities for virtually creating everything from scratch but also new perspectives and spaces for fashion. The Amsterdam-based 'digital-only' fashion house The Fabricant perhaps is one of the pioneering companies discovering the magical influence of this 'brave new world.' The Fabricant designs digital couture for virtual worlds, avatars and on-screen bodies. Digital fashion is a new field of fashion design. It relies on designer-specific 3D software. Hyper-realistic digital 3D garment simulations or digital models for physical products are fruits of

---

107 For the project 'Xenon' which these designs were produced see Synflux's website: www.synflux.io/projects/xenon.
108 IBM, 'Marchesa and Watson Worked Together to Create a Dress That Thinks' (2 May 2016) www.ibm.com/watson/stories/ca-en/dress.html.
109 Zalando's Project Muze: Fashion Inspired by You, Designed by Code, www.thinkwithgoogle.com/intl/en-cee/consumer-insights/consumer-trends/zalandos-project-muze-fashion-inspired-you-designed-code/.
110 Dave Gershgorn, 'Stitch Fix Is Letting Algorithms Help Design New Clothes – and They're Allegedly Flying off of the Digital Racks' (*QUARTZ*, 16 July 2017); Tom Davenport, 'The Future of Work Now: AI-Assisted Clothing Stylists at Stitch Fix' (*Forbes*, 12 March 2021) www.forbes.com/sites/tomdavenport/2021/03/12/the-future-of-work-now-ai-assisted-clothing-stylists-at-stitch-fix/?sh=50e71bd63590.

this new understanding of fashion designing. Digital fashion brings an alternative fashion culture and challenges the conventional norms of fashion. The Fabricant produces 'thought couture,' which is 'no longer tied to physical space,' and their audience are 'digi-sapiens.'[111] In 2016, Amber Jae Slooten – fashion designer, creative director and co-founder of the company – decided to experiment with AI. With a software developer, she used a dataset of thousands of Paris Fashion Week pictures as input for a GAN model that generated images. This AI created styles, shapes and colour options that could be translated into designs by human designers. The Deep Collection was eventually exhibited in 2018.[112]

1.6 Capabilities of AI

On 5 April 2016, four centuries after the death of Dutch painter Rembrandt van Rijn, a new Rembrandt was born: 'Next Rembrandt.'[113] *Next Rembrandt* is the name of an AI-generated portrait. The portrait is the result of a project aiming at the production of new works of art by the computer. In this project, data scientists, engineers and art historians collaborated in association with Microsoft. The project team examined Rembrandt's painting technique, style, objects and persons he used on approximately 350 works. Subsequently, they used GANs to copy existing works and create completely new and innovative works of art as well. Technical and aesthetic elements such as lighting, colouring, brush strokes and geometric shapes in Rembrandt's works were identified and digitised in the project. GANs were trained by exposure to such data digitally. Later, the program was instructed to generate a portrait of a 30/40-year-old white male looking to the right, wearing black clothes and a hat with a white collar and beard. The painting generated by the program did not resemble the people in Rembrandt's portraits. The program generated a brand-new face that was unknown to the project team but was bearing the artistic style of Rembrandt.[114]

Although the AI systems AARON,[115] developed by Harold Cohen in the 1970s, and The Painting Fool[116] by Simon Colton were the pioneers in this field, the portrait *Next Rembrandt*, printed by a special 3D printer, has the features of a real painting. The portrait sparked mixed reactions from critics, both positive and negative.[117] What are the limits of the technological capacity of these systems?

---

111 Särmäkari and Vänskä (n 76) 5–6.
112 Ibid 6. For the designs see; www.thefabricant.com/deep.
113 ING Bank, the J. Walter Thompson Agency, Microsoft, TU Delft University, Mauritshuis ve Rembrandthuis museums jointly conducted the project. Steve Schlackman, 'The Next Rembrandt: Who Holds the Copyright in Computer Generated Art' (22 April 2016) *Art Law Journal*, http://artlawjournal.com/thenext-rembrandt-who-holds-the-copyright-in-computer-generated-art.
114 www.nextrembrandt.com/.
115 Harold Cohen, 'Parallel to Perception, Computer Studies in The Humanities and Verbal Behavior' IV-3/4 (1973) Reprinted in 'Aspects: The Computer in the Visual Arts' (1981).
116 For information on this AI, see; www.thepaintingfool.com/.
117 For a review of the portrait as fan-fiction by Rembrandt fans, see; Peter Schjeldahl, 'A Few Words About the Faux Rembrandt' (*The New Yorker*, 8 April 2016) www.newyorker.com/culture/

Natalia Särmäkari and Annamari Vänskä explain that 'the umbrella term *algorithmic fashion design* was used for a design approach that uses algorithms to process data and generate images, structures, digital models, and entire design processes in the context of fashion design.'[118] They suggest that 'this approach be defined as the 'cyborg designer,' a contemporary figure of the fashion designer 4.0 that is enmeshed with technologies and complex human networks.' For them 'algorithmic fashion design entails hominisation of computers and computerisation of humans.'[119]

Is just hitting a button enough to create fashion design? Andrew Burgess argues that the current AI technologies can perform the following limited tasks: the first task is 'capturing information.' This means that AI can extract useful information from large datasets.[120] The second task has to do with trying to figure out 'what is happening.'[121] AI can also do 'optimisation' and 'prediction.' *Optimisation* means identifying patterns/models. *Prediction* refers to the ability to calculate what will happen at the next stage.[122] But the AI technologies known today simply lack an important human attribute: 'cognition.' This means that AI technologies are not capable of understanding 'why a certain thing is occurring.' That is to say, the human ability to understand does not exist in AI.[123] This raises questions as to AI's ability to create, a question that will be revisited in the following sections.[124]

1.7 Conclusion

AI systems have achieved numerous goals that seemed impossible a generation ago. The inclusion of AI in our lives with its ever-expanding capacity is the result of tremendous human effort. AI has also assumed several tasks performed by humans. Given its current trajectory, it appears to have an infinite reach. Along with these broad horizons, AI systems are currently used in the creation of a plethora of subject matter.

Has AI fundamentally changed fashion designing? AI in fashion designing is a topic that is currently being explored by designers and the research community. The field has gone from inconceivable to quite possible at a dizzying speed. Still, generative AI models are not quite ready for commercial use.[125] For that reason, Leanne Luce describes the promise of an 'AI fashion designer' as hype rather than

---

culture-desk/a-few-words-about-the-faux-rembrandt. James Grimmelmann states that *Next Rembrandt*, generated using GANs, is nothing but a *mash-up*. See; James Grimmelmann, 'There's No Such Thing as a Computer-Authored Work – And It's a Good Thing, Too' (2016) 39 *Columbia Journal of Law & Arts* 403.

118 Särmäkari and Vänskä (n 76) 8 (Emphasis original).
119 Särmäkari and Vänskä (n 76) 8.
120 Burgess (n 17).
121 Ibid 31.
122 Ibid 31.
123 Ibid 31.
124 See Chapter 5.
125 Luce (n 79) 131.

anything production ready.¹²⁶ Yet, as the aforementioned examples illustrate, they have at least some potential in designing.

At its current stage of development, AI is used more as a stylist assistant for designers rather than an independent designer. This does not, however, necessarily mean that AI has no role in creating fashion designs: it can make many of the decisions involved in the creative process with minimal human intervention. In GANs, the images and designs are produced, at least in part, by a process not under the direct control of the human artist or designer. Following the classification of computer art given by Margaret Boden, designs thus created can be called 'generative designs.'¹²⁷ As Susana Navas puts it, a generative design 'features randomness in its composition, evolution and constant change in a complex or even chaotic environment created exclusively by the software.'¹²⁸ In some other AI models, the program is designed to interact with the consumers and, in particular, to take external human choices into account. The result in these models is 'interactive designs.'¹²⁹

It must be noted, however, that the current AI technologies that are used in the fashion industry have limited capacity of intelligence. They still do what their operators instruct them to do, though with remarkable speed and accuracy. After all, they can only imitate creative works that they are trained to perform.¹³⁰ As Dave Gershgorn explains, although 'software might be able to make a mathematically perfect piece of clothing, . . . it still can't evaluate the cultural context that makes said piece fit (or not fit) into this season's fashion zeitgeist.'¹³¹ Nevertheless, using generative models in fashion designing might be a sensible strategy for fashion companies, because employing human fashion experts, stylists and fashion designers is costly.¹³²

So, who will own rights over AI-generated designs under EU design and copyright law? Who will be liable when AI-generated designs give rise to the infringement of design rights and copyright? The following two chapters will deal with these questions.

---

126 Ibid 137.
127 Margaret Boden, 'Computer Models of Creativity' (2009) 30(3) *AI Magazine* 23–34, 31. For a more expansive taxonomy of generative art see; Margaret Boden and E A Edmond, 'What Is Generative Art?' (2009) 20(12) *Digital Creativity* 21–46. For Philip Galanter: 'Generative art refers to any art practice where the artist cedes control to a system that operates with a degree of relative autonomy, and contributes to or results in a completed work of art.' See; Philip Galanter, 'Thoughts on Computational Creativity', Dagstuhl Seminar Proceedings 09291. Computational Creativity: An Interdisciplinary Approach https://drops.dagstuhl.de/opus/volltexte/2009/2193/pdf/09291.GalanterPhilip.Paper.2193.pdf.
128 Susana Navas, 'Creativity of Algorithms and Copyright Law' in Martin Ebers and Susana Navas (eds), *Algorithms and Law* (CUP, 2020) 226.
129 Boden (n 127) 23.
130 Luce (n 79) 127.
131 Gershgorn (n 110).
132 Härkönen (n 80) 167.

2 Artificial intelligence and EU design protection

2.1 Introduction

Fashions change. Fashion can change lives. In 1981, a designer with her partner bought bolts of cotton with a £100 loan. The couple's goal was making and selling white shirts. Their first customers were their friends. The enterprise worked well, and the white shirts became their early bestsellers. They opened their first fashion store two years later in Kent, United Kingdom (UK). The couple managed to turn their modest fashion enterprise into a successful company.

The following years brought new branches to the company across the UK. The fashion company continued to expand throughout the 1990s. By the time they sold out in 2004, the fashion brand became a chain of hundreds of stores with a global presence stretching from the UK to Europe, Asia and Australia. The designer who created an iconic fashion brand from piles of cotton was Karen Millen.[1]

The significance of Karen Millen does not lie in a fashion fairy tale. It transcends the designer's success story and narrates the reality of fashion. From selection of cotton to production of final wearable outfits, human beings stitch by stitch *design* fashion, because fashion is a cultural invention for human beings. Karen Millen is also a quintessential example to show how fashion designs are protected in the EU: in January 2007, the popular British brand Karen Millen sued Dunnes Stores based on an unregistered EU design rights on its clothing and began proceedings for injunctions and damages in the Irish High Court. Dunnes Stores appealed, and the Supreme Court referred two questions to the Court of Justice of the European Union (CJEU). The CJEU decision in *Karen Millen v. Dunnes Stores*.[2] considered the related questions and held once more that fashion designs can be protected as 'designs.'

---

1 Zoo Wood, 'How Karen Millen Lost the Battle for Her Name – and Her Fortune' (*Guardian*, 1 April 2017) www.theguardian.com/business/2017/apr/01/karen-millen-how-lost-battle-name-fortune; Alex Lawson, 'Karen Millen Hits out at "Greed" of Fast Fashion in Wake of Boohoo Scandal' (*Evening Standard*, 10 July 2020) www.standard.co.uk/business/karen-millen-slams-fast-fashion-boohoo-a4494756.html.
2 Case C-345/13 *Karen Millen Fashions Ltd v. Dunnes Stores and another* EU:C:2014:2013.

DOI: 10.4324/9781003355922-3

Design refers to the appearance of an article under EU law. It may consist of three-dimensional features, such as the shape of an article. It may represent two-dimensional features, such as patterns, lines or colour combinations. It can in this sense be any preliminary drawings or models used.

Design is applied to a wide variety of fields. Although it can sometimes be underacknowledged, it affects every aspect of our lives. It for instance covers product design, packaging design, web design, software design, graphic design, theatrical design, colour design, architectural design, automotive design, environmental design, furniture design, garden design, industrial design, interior design and urban design. As a widely used concept, it is one of the key factors that attracts consumers to a product or leads them to prefer using one product over another.

Designs are indeed at the heart of the European fashion industry. Fashion design emerges where function meets form. Covering both aesthetic and functional features, how can fashion designs be protected in EU law? Legal tools that are available for protection of fashion designs are multi-layered.[3] First and foremost, as the *Karen Millen* case illustrates, there is the specific legislation in the EU for protection of industrial designs. The Design Directive 71/1998/EC (Directive – DD)[4] and the Community Design Regulation (EC) No 6//2002 (Regulation – CDR)[5] governs the design regime. In this two-tiered system, the Directive harmonises the design protection in the EU. The overarching framework of a unitary Community right further complements the system. Like EU trademarks (EUTMs), Community designs (CDs) are unitary rights with equal effect throughout the EU. This means that they can be registered, transferred, surrendered or declared invalid with respect to the entire Union. The same applies to prohibition of use, unless the CDR itself stipulates otherwise.[6] Just like EUTMs, the European Union Intellectual Property Office (EUIPO) at Alicante administers design registrations at the EU level. However, the CDR provides for short-term Community-wide protection of unregistered rights (unregistered Community designs, UCDs).

Like EU trademark law, the functioning of the industrial design system has been subject to a comprehensive review. A series of economic[7] and legal[8]

---

3 For a practical book on these different protection regimes see; Rosie Burbidge, *European Fashion Law: A Practical Guide from Start-up to Global Success* (Edward Elgar, 2019).
4 Directive 98/71/EC of the European Parliament and of the Council on the legal protection of designs, [1998] OJ L 289/28.
5 Council Regulation 6/2002 on Community Designs; [2002] OJ L 3/1; consolidated version with subsequent amendments available at the EUIPO website, https://euipo.europa.eu/ohimportal/en/communitydesign-legal-texts (Regulation – CDR).
6 CDR Art 1(3).
7 The Economic Review of Industrial Design in Europe (January 2015) available at https://ec.europa.eu/docsroom/documents/10463/attachments/1/translations/en/renditions/native.
8 Legal review on industrial design protection in Europe (15 April 2016) available at https://op.europa.eu/en/publication-detail/-/publication/43fd4a5c-6c26-4639-ac9a-281ab57687de; The Intellectual property implications of the development of industrial 3D printing https://op.europa.eu/en/publication-detail/-/publication/e193a586-7f8c-11ea-aea8-01aa75ed71a1/language-en/format-PDF/source-124493516.

reports were delivered. These initiatives recently yielded some concrete Commission proposals in 2020 without any solution for AI-generated designs.[9]

While most fashion trends come and fade in the blink of an eye, some are timeless. UCD constitutes a great innovation for short-cycled products that need urgent protection from imitation for usually one or two seasons. For fashion items with a long lifespan, such as a Hermès classic Birkin or a Chanel suit, RCD regime offers much broader and longer protection.

Fashion designs can also attract protection under other fields of IP law, such as copyright, trademark or unfair competition law. Regarding copyright, the DD provides that such protection should be possible or even mandatory pursuant to Article 17: (a) design protected by a design right registered in or in respect of a Member State in accordance with this Directive shall also be eligible for protection under the law of copyright of that State as from the date on which the design was created or fixed in any form. Copyright protection of fashion designs will be explained in Chapter 3.

This chapter explores the legal framework of protection under EU design law when examining two questions: who will own design rights on an AI-generated fashion design? Who will be liable when an AI-generated fashion design infringes a third-party design? The relevant elements chosen for the analysis are the related design law concepts, including the design registration process; the definition of design; the requirements of novelty and individual character; the design authorship, invalidity, assignment and licences, duration and special protection of UCDs. Likewise, this chapter depicts three main circumstances in which using an AI system in fashion designing could potentially infringe design right while addressing the legality of these uses and liability regimes within the current scope of the protection under EU design law.

2.2 Registration process

2.2.1 Application

RCD is best for designs of classic fashion products or accessories that can have a longer market life. It is also a better option for fashion logos and patterns, as it gives a different line of protection for fashion designers.

RCD protection is acquired directly by application to the EUIPO or indirectly through the one of the national offices.[10] From 1 January 2008, applicants have

---

9 AI is mentioned only once; see: EU Commission, 'Evaluation of EU Legislation on Design Protection' (2020) 16, https://ec.europa.eu/info/law/better-regulation/have-your-say/initiatives/1846-Evaluation-of-EU-legislation-on-design-protection_en.

10 CDR Art 35(1). The application procedure is governed by the CDR and the Community Design Implementing Regulation (Commission Regulation (EC) No. 2245/2002 of 21 October 2002 implementing Council Regulation (EC) No. 6/2002 on Community designs [2002] *OJ L* 341/28 (17 December 2002) (CDIR). These are supplemented by EUIPO's *Guidelines for Examination of Registered Community Designs* (*Examination of Applications for Registered Community Designs* (1 March 2021). See also EUIPO, *Convergence on graphic representation of designs* (15 May 2018) ('Common Practice Guidelines') and Community Design (Fees) Regulations 2002

also been able to use the international registration system for industrial designs to obtain registration of a Community design.[11] This application procedure is established under the Hague Agreement and administered by WIPO.

The application must contain a request for registration, the name and address of the applicant (and their representative, if any), a representation of the design, an indication of the products in relation to which the design is intended to be used,[12] and payment of the registration fee. The application *may* also include a description, a request for deferment of publication, an indication as to classification and a citation of the designer.[13]

The application can be made in any of the official languages of the EU. It must, however, specify a second language from one of the five languages of the EUIPO.[14]

The most significant part of the application is the 'representation' of the design. The representation should consist of a 'graphic or photographic reproduction of the design in black and white or colour.'[15] The most common types of representation are drawings, photographs (except slides), computer-assisted graphic images or any other graphical representation, provided they are suitable for reproduction.[16] As the case of *PMS International Group* v *Magmatic* concerning the Trunki ride-on suitcase for children shows, the scope of protection of an RCD is determined by the representation of the design.[17] The CJEU has held that for obtaining a date of filing the application must contain a representation that clearly identifies the subject matter for which protection is claimed.[18]

Fashion designs can be registered in three distinct ways. These can be (i) a line drawing of the whole product and any unusual parts of the product such as a collar, sleeve or bag handle or clasp; (ii) a computer-aided drawing of the same item with shading to show depth, tone and colour contrasts; and (iii) a photograph of the actual product without branding.

The representation should cover only one design.[19] It may contain at least one view and a maximum of seven views of that design.[20] Especially when a fashion design is three-dimensional, it would be better to register each possible face by

---

(SI 2002/2942). Martin Schlotelburg, 'The Community Design: First Experience with Registrations' (2003) *EIPR* 383.

11 The Hague Agreement Concerning the International Deposit of Industrial Designs 1999 allows applicants to make a single application to WIPO for several countries.
12 CDR Art 36(2); CDIR Art 1(d). The indication of a product must clearly state the nature of the product and EUIPO requests applicants to use the 'Euro-Locarno List'. This takes Locarno's 32 classes and elaborates in the region of 4,000–5,000 products: CDIR Art 1(d).
13 CDR Art 36(3); CDIR Art 1(2).
14 Spanish, German, French, English, and Italian.
15 CDIR Art 4(1).
16 CDR Art 36(1); RCD Guidelines 3.3.1.
17 [2016] UKSC 12.
18 C-217/17 P, *Mast-Jägermeister v. EUIPO* ECLI:EU:C:2018:534 para 59.
19 Catherine Seville, *EU Intellectual Property Law and Policy* (2nd edn, Edward Elgar Publishing, 2016) 223; Lionel Bently, Brad Sherman, Dev Gangjee and Phillip Johnson, *Intellectual Property Law* (5th edn, OUP, 2018) 734. Also see; Case T-9/15 *Ball Beverage Packaging Europe v. EUIPO* EU:T:2017:386 (General Court, First Chamber).
20 CDIR Art 4(2). For further details see RCD Guidelines 5.1.

including up to seven views of a product in a design application. For registration of a repeating surface pattern, 'the representation of the design shall show the complete pattern and a sufficient portion of the repeating surface.'[21] Where registration is sought for a 'typographic typeface,' the representation must contain the complete alphabet, all the Arabic numerals and five lines of text.[22]

The representation may also contain a disclaimer. The EUIPO Design Guidelines offer a few techniques for demarcating the representation. These are 'broken lines,' 'colouring,' 'blurring' or 'boundaries.'[23] Broken lines indicate elements for which no protection is sought.[24] Where broken lines are a feature of the (fashion) design, such as stitching on clothing, the representation must clearly show this nuance.[25] In such circumstances, the use of a magnified view can be helpful. A design in black and white will protect against the use of the design in any colour.[26] Blurring is obscuring the features for which protection is not claimed.[27] Where a design is clearly shown within the boundary, all the features outside the boundary are disclaimed. When one wishes to register only the shape of the sole of shoes, for correctly applied boundaries the sole must be covered with broken lines.[28]

The application may also include a single description per design (not exceeding 100 words) explaining the representation of the design or specimen.[29] The description is used in two ways. It can explain aspects of the representation. It may also be used to disclaim features for which protection is not desired. However, it must not refer to the design's purported novelty, individual character or technical value.[30] For instance, the statement 'The novel part of the design is the pattern' is not suitable. Rather, the applicant should state that 'The design for which protection is sought is the pattern, the shape of the handbag being disclaimed.'[31]

---

21 CDIR Art 4(3); RCD Guidelines 5.3.8.
22 CDIR Art 4(4); RCD Guidelines 5.3.9.
23 RCD Guidelines 5.4.
24 Seville (n 19) 223; David Stone, 'Transparency Over Dotted Lines?' (2013) 8(6) *Journal of Intellectual Property Law & Practice* 437–440. On broken lines see cases: Case T-68/10 *Sphere Time v. Punch*; Case R 978/2010–3 *The Procter & Gamble Company v. SCA Hygiene Products AB* (Board of Appeal, 25 October 2011) para 19; and Case R 91/2010–3 *Svedbergs i Dalstorp v. Gofab Design*. The EUIPO does not recommend using of broken lines to indicate portions of the design which are not visible in that view. RCD Guidelines 5.4.1.
25 RCD Guidelines 5.4.1.
26 David Stone, *European Union Design Law: A Practitioners' Guide* (2nd edn, OUP, 2016) 51; Seville (n 19) 223. Also see; Case T-68/10 *Sphere Time v. OHIM – Punch SAS* ECLI:EU:T:2011:269 (General Court, 14 June 2011) para 82. If a design is coloured, the colours are regarded as claimed. See; Case R 965/2004–3 *Meterex Karl Kuntze (GmbH & Co)* (Board of Appeal, 31 March 2005); Case R 1583/2007–3 *DPD Dynamic Parcel Distribution GmbH & Co KG* (Board of Appeal, 12 November 2009).
27 RCD Guidelines 5.4.2.
28 RCD Guidelines 5.4.4.
29 CDIR Art 1(2)(a); CDR Art 36(3a).
30 CDIR Art 1(2)(a); RCD Guidelines 6.2.2.
31 For useful examples see; David Musker, *Community Design Law: Principles and Practice* (Sweet & Maxwell, 2002) 156–158.

A simple drawing is likely to offer a broader protection. If an image shows details such as the surface of the fabric or material of the design, this will narrow the scope of protection. Applications showing many views may also limit protection.[32]

It is possible to register multiple designs in a single application at the EUIPO. This is the case so long as these designs are all within the same class of the Locarno Convention.[33] This a standard classification system for designs and provides consistency in the description of designs worldwide.[34] In the case of ornamentation, designs do not need to be in the same class.[35] The most relevant classes for the fashion industry are class 2 (articles of clothing and haberdashery), class 3 (travel goods, cases, parasols and personal belongings, not elsewhere specified), class 5 (textile piece goods, artificial and natural sheet material), class 11 (articles of adornment – including jewellery) and class 32 (graphic symbols and logos, surface patterns, ornamentation).

In short, the EUIPO's practice of registering computer-aided designs indicates that it is also possible to register AI-generated fashion designs if the substantive requirements (section 2.3) are met with the question of who the owner of design right will be (which will be discussed in sections 2.5 and 2.6) remaining.

2.2.2 Priority

Priority may be claimed either together with the filing of the application or within one month after the date of filing. This can be made based on a previous (first) application of a design or utility model (but not based on a patent application) or certain exhibition of that design. To utilise priority, these previous applications must be filed in or for a state that is party to the Paris Convention or a member of the WTO. The exhibition of the design must also be a certain type. Priority can only be claimed where the application for a Community design is filed within six months from the date of filing of the first application or disclosure of such product.[36]

2.2.3 Secret designs and deferred publication

A design can be registered secretly. This is because publication can 'destroy or jeopardise the success of a commercial operation involving the design.'[37] The registration of secret designs can remain unpublished for 30 months.[38]

---

32 Schlotelburg (n 10) 383–387.
33 CDR Art 37(1); CDIR Art 2. This is known as the 'unity of class' requirement.
34 The Locarno Agreement Establishing an International Classification for Industrial Designs, 1968, is administered by WIPO. The Locarno classification system is now in its 13th edition, which entered into force on 1 January 2021.
35 CDIR Art 2(2).
36 CDR Arts 41–44; CDIR Art 8; RCD Guidelines 6.2.1.
37 CDR Recital 26; EC Green Paper 8.11.3.
38 CDR Art 50; CDIR Art 1(2)(b).

2.2.4 Grounds for refusal and examination

EUIPO essentially examines whether the application meets the formal requirements for filing.[39] The aim is to minimise the procedural burdens on applicants, to reduce the costs and render registration process more accessible.[40] The idea is that examination is difficult, expensive and inconclusive. Thus, the validity of a design can be best decided in *inter partes* disputes only over those designs with significant market value, where both parties will have a genuine interest. These disputes can for instance be a request for a declaration of invalidity or infringement proceedings.[41]

Normally, no substantive examination is made as to compliance with the requirements for protection, such as subject matter, novelty or individual character. However, EUIPO examines substantive grounds in two circumstances: first, whether the subject matter of the application satisfies the definition of a design; and second, whether the design is contrary to public policy or accepted principles of morality. In these cases, if the applicant fails to remedy the shortcoming upon notification, EUIPO shall refuse the application.[42] EUIPO cannot, however, refuse obviously old designs.[43]

2.2.5 Registration and publication

Once the application meets the formal requirements, EUIPO is obliged to register the design and publish it in the Community Design Bulletin.[44] Deferment of publication can be requested in the application and results in a delay before publication of up to 30 months.[45]

Registration is treated as being made as of the date of application, despite a typical processing period of a couple months.

Finally, if a design is very commercially sensitive, it is possible to delay publication of the design for up to 30 months.

2.3 Requirements for protection

To be protected as registered and unregistered community designs under EU law, a fashion design must meet the following criteria:

- There must be a 'design.'
- The design must be 'new.'

---

39 CDR Art 45; CDIR Arts 10–11. These requirements are provided by Article 36, Article 37 (for multiple applications), and Articles 41–44 (if a priority is claimed). See also; Case C-448/10 *Celaya Emparanza y Galdos Internacional SA v. Proyectos Integrales de Balizamientos SL* (2012) ECDR 17 (ECJ, First Chamber) para 43.
40 CDR Recital 18.
41 EC Green Paper 2.3.4, 4.3.10–4.3.11.
42 CDR Art 47; CDIR Art 11; RCD Guidelines 4.
43 Musker (n 31) 177.
44 CDR Arts 48, 49, and 73; CDIR Art 13.
45 CDR Art 50(1).

- The design must have 'individual character.'
- The applicant or right holder must be 'entitled to design.'
- The design must not conflict with 'earlier rights' (which include earlier design applications, trademark rights, copyright, rights relating to certain types of emblems).
- The design must not be among three types of 'excluded subject matter,' namely:
  - designs dictated solely by technical function,
  - designs for products that must be produced in a specific way to enable them to connect to another product,
  - designs that are contrary to morality.

2.3.1 Design

2.3.1.1 Appearance, features and product

Design is defined as 'the appearance of the whole or a part of a product resulting from the features of the lines, contours, colours, shape, texture and/or materials of the product itself and/or its ornamentation.'[46] This definition is highly broad and has three key elements; namely, 'appearance,' 'features' and 'product.'[47]

The definition of design first refers to the *appearance* of products. Since the focus is on the look of products, a design does not need to be appealing, decorative, ornamental or aesthetically pleasing. It is possible to protect functional designs, so long as the look of the product is significant.[48] The concept of appearance covers moving designs (such as symbols or lines moving across computer screens), microscopic designs (such as patterns in nanotechnology).[49] It is unlikely to register single colours. Complex colour patterns and combinations can be registered.[50] An ornamentation can be protected independently of the product to which it is attached. It has however been held that 'words written in black standard script' cannot be registered 'because they do not contain any features of appearance and therefore cannot be considered as ornamentation.'[51]

Design law is centred on the visual appearance of objects.[52] In order to be protected, a design must be in physical form. This means design rights do not protect

---

46 Designs Directive Art 1(a); CDR Art 3(a).
47 Bently *et al* (n 19) 742.
48 Designs Dir., Recital 14; CDR, Recital 10.
49 Bently *et al* (n 19) 742.
50 Stone (n 26) 51.
51 Case R 1266/2016–3 *Baw London v. EUIPO* (17 February 2017) para 10.
52 For arguments that 'appearance' is limited to the visual, see David Musker, *The Design Directive* (CIPA, 2001) 12.

ideas,[53] design concepts[54] or methods of use or operation.[55] The reference to 'texture' and 'materials' in Article 3(a) of the Regulation suggests that appearance includes tactile as well as visual designs.[56] For example, a conventional style of clothing might be protected when it is made of a new material with a distinct texture, as Lycra once was.[57] It must be noted that texture and feel will only be protected when they can be seen.[58] In this sense, sounds, smells and taste fall outside the definition of design because they do not relate to the appearance of products.[59] In a similar vein, it was held that because the layer of chocolate filling inside a cookie was only visible after it was broken open, 'this characteristic does not relate to the appearance of the product.'[60]

According to the definition of design used in the CDR and the Designs Directive, the appearance that is protected must derive from the *features* of a product.[61] This definition provides a non-exhaustive list of characteristics that can produce the appearance. The list includes lines, contours, shape, texture or materials. It refers to any aspect of appearance that could add economic value,[62] including aspects of conventional graphic design, industrial design, product and packaging design, and fashion design.[63] For an item of clothing, the protected features would include the shape of the collar, the proportions, pattern, embroidered features (such as buttonholes) and possibly also the colours.

The third notable feature of the definition of design focuses on the appearance of *products* or *parts of products*. Product is defined exhaustively and very broadly in Article 3(b) of the Regulation as 'any industrial or handicraft item, including inter alia parts intended to be assembled into a complex product, packaging, get ups, graphic symbols and typographical typefaces, but excluding computer programs.'[64] Clothes, fabric, furniture, electrical goods and motor vehicles are registrable products. The definition of product also includes packaging, get-up, graphic symbols and typefaces.

---

53 Case T-68/11 *Erich Kastenholz v. OHIM – Qwatchme A/S*, ECLI:EU:T:2013:298 (General Court, 6 June 2013) para 72. See also Opposition Case No 2011/0001D/01 *Wheelbarrows* (Patent-och Registeringsverket, 27 October 2011); affirmed on appeal as Case 12–020 *Åke Gustafson v. Alexander Söderholm* (Patentbesvärsrättens Dom, 12 April 2013).
54 Seville (n 19) 226.
55 Case T-337/12 *El Hogar Perfecto del Siglo XXI SL v. OHIM – Wenf International Advisers Limited* ECLI:EU:T:2013:601 (General Court, 21 November 2013).
56 Charles-Henry Massa and Alain Strowel, 'Community Design: Cinderella Revamped' (2003) 25 *EIPR* 71; Musker (n 52) 12; Seville (n 19) 226.
57 Bently *et al* (n 19) 742.
58 Stone (n 26) 52.
59 Ibid 49.
60 Case T-494/12 *Biscuits Poult SAS v. OHIM – Banketbakkerij Merba BV* ECLI:EU:T:2014:757 (General Court, 9 September 2014) para 24. For a view that the case was inaccurately decided, see; Stone (n 26) 57.
61 Stone (n 26) 50.
62 See; Uma Suthersanen, *Design Law: European Union and United States of America* (2nd edn, Sweet and Maxwell, 2010) 95.
63 Bently *et al* (n 19) 744.
64 Designs Directive Art 1(b); CDR Art 3(b).

The Regulation deliberately omits the requirement of 'industrial character.' This means that a product can be the result of traditional craftsmanship such as hand-made *haute couture* designs.[65] EU design law protects both two-dimensional (such as logos, patterns and textures) and three-dimensional designs (such as the cut of a dress or the shape of a hat or a handbag).[66] However, fashion 'styles' (such as mini-skirts or boot cut/flare/skinny jeans) on their own are not protectable. This relies on the fact that they lie closer to non-protectable idea as opposed to its protectable embodiment.[67]

Artwork (such as paintings, photographs and sculptures),[68] buildings,[69] graphical user interface,[70] computer icons,[71] certain elements of web design,[72] the topographies of semi-conductor chips,[73] adornments or additions to the body (such as surgical implants; artificial limbs, teeth, and eyes; tattoos; false eyelashes and nails; and wigs),[74] types of packages (such as bags, boxes, cartons, bottles, sachets, blister packs, crates and pallets)[75] and sets (such as a chess board and a set of tableware)[76] are examples of products that are all capable of design protection.

Design protection does not, however, extend to computer programs,[77] mere words,[78] music and sounds,[79] and living organisms (such as heart-shaped tomatoes[80] and animals[81]).

---

65 Suthersanen (n 62) 96.
66 Eveline Van Keymeulen, 'Copyrighting Couture or Counterfeit Chic? Fashion Design: A Comparative EU – US Perspective' (2012) 7(10) *Journal of Intellectual Property Law & Practice* 730.
67 Ibid 730.
68 Stone (n 26) 65 (noting that the EUIPO has accepted more than 400 RDCs for 'sculptures,' and more than 50 'paintings').
69 Massa and Strowel (n 56) 71 (arguing that environmental designs, whether internal or external, are protectable). Euro-Locarno Classification System includes houses, buildings, and buildings (transportable) in Class 25, 'Building Units and Construction Elements.'
70 Also note C-393/09 *Bezpecnostni Softwarova Asociace – Svaz Softwarove Ochrany v. Ministerstvo Kultury* (2011) FSR (18) 465 (ECJ, Third Chamber) (graphic user interface is not software protected under the Software Directive but may be a graphic work protected by copyright).
71 RCD Guidelines 4.1.3. See; Schlotelburg (n 10) 386.
72 Stone (n 26) 67.
73 This creates an overlap in protection with the Directive 87/54 on the legal protection of semiconductor chips OJ L24/36.
74 Bently *et al* (n 19) 746 (making distinction with the case of tattoo).
75 Stone (n 26) 66.
76 Stone (n 26) 67.
77 These are protected as literary works by the Computer Programs Directive. See; Council Directive 91/250/EEC on the legal protection of computer programs ('Computer Programs Directive') [1991] OJ L122, Art 1. The exclusion here was intended to prevent interference with that protection. See Musker, 16 (suggesting the scope of the exclusion should be confined to what is protected by copyright). See also; Annette Kur, 'Protection of Graphical User Interfaces under European Design Legislation' (2003) 34 *IIC* 50.
78 RCD Guidelines 4.1.4. See; Stone (n 26) 65. Use of fanciful characters or a figurative element may render the design eligible for protection.
79 The graphic representation of a musical phrase could qualify. RCD Guidelines 4.1.5.
80 Case R 595/2012–3 *ACJ Ammerlaan* (Board of Appeal, 18 February 2013).
81 RCD 1982380 (23 February 2012).

The reference to *part of a product* enables designers to claim protection over a product, such as a handle of a cup or the shape of a collar. The CJEU considered the protection of 'partial design' in a recent case of *Ferrari v. Mansory Design*.[82] Mansory Design is a German company that manufactures and sells tuning accessories for luxury cars. Ferrari sued Mansory Design for copying several UCDs, for which it claims to be the owner. The disputed designs were the accessories designed by Mansory Design to make a previous model of Ferrari car resemble a new model. The CJEU noted that the disclosure of the complete product potentially also gives rise to making available of the design of a part of that product. However, the Court confirmed that, for this protection to arise, the appearance of part of the product must be 'clearly identifiable' when the design is made available, and it must satisfy the condition of individual character. It must also constitute a 'clearly visible' section of the product, clearly defined by lines, contours, colours, shapes or texture.[83]

Part of a product should be distinguished from a 'component part of a complex product,' which needs to satisfy different criteria to be valid. A 'complex product' means 'a product which is composed of multiple components which can be replaced permitting disassembly and reassembly of the product.'[84] Designs applied to a component part of a complex product must reach a higher threshold of protection.[85] To be protected, the component part of the complex product must remain visible while the complex product is in normal use. Normal use is defined to be use by the end user.[86] Normal use specifically excludes maintenance, servicing or repair work.[87] The novelty and individual character requirements clearly must be met by the visual features of the component part.[88] All other features are ignored. A component part does not need to be clearly visible at every moment of use.[89] These provisions were intended to limit design protection of spare parts for cars.[90] For instance, the interior of a handbag could be protected, but any features hidden beneath the lining could not be registered.

---

82 Case C-123/20 *Ferrari SpAn v. Mansory Design & Holding GmbH* (28 October 2021).
83 Ibid 52.
84 Designs Directive Art 1(c); CDR Art 3(c).
85 Designs Directive Arts 3(3) and 14; CDR Arts 4(2) and 110.
86 Designs Directive Art 3(4); CDR Art 4(3). In a case which concerned the design for an internal combustion engine the General Court said that the end-user was the person who used the mower to cut lawns and that normal use was the cutting of lawns. As a result, the design was limited to the top upper side of the engine. Case T-11/08 *Kwang Yang Motors v. OHIM* (2011) ECR II-265 (GC).
87 Designs Directive Art 3(4); CDR Art 4(3). This is confirmed by Case R 1276/2008–3 *Albright France (SARL) v. Schaltbau GmbH* (Board of Appeal, 4 August 2009).
88 Designs Directive Art 3(3); CDR Art 4(2).
89 Case R 690/2007–3 *Lindner Recyclingtech v. Franssons Verkstäder* (2010) ECDR 1 para 21.
90 Seville (n 19) 228. See also Stone (n 26) 76 (arguing that car hubcap *can be registered as a design while car engine cannot*) and Bently et al (n 19) 749 (noting that 'complex technical objects' – such as cars, machines for shredding materials for recycling, and lawnmowers – and several 'less technical objects' – such as a skirting board, a window blind system and a fireplace – have been found to be 'complex products').

2.3.1.2 Functionality exception

A design 'shall not subsist in features of appearance of a product which are solely dictated by its technical function.'[91] The task of judging whether design features are dictated by function is 'assessed from the standpoint of a reasonable observer.'[92] A reasonable observer is the person 'who looks at the design and asks ... whether anything other than purely functional considerations could have been relevant when a specific feature was chosen.'[93] The exclusion aims to prevent design rights from being used to obtain 'monopolies over technical solutions without meeting the more stringent conditions laid down in patent law.'[94] In so doing, it aims to prevent technological innovation from being hampered.[95]

This exclusion does not mean that these features are not designs. Rather, a design right shall not subsist in features that are solely dictated by technical function. Thus, it is possible to register a design that includes some functional features.[96] A design will only be excluded where the design was dictated by function.[97]

Regarding the meaning of features that are 'solely dictated' by technical function, there are two main interpretations. The first is that the exclusion does not apply if alternative designs exist. This is known as the 'multiplicity of forms' test or mandatory approach.[98] The second is that the exclusion applies where the various features of appearance of the product are dictated solely by the need to achieve a technical solution and aesthetic considerations are entirely irrelevant. This is often referred to as the 'no aesthetic considerations' test or causative approach.[99] EUIPO and national courts initially appeared to favour the former approach. However, the latter approach has been embraced in more recent decisions. For instance, the designs of chaff cutters[100] and cylindrical centring pins[101] were found to be solely dictated by their technical function and invalid.

---

91 Designs Directive Art 7(1); CDR Art 8(1).
92 Case R 1997/2012–3 *TrekStor v. Zagg* (12 May 2014) para 28.
93 Ibid.
94 Case R 690/2007–3 *Lindner Recyclingtech v. Franssons Verkstäder* (2010) ECDR 1 para 28.
95 Designs Directive Recital 13; CDR Recital 10.
96 Bently *et al* (n 19) 751.
97 Case R 998/2013–3 *Austrotherm v. Termo Organika* (12 February 2015) para 45.
98 Bently *et al* (n 19) 752–753; Jason J Du Mont and Mark D Janis, 'Trends in Functionality Jurisprudence: U.S. and E.U. Design Law' in Henning Hartwig (ed), *Research Handbook on Design Law* (Edward Elgar Publishing, 2021) 51.
99 Ibid.
100 Case R 690/2007–3 *Lindner Recyclingtech v, Franssons Verkstäder* (2010) ECDR 1 paras 31, 42 (referring to the 1971 English decision of *Amp Inc v. Utilux Pty Ltd (1971) FSR. 572*, where the House of Lords interpreted a similar provision and adopted the causative approach).
101 Case C-395/16 *Doceram v. CeramTec* EU:C:2018:172 paras 22–23 (the CJEU rejected the multiplicity-of-forms approach and essentially adopted the approach in *Amp v. Utilux*). Also see; Jonathan Dobinson, 'Rethinking the Functionality Exclusion in EU Community Design Law' (2019) 41(10) *European Intellectual Property Review* 639–653 (arguing to repeal the exclusion and amend the CDR and Design Directive to determine the technical function of a product when assessing individual character, as is the case in Australian law).

50 *Artificial intelligence and EU design protection*

Thus, for this exception to apply, technical function must entirely dictate the features of the appearance of the product. As the function of a clothing article (covering the body and keeping a person warm) can be achieved by many aesthetical or stylistic configurations, this exception does not prevent the protection of fashion design under EU law.

2.3.1.3 Designs of interconnection

A design right

> shall not subsist in features of appearance of a product which must necessarily be reproduced in their exact form and dimensions in order to permit the product in which the design is incorporated or . . . applied to be mechanically connected to or placed in, around or against another product so that either product may perform its function.[102]

Design features that are required for connectivity are also denied protection. While the functionality exclusion broadly applies to all design features, the connectivity exclusion is tailored to features that might limit the standardisation and interoperability of products.[103] Like the functionality exclusion, it is applied on a feature-by-feature basis. This means that designs with some excluded features might still be protected if their non-excluded features meet the remaining validity requirements.[104]

The aim is not to extend protection to the features that allow mechanical parts to fit together. Such protection, if provided, might give rise to restrict competition in secondary markets, for instance for accessories or consumables. Therefore, such features are not taken into consideration in assessing whether other features of the design fulfil the requirements for protection (novelty and individual character).[105]

The exception does not apply to 'modular systems.' Features that allow 'multiple assembly or connection of mutually interchangeable products within a modular system' can be protected. It was adopted because of lobbying by the Danish government, in the hope of securing some continued protection for LEGO bricks. This is also important to the field of furniture design and more conventional products such as modular seating and shelving.

2.3.1.4 Designs contrary to morality or public policy

A design right 'shall not subsist in a design which is contrary to public policy or to accepted principles of morality.'[106] Importantly, this exclusion operates

---

102 Designs Directive Art 7(2); CDR Art 8(2).
103 Du Mont and Janis (n 98) 61.
104 Ibid 62.
105 Designs Directive Recital 14; CDR Recital 10.
106 Designs Directive Art 8; CDR Art 9.

as a ground for refusal of registration (both at national and EU levels) and as a ground for invalidity.[107] Morality can only be invoked, where according to the moral principles of right-thinking members of society it would be inappropriate to grant protection to a design. Thus, the fact that some people might find the design unpleasant is not sufficient. It has been suggested that designs that contain racist or homophobic messages[108] or textile designs that utilised a swastika[109] might fall within the exclusion. Similarly, obscene fashion designs cannot be registered.

2.3.2 Novelty

To be valid, a design must be new.[110] Novelty in design law is at a lower threshold than in patent law. A design is deemed to be new if no identical design has been made available to the public. However, designs are identical if their features differ only in immaterial details. There is no need to have to come up with a new concept, it is enough to make a new design.

Assessment of novelty is an objective test that requires the design to be compared with the body of existing materials (prior art).[111] Novelty is different from non-obviousness. A design is novel if no one has previously made a similar design. A design is nonobvious if no one has even considered making the design. Thus, it is possible for a design to be new and obvious at the same time. As such, novelty can be contrasted with copyright's originality test. Originality is a subjective test that focuses on the relationship between the creator and the creation.[112]

The first point that needs to be clarified in terms of novelty is the 'relevant date,' namely the date on which the state of the art is assessed. For a registered design, novelty is assessed against designs made available to the public before the date on which the application for protection is filed. If priority is claimed, the relevant date is the date of priority.[113] In the case of UCDs, it is assessed at the date on which the design was first made available to the public.[114]

Novelty prevents a business from obtaining a monopoly right over standard fashion products such as a white T-shirt or boot-cut jeans. It is, however, possible to get design protection for a T-shirt or jeans if the design is 'new' and has 'individual character' in the design field.

The state of the art consists of all designs disclosed to the public before the relevant date. Disclosure, or making a design available to the public, may occur through publication (either after registration or in a magazine), exhibition, use in

---

107 Bently *et al* (n 19) 756.
108 Ibid.
109 EC Green Paper, para 8.9.2.
110 Designs Directive Art 4; CDR Art 5.
111 Stone (n 26) 195.
112 For discussion of originality under EU copyright law see Chapter 3.
113 Designs Directive Art 4; CDR, Arts. 38 (date of filing), 41 (right of priority).
114 CDR Art 5(1)(a).

trade or any other form of disclosure.[115] Disclosure of a design by any means and anywhere in the world – subject to the exceptions discussed later – thus constitutes part of the prior art against which a design's novelty will be assessed. Any design that is already available to the public will no longer be new and cannot be protected, because it is part of the prior art.[116]

Certain disclosures are disregarded when novelty is examined.[117] These also apply in relation to the requirement of individual character. First, any disclosure that is made in confidence to outsiders is not considered.[118] Second, unlike in patent law, in a certain sense, novelty is limited to the EU. In this sense, the prior art does not include events that could not reasonably have become known in the normal course of business to the circles specialised in the sector concerned operating within the EU and who specialise in the relevant design area.[119] This 'safeguard clause' is intended to exclude obscure disclosures from the state of the art.[120] The relevant sector here is the one that consists of the sector of the alleged prior art.[121] The *circles specialised* in the sector refer to all individuals doing business in that sector – such as designers, advertisers, producers, distributors, wholesalers, importers and retailers.[122] Third, other disclosures that do not make the design available to the public cover disclosures that are confidential,[123] disclosures that are a consequence of a breach of confidence[124] and disclosures by the applicant within the 12-month grace period.[125]

It is also important to note that novelty is examined by comparing *appearance*, not function or, most of the time, the products to which the appearance is applied. Comparison is made with earlier individualised and defined designs and not with a combination of designs that had already been made available to the public.[126] The issue here is whether the appearance is precisely the same. In these cases, novelty will often depend on the way the design is represented.

---

115 Designs Directive Art 6; CDR Art 7(1).
116 See; Case T–450/08 *Coverpla v. OHIM – Heinz-Glas* EU:T:2012:117; Case T–651/16 *Crocs, Inc v. EUIPO, Gifi Diffusion, intervener*, EU:T:2018:137.
117 Designs Directive Art 6; CDR Art 7.
118 Private business correspondence in the form of email was a private communication and thus not part of the state of the art. See; Case R 1103/2012–3 *CTA Digital v. Bigben Interactive* (6 August 2015).
119 Designs Directive Art 6(1); CDR Art 7(1).
120 Seville (n 19) 233.
121 Joined cases C–361/15 P and C–405/15 P *Easy Sanitary Solutions BV and EUIPO v. Group Nivelles* EU:C:2017:720.
122 Case C-479/12 *H. Gautzsch Großhandel v. Münchener Boulevard Möbel Joseph Duna* EU:C:2014:75.
123 Designs Directive Art 6; CDR Art 7.
124 Designs Directive Art 6(3); CDR Art 7(3).
125 Designs Directive Art 6(2); CDR Art 7(2)(b). See; E Ferrill and J Roorda, 'Amazing Grace Periods for Registered Designs and Design Patents' (2016) 11 *Journal of Intellectual Property Law & Practice* 762.
126 Joined cases C–361/15 P and C–405/15 P *Easy Sanitary Solutions BV and EUIPO v. Group Nivelles* EU:C:2017:720.

Whether two designs are identical is a question of fact, to be determined by the tribunal. The main difficulty that arises in this context is determining whether, when two designs differ slightly, the difference is immaterial. Tribunals begin by identifying the differences between the prior art and the registered design. Once this is done, they then need to decide whether the identified differences are material. In most cases, there is little guidance from the tribunal as to this examination. However, there is a very strict approach that seeks for almost exact similarity between the registered design and the prior art for the design to be declared invalid. There are already several examples where differences in details have been held to be material, and therefore the designs were not identical. For instance, the difference in colours,[127] trademarks[128] and stems of wine glasses[129] have been found to be material, while the difference in surface decoration[130] has not. A key consideration is whether the differences contribute to the overall appearance of the product.

One question that arises is the perspective from which the differences are identified. The legislation remains silent in relation to whom the differences must be immaterial. This assessment can be made from the eyes of the designer, the design expert, the consumer, the informed user and relevant circles. The General Court said that this should be addressed from an objective point of view.[131] It is still uncertain, although the Court did suggest that it would not include the informed user.[132]

2.3.3 Individual character

In addition to being new, to be valid a design must also have 'individual character.'[133] The test of individual character is related to determine whether 'the overall impression (the design) produces on the informed user differs from the overall impression produced on such a user by any design which has been made available to the public.'[134]

The main rationale for design protection is not to prevent consumer confusion or deception. It is not strictly about innovation either. Nor is it completely oriented on individual creativity. Rather, the goal of design law is to protect the design as

---

127 Case R 1942/2007-3 *Detumando SL v. Aroco-Comercio e Distribução de Materias Sergurança LDA* (Board of Appeal, 26 February 2009).
128 Case ICD 867 *Ampel 24 Vertriebs-GmbH & Co KG v. Daka Research Inc* (Invalidity Division, 1 December 2005). For an opposite ruling see; Case ICD 1329 *Martin Saulespurens v. SIA Scruples* (Invalidity Division, 23 August 2006).
129 *Guy Jackson-Eben v. Wine Innovations*, ICD 8610 (27 February 2013) (Invalidity Division).
130 Case ICD 9094 *Glaxo Group Limited and Another v. Celon Pharma Sp zoo* (Invalidity Division, 21 May 2014).
131 Case T-68/11 *Erich Kastenholz v. OHIM* EU:T:2013:298 (GC) para 40.
132 See; Bently *et al* (n 19) 771 (arguing the novelty assessment 'will almost always be overshadowed by the more exacting inquiry into individual character').
133 Designs Directive Art 3(2); CDR Art 4(1).
134 Designs Directive Art 5.

a *design*.¹³⁵ The overall impression created by the design is the defining feature of the protection. What matters here is whether the informed user prefers an article for its individual character.¹³⁶

One of the notable features of the test for individual character is that it mirrors the test used to determine the scope of design protection and thus infringement.¹³⁷ There is a difference in terms of timing of the assessment; nonetheless, the concepts used are the same. Individual character is a retrospective test from the design in question to relevant designs in the prior art. Infringement is forward-looking from the design in question to subsequent designs.

Like novelty, to determine whether a design has individual character, it is necessary to compare the design in question with relevant designs in the prior art. However, the distinguishing feature of the inquiry into individual character is that it is undertaken from the perspective of a particular person, namely the 'informed user.' The informed user is a legal fiction.¹³⁸ It is used to set the standard by which the designs are judged for deciding individual character and infringement. It is also used when deciding whether an application contradicts earlier rights.¹³⁹

The CJEU defined the concept of the informed user in the *PepsiCo v. Grupo Promer* case.¹⁴⁰ The CRD related to small collectible children's toys, known as pogs. These toys were often distributed as free gifts with other products. A declaration of invalidity of the design was claimed on the basis that the PepsiCo design lacked novelty and individual character and on the existence of a prior right. According to the CJEU, the informed user is not an average consumer. They are not an expert in the sector who would be quite knowledgeable and identify every detail either. In this sense, they are not a designer, technical expert or manufacturer, nor a seller of the products in which the designs are incorporated.¹⁴¹ Instead, the informed user is a regular user of products of the same sort upon which the

---

135 Annette Kur and Marianne Levin, 'The Design Approach Revisited: Background and Meaning' in Annette Kur, Marianne Levin and Jens Schovsbo (eds), *The EU Design Approach: A Global Appraisal* (Edward Elgar Publishing, 2018) 1–27 (noting that 'the design is not meant to convey any message beyond its own appearance').
136 Justine Pila and Paul Torremans, *European Intellectual Property Law* (2nd edn, OUP, 2019) 466 (suggesting that 'the requirement of individual character is much more in the eye of the particular beholder').
137 Bently *et al* (n 19) 773.
138 Case T-209/18 *Dr. Ing h c F Porsche AG v. EUIPO* ECLI:EU:T:2019:377 (General Court, 6 June 2019) para 37 (noting that informed user is a 'hypothetical person').
139 Bently *et al* (n 19) 774.
140 Case C-281/10 P *PepsiCo Inc v. OHIM – Grupo Promer Mon Graphic SA* ECLI:EU:C:2011:679 (Court of Justice, 20 October 2011) (Hereinafter 'PepsiCo').
141 Case T-53/08 *Shenzhen Taiden v. OHIM – Bosch Security Systems* (2010) ECR II-2517 paras 46–48 (Hereinafter '*Shenzhen*'); Case T-10/08 *Kwang Yang Motor Co, Ltd v. OHIM* (Honda Giken Kogyo Kabushiki Kaisha intervening) (2012) ECDR 2 paras 23–25 (Hereinafter 'Kwang Yang Motor'); *PepsiCo* (n 140) paras 53, 59; Case T-68/11 *Kastenholz v. OHIM* (6 June 2013) paras 57–59.

protection is claimed.¹⁴² The concept of the informed user does not refer 'to a user of average attention.'¹⁴³ The informed user shows a high degree of attention and is particularly observant. The informed user has a relatively high degree of knowledge of the sector in question.¹⁴⁴ The informed user is reasonably discriminatory in that they show a relatively high degree of attention when they use the product.¹⁴⁵ The informed user also has some awareness of the existing designs in the sector 'without knowing which aspects of that product are dictated by technical function.'¹⁴⁶ The informed user is someone who has 'become informed on the subject . . . by browsing through catalogues, visiting (the relevant) stores, downloading information from the Internet.'¹⁴⁷ Thus, the informed user lies somewhere between the average consumer in trademark law and the sectoral expert from patent law.¹⁴⁸

Specifically regarding fashion design, for example, all black pumps may look the same to a casual buyer. The experienced fashion connoisseur will however immediately notice the difference between D'Orsay pumps, stilettos, kitten heels and platform soles. In *Karen Millen v. Dunnes Stores*, an Irish court defined an informed user as

> a woman with a keen sense of fashion, a good knowledge of designs of women's tops and shirts previously made available to the public, alert to design and with a basic understanding of any functional or technical limitations on designs for women's tops and shirts.¹⁴⁹

With regard to handbags, the informed user can be 'someone with more knowledge of handbag design than the average purchaser, i.e. not just 'a woman in the street' but not an industry expert either.'¹⁵⁰

The knowledge of the fictional informed user over the article in question is important. Where the informed user has more knowledge, they are more likely to identify small differences and conclude that the designs create a different overall impression. In contrast, where the informed user is less knowledgeable of the article, they are more likely to think that the designs are the same.¹⁵¹

---

142 See; *Woodhouse UK PLC v. Architectural Lighting Systems (t/a Aquila Designs)* [2005] EWPCC (Des) 25 (25 July 2005) para 50. It is not the user of the allegedly infringing product or any prior design.
143 *PepsiCo* (n 140) para 53.
144 *PepsiCo* (n 140) para 53. See also; Joined Cases C-101/11P and C-102/11P *Neuman v. OHIM* (2012) ECR I–641 (ECJ, Sixth Chamber) paras 53–54.
145 *Shenzhen* (n 141) para 47. See also *Dyson v. Vax* [2011] *EWCA Civ* 1206 para 15.
146 *Shenzhen* (n 141) para 48; *Kwang Yang Motor* (n 141) para 27.
147 Case R-915/2013–3 *Design Bruno Mathsson AB v. Temoto Production AB* (Board of Appeal, 13 May 2015) para 46.
148 *PepsiCo* (n 140) para 59.
149 *Karen Millen Ltd v. Dunnes Stores* [2007] IEHC 449 (21 December 2007).
150 Van Keymeulen (n 66) 733.
151 Bently *et al* (n 19) 775.

The test of individual character focuses on the impression made by the design on the fictional informed user. This is to see whether that differs from the impression made by the existing designs. At the end, this is a factual question that depends on the circumstances of the case. This factual question is examined according to the nature of the design in question. In some cases, the prominent feature of the design might be the lack of ornamentation, such as Apple products.[152] However, ornamentation may have an important role in influencing the overall visual impression created by a design.[153]

Another significant factor in evaluating overall impression is the degree of freedom that the designer had in developing the challenged design.[154] If the design freedom is limited, minor differences may be sufficient to create a different overall impression on the informed user.[155] In contrast, if the designer has a high degree of freedom in developing a design, the designs that do not have significant differences will produce the same overall impression.[156] Design freedom is objectively examined; constraints personal to the actual designer are irrelevant.[157] Fashion designers are often quite limited in their scope for creativity because of functional considerations. Clothing must fit the human body in the first place. Likewise, there is a social need to conform to accepted dress codes. Clothes are constrained by two-dimensional materials, patterns and cultural clothing archetypes.[158] A fashion designer will have more freedom – in terms of colour, material, design – when creating an extravagant night dress compared to a classical suit. Given that a few new designs on the market are truly exceptional in form, a single distinguishing feature can be enough to produce a unique overall impression. For instance, an embroidered jeans pocket, an oversized or coloured zipper or a big print can justify the protection of either the extraordinary feature or the item in its entirety.[159] Considering the limited amount of design freedom of the designer, The General Court in *Senz Technologies v. OHIM* concluded that two registered umbrella designs having minor differences with the prior art did have individual character and were valid.[160]

---

152 See; *Samsung Electronics (UK) v. Apple* [2012] *EWCA Civ* 1339, [2013] *FSR* 9 paras 15–16.
153 See; *PMS International Group v. Magmatic* [2016] *UKSC* 12.
154 Designs Directive Art 5(2); CDR Art 6(2).
155 *Kwang Yang Motors* (n 141) para 33; Case R 991/2011–3 *BS Studio v. Naturkram Giot* (27 September 2012) (Third BoA) para 28; *Case T 68/11 Erich Kastenholz v. OHIM* EU:T:2013:298 para 62.
156 *Kwang Yang Motors* (n 141) para 33; *BS Studio* (n 155) para 28.
157 Stone (n 26) 208.
158 Wang-Cheng Kang, Chen Fang, Zhaowen Wang, Julian McAuley, 'Visually-Aware Fashion Recommendation and Design with Generative Image Models' (2017) *IEEE International Conference on Data Mining* 207 ff, https://ieeexplore.ieee.org/abstract/document/8215493.
159 Van Keymeulen (n 66) 732.
160 Joined Cases T-22 and 23/13 *Senz Technologies BV v. Office for Harmonisation in the Internal Market (Trade Marks and Designs) (OHIM) (Impliva BV, intervening)* EU:T:2015:310 paras 56–59 (Hereinafter 'Senz Technologies').

A designer would be subject to the various constraints when developing the design. These might include technical constraints (such as product safety or industry standards), created by the fact that the product needs to perform a particular function,[161] legal requirements[162] or economic considerations (such as the need for the item to be inexpensive).[163] However, expectations of the market and fashion do not restrict the freedom of the designer.[164]

When considering individual character, the assessment is made side by side. The comparison is made between the design at issue (registered or unregistered) and an individual earlier design. It is not possible to combine a hypothetical amalgam of features from a range of earlier designs for this comparison.[165]

Small differences that do not change the overall impression should be ignored, even if they are by no means insignificant details.[166] It is necessary to search for differences that may sufficiently conclude that the overall impression is different.[167] The focus of the comparison is limited to the aspects that are protected. The products to which the design will be applied in trade can only be considered by way of illustration.[168]

The issues of novelty and individual character are examined only when design rights are challenged. The validity of an unregistered design has not been tested until this point. Likewise, there is no substantive examination of these matters on application for a registered design. An RCD may be declared invalid either in invalidity proceedings before the EUIPO or as a counterclaim in proceedings for infringement before a Community design court. Community design courts have sole jurisdiction to determine invalidity with respect to UCDs.[169]

As Chapter 1 sections 1.5.2 and 1.5.3 illustrate, AI can produce fashion designs that have the features described in this section. Thus, AI-generated fashion designs are no different from human-generated designs bearing these requirements (being a design, novelty and individual character).

---

161 For example, a handle must have a grip and be fixed onto a door: Case R 1083/2011–3 *Neves & Fihos v. Alcides de Sá Pinto Castro* (31 October 2012) (Third BoA) para 37.
162 Case T-9/07 *Grupo Promer Mon Graphic v. OHIM-PepsiCo* (2010) ECR II–981 (GC) para 67.
163 Bently *et al* (n 19) 779.
164 EC Green Paper 5.5.8; *Senz Technologies* (n 160) para 58; *Shenzhen* (n 141) para 58.
165 *Karen Millen* (n 2) para 35.
166 Case T–666/11 *Danuta Budziewska v. OHIM (Puma SE intervening)* EU:T:2013:584; Case T–153/08 *Shenzen Taiden v. OHIM (Bosch Security Systems)* [2010] ECR II-2517.
167 *Danuta Budziewska* and Case T–513/09 *Baena Grupo v. OHIM (Neuman and Galdeano del Sel)* (16 December 2010).
168 *PepsiCo* (n 140) para 73.
169 CDR Art 24. Community design courts are national courts and tribunals designated by member states to perform the functions assigned to them by the Regulations. They have exclusive jurisdiction to deal with actions for the infringement of a Community design, whether registered or unregistered; actions for a declaration of invalidity of an unregistered Community design; and counterclaims for a declaration of invalidity of a Community design (whether registered or unregistered), in the context of an infringement action: CDR, Arts. 80, 81. CDR Art 82 determines which Member State's Community design courts have jurisdiction in the proceedings.

2.4 Scope of protection

2.4.1 Design rights and infringement

Fashion companies working with AI in designing and trend forecasting often use a huge database of images taken from photo-sharing websites such as Instagram, Twitter, Pinterest and Flickr. They can also sometimes use fashion photos to train AI (for such uses see Chapter 1 section 1.5). This is because AI learns based on what it is fed. Data is vital for AI's learning and creativity. In these circumstances, many might focus on the implications of data protection. But what is the position about training AI by using third-party design (copyright) works in the EU generally? Who will be liable if AI designs infringe prior designs?

There are three main ways in which using an AI system in fashion designing could potentially infringe design right (and copyright): (i) gathering a digital corpus of training data, where a selection of fashion designs (or copyright works) is digitised and/or reproduced in preparation phase for training (Use 1), (ii) making unauthorised intermediate copies of images during training in neural networks (Use 2), (iii) generating a derivative work that reproduces elements of an original design (or work) by AI (Use 3).

Before concluding which of these uses would amount to a design infringement, it is necessary to understand the nature of the design protection. It must first be noted that RCDs enjoy full monopoly rights. The right holder has the exclusive right to use the design and to prevent any third party from using it without consent. The concept of use specifically includes 'the making, offering, putting on the market, importing, exporting or using of a product in which the design is incorporated or to which it is applied, or stocking such a product for those purposes.'[170] The exclusivity also covers the mere using of a design.[171] Recital 21 of the Regulation states that the right 'should also extend to trade in products embodying infringing designs.' This suggests that the meaning of *use* is to be confined to 'trade in products.' On this account, *use* would not cover broadcasting.[172] Also, it could be argued that the immaterial use of a physical product is not infringing, as there is no product.[173]

Infringement is not confined to dealings with the same product to which the design is applied or that is mentioned in the application. Rather, the rights are

---

170 Designs Directive Art 12; CDR Art 19.
171 CDR Art 19(1).
172 Bently *et al* (n 19) 792. Compare; Thomas Margoni, 'Not for Designers: On the Inadequacies of EU Design Law and How to Fix It' (2013) 4(3) *JIPITEC* 232 (arguing that broadcasting only covers 2D designs).
173 Margoni (n 172) 232; Mark P McKenna and Lucas S Osborn, 'Trade Mark Protection for Digital Goods' in Tanya Aplin (ed), *Research Handbook on Intellectual Property and Digital Technologies* (Edward Elgar Publishing, 2020) 395; Danusha Mendis, 'Fit for Purpose? 3D Printing and the Implications for Design Law: Opportunities and Challenges' in Tanya Aplin (ed), *Research Handbook on Intellectual Property and Digital Technologies* (Edward Elgar Publishing, 2020) 456; Viola Elam, 'CAD Files and European Design Law' (2016) 7(2) *JIPITEC* 151.

infringed using *any* product in which the design is incorporated.[174] Once a design is registered, it is not only protected in relation to the products specified in the application but also in relation to *any* product in which the design is used. A pattern design on a handbag might be infringed by making curtains bearing a similar pattern. Design rights extend to any third party who uses a design that does not produce on informed users a different overall impression.[175]

In contrast to registered national designs and RCDs, the rights conferred by UCDs are confined to cases where the defendant copied the protected design. In other words, the right holder's exclusive right to use can be exercised only against copying the protected design.[176]

The scope of the protection conferred by design rights is defined to include 'any design which does not produce on the informed user a different overall impression.'[177] As previously mentioned, the test for whether a design is infringing mirrors the test to determine individual character. Under EU design law, designs will accordingly infringe when they create the 'same overall impression' on the informed user. In assessing the scope of protection, these two reference points, namely 'the informed user' and 'the degree of freedom of the designer,' create a precise line between entitlement to protection and infringement. A similar design that provides a different overall impression will not infringe and may thus be entitled to protection. For registered designs, the representations are the starting point for comparison.

When comparing the defendant's allegedly infringing design with the claimant's design, the informed user will disregard aspects of the design that are optional accessories, such as the heel strap on a shoe.[178]

Following a general logic in intellectual property law, the ideas or concepts that lie behind a design are not protected. Protection is limited to appearance that is embodied either in an article or a design document.[179] A design for a three-dimensional product, such as the design of a clothing, would not be infringed by use on two-dimensional products, such as posters. This is because, the design – that is, the shape – has not been applied to the poster. However, this may not be the case if the designer not only claimed shape but also features of colour, line or pattern.[180]

A casual buyer (observer) may think that differences between two designs concerning the arrangement of buttons, the shape of a collar or the colour palette of a garment has minor importance. These differences may, however, produce a different overall impression in the eye of an informed *fashionista* (user).[181] In a

---

174 Bently *et al* (n 19) 792.
175 Seville (n 19) 248.
176 CDR Art 19(2), (3).
177 Designs Directive Art 9(1); CDR Art 10(1).
178 Case R 9/2008–3 *Crocs v. Holey Shoes Holdings* (26 March 2010) (BoA) paras 102–103.
179 EC Green Paper 5.4.3.1–5.4.3.4 (design law does not protect the idea or overall concept).
180 Bently *et al* (n 19) 796.
181 Van Keymeulen (n 66) 734.

fashion-related design case of *Jose Manuel*, the General Court pointed out that the sentimental differences between the two characters depicted on the T-shirts (angry versus relaxed goblins) would be highly significant for the informed users. In the case, teenagers buying the T-shirts were accepted as such informed users. On that basis the Court held that the overall impression generated by each of these cartoon silhouettes on such informed users was different.[182]

In *Karen Millen v. Dunnes Stores*, the CJEU drew a fashion designer-friendly interpretation of the concept of individual character. By relying on this construction, the Irish Supreme Court upheld the judgment of the High Court holding that the slavish copying of two striped shirts (one blue, one stone brown) and a black knit top were clearly an infringement.[183]

These decisions illustrate that courts may be willing to accept a great deal of similarity without finding infringement. This is in line with case law of national courts in which relatively minor differences between competing designs were sufficient to establish a 'different overall impression on the informed user.'[184]

Consequently, both UCDs and RCDs protect against identical or virtually identical copies of a fashion design, such as the type of copies made by a counterfeiter or knockoff designer. However, they generally do not prohibit the derivative work of a lower-end retailer seeking to reference a new trend, such as the colour of the season, the length of skirts and leg width of jeans that is currently 'in,' etc.[185]

There remains the initial fundamental question: are AI uses of previous fashion designs infringement? The issues here concern specifically whether the protection is tied to the reproduction of physical products and whether the scope of protection covers dimensional change (such as digitisation). In the EU, there are two sets of views regarding the dimensional conversion: the 'abstract' and the 'concrete' view of protection. In the 'abstract' view, the protection is granted for the 'form as such,' regardless of the object's dimensions. In the 'concrete' view, again, the protection is conferred on the product's actual dimensions. Thus, if the design protection is originally registered for a 2D shape, its use in 3D would not be seen as infringing, or vice versa.[186]

The CJEU in *Nintendo v. Bigben*[187] had to deal with the question of whether the use of a 2D image of a 3D design on a webpage may be an act of reproduction, subject to exceptions such as citation right. Mikko Antikainen argues that the

---

182 T-153/09 *Jose Manuel Baena Grupo v. OHIM* (General Court, 16 December 2010).
183 *Karen Millen* (n 2).
184 For the recent overviews on the national fashion-related cases see; The Bird & Bird IP Team, 'Fashion-related IP Decisions Round-up 2020' (2021) 16(6) *Journal of Intellectual Property Law & Practice* 595–625; The Bird & Bird IP Team, 'Round-up of Fashion-related IP Decisions 2021' (2022) 17(3) *Journal of Intellectual Property Law & Practice* 260–296.
185 Van Keymeulen (n 66) 734.
186 Mikko Antikainen, 'Differences in Immaterial Details: Dimensional Conversion and Its Implications for Protecting Digital Designs Under EU Design Law' (2021) 52 *IIC* 138–139.
187 Joined cases C-24/16 and 25/16 *Nintendo v. Bigben* ECLI:EU:C:2017:724.

CJEU has adopted the abstract view, and both transformative use (of 3D design to 2D) and use on a web page count as infringement under EU design law.[188]

It is true that the CJEU's ruling in *Nintendo* indicated that the digital use of a CRD can be infringement under some circumstances. But one must bear in mind the circumstances and outcome of the case. In the case, the defendants made and supplied accessories compatible with Nintendo's Wii console and advertised these on a website alongside images of goods corresponding to the protected designs. Thus, Nintendo's CRD was used by setting up a link with the defendant's products. Eventually, the CJEU held that reproduction of designs by citation is permitted, provided there is no impression of a commercial connection between the design right-holder and the party citing the design. Likewise, mentioning the source of the design occurs when a reasonably well-informed and observant consumer can easily identify the origin of the product corresponding to the protected design.

From this perspective, infringement, as a principle, occurs where a fashion design is physically embodied on a *product*. Of course, to establish infringement it is also necessary to show that the infringing design does not create a different overall impression on the informed user. Uses 1 and 2 are not uses of a design on a *product*. Nor are they 'trade in products' and uses in design application documents. They are mere digitisation. The use of a physical (fashion) design appearance digitally and invisible to the informed user in cases of Uses 1 and 2 should not be seen as tantamount to an act of infringement.[189] In these cases, there is *only use of appearance* without the product. Further, even if it is assumed that there is a product, the overall impression on the informed user is different, as few would confuse a physical product.[190] Uses 1 and 2 are mere digitisations without commercial use of a design on a product, and therefore, these uses would not lead to design infringement under EU law.

In cases of Use 3, infringement can arise where the derivate design uses prior design as a whole or partially. For instance, AI can generate a dress with its entire design elements (such as its length, sleeve or collar types, etc.). Alternatively, it can incorporate a third-party design in a fashion creation (such as using identical patterns on a handbag, identical prints on a T-shirt or identical features or accessories of a garment for which design protection is claimed or registered). In both cases for Use 3 to count as an infringement, the derivate design generated by AI must produce a similar overall impression on the informed user. This can rarely happen because the current AI systems are automated to generate designs in spaces where prior art does not occupy. If this happens, the designer using the AI

---

188 Antikainen (n 186) 158, 160.
189 Margoni (n 172) 232.
190 Ibid. See also; Ana Nordberg and Jens Hemmingsen Schovsbo, 'EU Design Law and 3D Printing: Finding the Right Balance in the New e-Ecosystem' in Rosa Maria Ballardini, Marcus Norrgård and Jouni Partanen (eds), *3D Printing, Intellectual Property and Innovation – Insights from Law and Technology* (Wolters Kluwer, 2017) Chapter 13 (arguing that reproducing and converting a design into a digital format should constitute an infringement).

systems in this way can escape from liability by not applying the derivate design to a product. If not, this could be a design infringement under EU law, the legality of which requires an exception.

2.4.2 Exceptions

The exclusive rights of the rights holder are subject to certain limitations and exclusions.[191] These defences include: (i) acts done privately and for non-commercial purposes, (ii) acts done for experimental purposes, (iii) acts of reproduction for citations or teaching,[192] (iv) exceptions in relation to foreign-registered ships and aircraft, which are temporarily in the country, the repairing of these and the importation of spare parts for that purpose, (v) freedom of expression.[193]

The Directive and Regulation also contain provisions on exhaustion of rights and the repair of complex products. Spare parts are a particularly contentious matter. No final agreement could be reached when the Regulation was put in place. It therefore contains the following transitional provision:

> Until such time as amendments to this Regulation enter into force on a proposal from the Commission on this subject, protection as a Community design shall not exist for a design which constitutes a component part of a complex product used within the meaning of Article 19(1) for the purpose of the repair of that complex product so as to restore its original appearance.[194]

Another limitation to design rights is exhaustion of those rights. The rights conferred by a design cannot be exercised when the product has been 'put on the market in the [EU] by the holder of the Community design or with his consent.' The exhaustion rule applies at the EEA level.[195]

These exceptions provide very little room for fashion designers who use AI. Only developing a fashion design for experimental purposes can play a role to exempt the designer form the liability in exceptional circumstances.

---

191 Designs Directive Art 13; CDR Art 20.
192 This is the case, 'provided that such acts are compatible with fair trade practice and do not unduly prejudice the normal exploitation of the design, and that mention is made of the source.'
193 For instance, see the case on the protection of freedom of expression over a painting called *Simple Living*, which depicts an African child holding a pink Chihuahua and a Louis Vuitton handbag; *Nadia Plesner Joensen v. Louis Vuitton Malletier*, Case 389526/KG ZA 11–294 (4 May 2011) (District Court of The Hague). For the English translation of the case see; Lucie Guibault, 'The Netherlands: Darfurnica, Miffy and the Right to Parody!' (2011) 2(3) *JIPITEC* 236.
194 CDR Art 110.
195 Designs Directive Art 15; CDR Art 21. See; Case 144/81 *Keurkoop BV v. Nancy Kean Gifts BV* [1982] ECR 2853, [1983] 2 CMLR 47.

2.5 Designer's attribution

Another feature of the EU design law is the designer's right of attribution. Under the Regulation, the designer (or the design team) has the right to be 'cited as such before the Office and in the register.'[196] The designer is conferred due recognition for their creative effort by way of a note in the application and the register.[197] This derives from the fact that the citation of the designer or the team of designers is one of the optional elements of the application for an RCD.[198] This right is particularly important given the controversy surrounding the DABUS patent. Is this right equivalent to moral right of attribution as provided for in copyright law?

The concepts of authorship in design and copyright laws are different. The author has a central role in copyright law.[199] Design law by contrast focuses mostly on designs rather than on designers. The authors of designs often remain behind the design, since the law sees it as an asset and marketing instrument.[200] As Annette Kur reminds, the rationale for design protection is detached from the foundation of copyright protection, that is, 'the creator's personal expression and the relationship between author and work.'[201] The role of modern design as a marketing instrument shapes the legal framework of *sui generis* design protection.[202] As a result, it is the perception of the design in the public eye that matters in the design regime, and the personal contribution of authors to designs as a form of expression is irrelevant.[203]

The market, the laws of physics, the needs of users and even fashion constrain the process of creating designs. The designer is then seen to have a more distant relationship with their design than an artist has with their creations.[204] This fundamental premise leaves little space for protecting a designer's special link to the created subject matter under a moral rights scheme within the *sui generis* design regime.[205] Therefore, the Regulation leaves the protection of moral rights of the designer ultimately to the national copyright regimes or to other national laws protecting the designers' non-economic interests.[206] Article 18 of the CDR, however, is the only provision in EU design law that provides some right that is closed

---

196 CDR Art 18.
197 Ibid.
198 CDR Art 36(3)(e).
199 Bently *et al* (n 19) 125.
200 Bently *et al* (n 19) 720; Margoni (n 172) 224.
201 Annette Kur, 'The Green Paper's 'Design Approach' – What's Wrong with It?' (1993) 10 *EIPR* 376.
202 Kur and Levin (135) 7.
203 Kur (n 201) 377.
204 Bently *et al* (n 19) 720; Margoni (n 172) 233.
205 Anna Tischner, 'Design Rights and Designer's Rights in the EU' in Henning Hartwig (ed), *Research Handbook on Design Law* (Edward Elgar Publishing, 2021) 171.
206 CDR Art 96. EC Green Paper 7.1.3. et seq.

to the attribution of the design.²⁰⁷ Anna Tischner thinks that even though Article 18 of the CDR refers to a *right* ('the designer shall have the right to be cited'), this is not a moral right in traditional sense in copyright law.²⁰⁸

Under Article 20(1)(c) of the CDR a design can be reproduced for citations or teaching, provided that the source should be mentioned. It is unclear, however, whether such mention of the source must include the designer's identity in addition to the right holder's name.²⁰⁹ The CJEU clarified this condition in *Nintendo v. Bigben* when interpreting a design citation in referential use.²¹⁰ According to the CJEU, 'in order to fulfil the condition that the source be mentioned, it is necessary, *inter alia*, that the type of mention chosen for that purpose enables a reasonably well-informed and reasonably observant and circumspect consumer easily to identify the commercial origin of the product corresponding to the Community design.'²¹¹ In *Nintendo*, the notion of transparent market communication prevailed over the designer's right to be identified.

Consequently, the identity of the designer may be declared in the application or remain anonymous. If the designer prefers to stay anonymous, the applicant should include a statement that the designer or the team of designers waived the right to be cited. However, the applicant can sometimes indicate the designer's identity inaccurately or may not declare it despite the designer's wish. In these circumstances, the dispute concerning accurate attribution of the designer – between the applicant and the designer – must be resolved by the national courts.²¹² The designer cannot bring this matter through invalidity proceedings before EUIPO.²¹³ This is because they cannot be a party to the registration proceedings before EUIPO.²¹⁴ These procedural obstacles diminish the significance of the designer's right of attribution.²¹⁵

The provision on designer's attribution under EU law is unclear whether to prohibit or allow the applicants to mention AI as the designer. Since inclusion of the name of the designer in the RCD application is not mandatory under the CDR,²¹⁶ the problem of authorship of AI-generated design may not arise in near future. Instead, this may be an incidental issue in invalidation or infringement

---

207 Some vague norms for protecting the right of paternity of the designer can be found in international IP law. For instance, Article 5(2)(b)(i) of the Hague Agreement Concerning the International Registration of Industrial Designs requires the 'indications concerning the identity of the creator of an industrial design that is the subject of an international application.'
208 Tischner (n 205) 172.
209 Ibid.
210 *Nintendo* (n 187) paras 83–86.
211 Ibid para 84.
212 Bently *et al* (n 19) 736 (noting that this is for an order of 'a declaration as to who has the right to be cited as the designer before the Office and in the register').
213 Bently *et al* (n 19) 736 (claiming that that where a designer 'has not been named by the legitimate proprietor,' it is possible for the designer to bring an action against EUIPO).
214 Tischner (n 205) 172.
215 Bently 736. See also; Tischner (n 205) 172; Stone (n 26) 133.
216 CDR Art 36(3)(e).

proceedings.[217] Just like the patent application for DABUS's invention, some IP offices or courts could welcome AI as designer. However, does EU design law really recognise AI authorship of a fashion design? The next section will look at this question.

2.6 Initial entitlement to and ownership of a design

The Design Directive leaves the questions of initial entitlement and ownership of a registered design to the national laws of the Member States. The CDR, by contrast, includes detailed rules on these questions. Under the CDR, the right to both a registered and an unregistered Community design vests in the 'designer' or the 'designer's successor in title.'[218] More specifically, The CDR provides that the right to a design is attributed to the individual who *developed* the design.[219] This approach is called 'designer doctrine,' under which the right to a design is conferred on its creator.[220] Thus, designers are the first owners of the rights to the designs they created.[221]

The concept of the designer plays a central role in conferring design rights. The Regulation uses the term *designer* several times but does not define it.[222] The CJEU emphasised that the term must be interpreted in an autonomous and uniform manner throughout the EU.[223] The concept of the designer has autonomous meaning in two respects. First, it is different form notions of authorship and inventorship in copyright and patent laws.[224] The subject matter of design protection is not an invention or a work featuring originality. Rather, it is an appearance of a product that is new and has individual character, which is a result of human effort. Thus, it cannot be defined by direct analogies with copyright and patent law concepts. Second, the concept of the designer has some differences from national concepts of design authorship.[225]

For making sense of this concept, both the characteristics of EU design law (namely, design approach[226]) and the process of design development must be considered. The starting point then becomes the very definition of design. The

---

217 Tischner (n 205) 177.
218 CDR Art 14(1).
219 Gordian Hasselblatt, *Community Design Regulation: An Article by Article Commentary* (2nd edn, Beck/Hart/Nomos, 2018) 204.
220 Tischner (n 205) 174.
221 See the *Bolero* case, German Bundesgerichtshof I ZR 23/12 (2014) IIC 239.
222 See for example, Recitals 7, 14, 20, 21, and 24, and Articles 6, 7, 10, 14, 18, 19 and 36 of the Regulation; and Articles 1, 14 and 69 of the Implementing Regulation.
223 Case C-32/08, *Fundación Española para la Innovación de la Artesanía (FEIA) v. Cul de Sac Espacio Creativo, SL and Acierta Product & Position, SA* ECLI:EU:C:2009:418 paras 63–66.
224 Tischner (n 205) 175.
225 See Estelle Derclaye and Matthias Leistner, *Intellectual Property Overlaps: A European Perspective* (Hart Publishing, 2010) 38–39.
226 Kur and Levin (n 202) 1.

legal definition of design[227] under EU law hints at the identity of a designer. The designer is the person who *develops* the design.[228] This refers to a person who gives the specific appearance to a product, which is new and has individual character.[229] The act of development of a design denotes the intellectual effort of one or more individuals. The provisions on initial entitlement to a design and right ownership of employer gives further clues about the personality of the designer: they can conclude contracts over their designs and can work as an employee under contractual terms. Therefore, as Anna Tischner underscores, 'only natural persons may be designers in the light of Article 14(1) of the CDR.'[230]

Where two or more designers jointly develop design, the right to the Community design shall vest in them jointly.[231] For joint entitlement to a design, there must first be plurality of designers. In addition, there must be a common plan that combines the creative efforts of two or more designers who endeavour to solve one 'design problem' at different levels of the process. These joint designers must also have the intention to merge their creative efforts to form a unitary whole. Where joint creative efforts lead to the development of a design that is new and has individual character, joint design holdership occurs in the sense of Article 14(2) of the CDR. The contributions of joint designers may, however, have a different weight; they do not have to be in equal proportions and of equal significance.[232]

The 'successor in title' covers the cases of inheritance, succession, merger of companies and contractual assignment (transfer of the right to the Community design).[233]

The CDR brings an exception to the designer doctrine. This exception gives the ownership of a design right to the employer rather than its creator. An employer can be owner of a design right under two circumstances. Where an employee (designer) develops a design '*in the execution of his duties* the right to the Community design shall vest in the employer.'[234] An employer can also be owner of the design right where the designer creates the design *by following his employer's instructions*.[235] The exceptional ownership of a design is limited to a specific type of contractual relationship, that is, an employment relationship as defined by labour law.[236] The designer and their employer may, however, agree otherwise. In this case, the designer continues to be the right holder. Similarly, the

---

227 CDR Art 3(a): 'appearance of the whole or a part of a product resulting from the features of the lines, contours, colours, shape, texture and/or materials of the product itself and/or its ornamentation.'
228 See; CDR Arts 6(2), 10(2), 14(2)-(3).
229 Tischner (n 205) 176.
230 Ibid.
231 CDR Art 14(2).
232 See; Tischner (n 205) 177–183.
233 Opinion of Advocate General Paolo Mengozzi delivered on 26 March 2009 in C-32/08 *FEIA v. Cul de Sac* ECLI:EU:C:2009:200 para 43.
234 CDR Art 14(3) (Emphasis added).
235 CDR Art 14(3).
236 FEIA (n), para 51.

Artificial intelligence and EU design protection 67

national laws of the Member states may adopt different legal arrangements from the design right ownership of an employer. If national law gives the ownership of the design to the employee, this exceptional ownership becomes irrelevant. The CJEU has clarified that this exception only applies to 'employers and employees' and that it does not extend to include other relationships, such as designs that have been produced because of a commission.[237] Additionally, the EU design law provides no specification about commissioners. Thus, in case of a commission the initial rights are left to the designer: a commissioner who wishes to own design right must secure their prospective rights by assignment.[238] However, the designer shall in any case retain the right to be cited as such in the register.[239]

Under the CDR, the person named on a Community registered design is 'deemed to be the person entitled.'[240] This is a presumption that can be rebutted.[241]

The development of design may be performed by an independent designer, a design agency or a studio, separate from the commissioner and as such employing or commissioning the designers, or by a design development department which is an integral part of the company.

Thus, there is no specific article in the CDR provided to regulate AI-generated designs. However, the EU Commission in the Green Paper on the Legal Protection of Industrial Design states that:

> The question 'computer generated designs' is sometimes evoked. The Commission considers that the requirement that a design be the result of a human activity covers this type of designs and in the same time gives an answer to the question of the entitlement to the right on such designs. It should be admitted that the generation of a design by computer is just one untraditional method of operating which should entitle the person using the computer to this effect and choosing the design generated among the possible multiplicity of solutions given by the computer, to obtain protection if the design fulfils the objective requirement of distinctive character.[242]

EU design law envisages the designer as someone who can decide to develop a (fashion) design by making creative choices concerning style, ornaments, length,

---

237 Case C-32/08 *Fundacion Española para la Innovación de la Artesania (FEIA) v. Cul de Sac Espacio Creativi SL* [2009] ECR I–561 para 49.
238 Bently *et al* (n 19) 787–788.
239 CDR Art 18.
240 CDR Art 17.
241 There is an opportunity for challenge by 'the person entitled to it,' who may 'claim to become recognised as the legitimate holder of the Community design.' See; CDR Art 15(1). This matter will be decided by national courts with jurisdiction regulated by the Brussels Convention. There is a limitation period of three years from the date of publication of an RCD or the date of disclosure of a UCD, unless the person who is not entitled was acting in bad faith. Similarly, a Community design may be declared invalid if, by virtue of a court decision, it is known that the right holder is not entitled to the Community design.
242 EC Green Paper 5.6.2.

size, colours, shape and embodiment of several parts of a fashion design. This person, according to law, is also someone who can collaborate with their peers to create a design (joint authorship), who has legal capacity to make contracts (as an employer or employee, or with a commissioner or a representative of a merging company – contractual successor in title) or who can die and whose design can be inherited (successor in title). This shows that rights to a Community design may vest in a natural person or a group of natural persons (that is, a single designer or joint designers or a natural person being an employer or a successor in title) or in a legal person (as an employer or a successor in title including a commissioner). Consequently, EU design law does not recognise the AI authorship and ownership of a design right. At best, one can follow the proposal by the Green Paper and admit that the person using the AI should be the designer of AI-generated designs if it fulfils the objective requirement of distinctive character.

2.7 Invalidity

A design can be declared invalid.[243] A declaration of invalidity for a Community design can be made either by a Community design court based on a counterclaim in infringement proceedings. This can alternatively be done by EUIPO's Invalidity Division.[244] A similar option exists in many national laws.

The grounds for invalidity can be grouped into three general categories.[245] The first category relates to the intrinsic characteristics of the design that is the subject of protection and its ability to function as a design. The first ground for invalidity arises where an appearance of a product does not meet the statutory definition of a design. Designs may also be declared invalid when they are devoid of novelty and individual character.[246]

The second and more varied category of grounds for invalidity provides that designs shall be invalid if they are contrary to public policy or morality;[247] or include a protected emblem;[248] or where there are problems with disclosure requirements; or if the applicant or holder[249] is not entitled to it.[250]

---

243 Designs Directive Art 11; CDR Art 24–25.
244 CDR Art 24(1).
245 For the Design Directive, four grounds – not a design, lack of novelty and individual character, lack of entitlement and conflict with a prior design – are mandatory. The remainder are optional. See; Designs Directive Art 11(1)(2).
246 See Cases T–666/11 *Danuta Budziewska v. OHIM (Puma SE intervening)* EU:T:2013:584; T–10/08 *Kwang Yang Motor Co. Ltd v. OHIM* [2012] ECDR 2; T–68/10 *Sphere Time v. OHIM* [2011] ECDR 20; T–153/08 *Shenzhen Taiden v. OHIM* T:2010:248.
247 Designs Directive Art 11(1)(b); CDR Art 25(1)(b).
248 This is the case if the design give rise to an improper use of any of the items listed in Article 6*ter* Paris Convention, or of badges, emblems, and escutcheons other than those covered by the said Article 6*ter,* and which are of public interest in a Member State. Designs Directive Art 11(2)(c); CDR Art 25(1)(g).
249 Regarding this ground of invalidity, for the Regulation there must be a prior court decision (challenging design-holdership).
250 Designs Directive Art 11(1)(c); CDR Art 25(1)(c).

The third category for invalidity is divided into two subcategories: those related to earlier designs and those related to earlier rights. For the first subcategory, a design may be declared invalid[251] if the design conflicts with a prior design that has been made available to the public after the date of filing of the application or, if priority is claimed, the date of priority of the Community design, and which is protected from a date prior to the said date.[252] The second subcategory is the case where the design includes a 'distinctive sign'[253] (such as trademarks or other distinctive signs protected by passing off, unfair competition and possibly geographical indications and even some personality rights)[254] or copyright works.[255]

A Community design that has been declared invalid shall be deemed not to have had any effects from the outset.[256]

2.8 Assignment and licences

The right to an RCD can be transferred.[257] Since the RCD is a unitary right, it can only be transferred in its entirety, for the whole Community territory.[258] Where an RCD is transferred, one of the parties may request that the transfer be entered in the register and published. Until registration and publication, the rights arising from the registration of the Community design may not be invoked against third parties.[259]

An RCD may be shown as security or levied in execution. These rights may equally be entered in the register upon the request of one of the parties.[260] A Community design may only be involved in insolvency proceedings in the territory where the debtor's main interests are situated.[261]

A Community design may be licensed for the whole or part of the Community. Licences may be exclusive or non-exclusive. An exclusive licensee may initiate proceedings for infringement of a Community design if the right holder does not do so within an appropriate period, having been given notice. A non-exclusive licensee needs the consent of the right holder to bring infringement actions. A licence of an RCD may be entered in the register.[262] This means that, in practice,

---

251 On the application of the applicant for or the holder of the earlier right in the case of a Community design.
252 Designs Directive Art 11(1)(d); CDR Art 25(1)(d).
253 Designs Directive Art 11(2)(a); CDR Art 25(1)(e). This ground can be applied where there is confusion on the part of the relevant public. See; Case T-793/16 *Şölen Çikolata Gıda Sanayi ve Ticaret AŞ v. EUIPO, Elka Zaharieva, intervener* EU:T:2018:72.
254 Seville (n 19) 244. See; Case T-148/08 *Beifa Group Co. Ltd v. OHIM* [2010] ETMR 42.
255 Designs Directive Art 11(2)(b); CDR Art 25(1)(f). See Case; T-566/11 and 567/11 *Viejo Valle SA v. OHIM (Établissements Coquet intervening)* EU:T:2013:549.
256 CDR Art 26(1).
257 CDR Art 28.
258 CDR Art 27.
259 CDR Art 28.
260 CDR Arts 29 and 30.
261 CDR Art 31.
262 CDR Art 32.

it is sensible to conclude assignments and licences in writing, although this is, in theory, not an express requirement.

2.9 Duration

The Designs Directive harmonised the term of protection for national design rights at a maximum of 25 years, granted in five-year periods from the date of filing.[263] The term of protection of the RCD is set at the same maximum of 25 years. Again, it is granted in five-year periods.[264] The UCD is protected for three years. The three-year term starts on the date on which the design was first made available to the public by publication, exhibition, use in trade, or any other way of disclosing the design if it could be reasonably known in specialised Community circle.[265] The last way of disclosing should not be limited to designers in the relevant field and can include traders or retailers in the field.[266]

2.10 Community unregistered design right

The CDR also contains a Community *unregistered* design right. This complements the registered right. Fashion was a prominent industry when the UCD was brought, where trends change every couple of months. The need for UCD was also visible in those industries for which the registration process would simply last too long. There are also many cases in which the design holder would rather see the market reaction to the design before registration, which might be also quite costly.[267]

For the most part the Regulation treats both the RCD and the UCD in essentially the same manner. Thus, the meanings of a 'design,' 'product' and 'complex product' are the same for both EU designs. The UCD, however, arises automatically when certain conditions are met. To establish the existence of an UCD, the design holder must first show that the design was initially made available to the public within the Community.[268] If a design is first disclosed outside the EU, it will not be protected as an UCD. This also undermines the possibility of registering the design because of a lack of novelty. Second, no identical design must have been made available to the public before the date on which the UCD for which protection is claimed has first been made available to the public.[269] The third condition to establish the existence of an UCD, as accepted in *Karen Millen* is 'to

---

263 Designs Directive Art 10.
264 CDR Art 12.
265 CDR Art 11.
266 See; Case C–479/12 *H Gautzsch Großhandel GmbH & Co KG v. Münchener Boulevard Möbel Joseph Duna GmbH* [2014] ECDR 14 para 30.
267 See Victor M. Saez, 'The Unregistered Community Design' [2002] 24(12) *EIPR* 585.
268 CDR Art 11.
269 CDR Art 5(1)(a).

indicate what constitutes the individual character of their Community design.'[270] This means that a design holder also has to indicate those elements of the design that 'create a different overall impression on an informed user from any design that has been previously made available to the public.'[271] The rights holder is not, however, required to *prove* that the design has individual character.

Similarly, the rights given to proprietors are the same for both EU designs. The scope of protection extends to any design that does not produce on the informed user a different overall impression.[272] In assessing whether this is so, the designer's degree of freedom will be considered as well.[273] As a result, the CJEU's decision in *PepsiCo*, for example the informed user in relation to CRDs, should apply equally to UCDs. In addition, the limitations on the rights conferred by a design right also apply to both EU designs. Most notably, there will be no protection for designs dictated by their technical functions or their need to fit with a product that allows the product to function.[274]

There are, however, two key differences between the RCD and the UCD. First, a UCD will only be infringed if the contested use results from direct or indirect copying.[275] Second, the term of protection of an UCD is only for three years from the date of disclosure to the public within the Community.[276]

Jurisdiction to determine invalidity of an UCD is conferred to Community design courts, whether on an application for a declaration of invalidity or as a counterclaim to an infringement action.[277]

2.11 Conclusion

AI presents unique opportunities for designers, improving the design process and enabling user engagement and the creation of more personalised designs. The role of EU design law is stimulating investments in design creativity. The features of the design development and registration processes; morality exception; innate concepts such as 'designer,' 'informed user' and 'successor in title' all point to one certain direction: the entire EU design regime is human-centred. Under the current EU design standards, AI designers are not likely to be considered the owners of their fashion creations. This derives from the fact that the law is not 'designed' to grant the ownership of a design right to a machine-entity. The law is also not clear whom to give the ownership of a design right concerning AI-generated designs. Equally, the attribution of liability over AI creations causing design infringement bears uncertainties. In particular, the questions of authorship and liability may

---

270 CDR Art 85(2) (Emphasis added).
271 CDR Art 6.
272 CDR Art 10(1).
273 CDR Art 10(2).
274 CDR Art 8.
275 CDR Art 19(2).
276 CDR Art 11.
277 CDR Arts 24, 25.

demand a specific and more nuanced approach to crafting rules for the future. Any solutions proposed should consider the interests of the 'designer community' to have free access to the public domain material as well.

The impact of AI on design development also requires re-thinking the fundamental concepts of authorship of copyright protected (fashion) design and liability of copyright infringement. The following sections will explore these questions.

3 Artificial intelligence and EU copyright protection

3.1 Uncharted territories

Can a pair of jeans be protected by copyright in the European Union (EU)? Some say fashion is a 'wearable art.'[1] Others think fashion is 'a form of visual art.'[2] This question requires a broader inquiry into the meaning of craft in copyright law and the question of to what extent it differs from art.

Our incomplete history suggests that the line between art and craft, which has been prominent since romantism of the 19th century, was not drawn until the 18th century. Prior to this era, the concepts of artist and craftsman were used interchangeably.[3] However, from the end of the 17th century onward, the course of history for art and craft started to change. The influence of developing market economies gave rise to social and economic changes. This eventually brought a relative division between arts and crafts.[4]

The rising market economy fuelled the growth of a middle class. This new segment of society gradually became engaged with art. Art, the privilege of patrons during the Middle Ages and the Renaissance, began to reach to a wider audience in the 18th century. The new-art public sought to distinguish themselves from taste of 'lower' classes. This cultural and social division that the middle class attempted to establish led to a distinction between the 'refined' taste of the new fine art public and the 'vulgar' amusements of the populace.[5]

The emergence of the new art audience increased the demand for artworks and expanded the art market. This development transformed works of art into a commodity. Artists were emancipated from patronage systems, where works

---

1 Eveline Van Keymeulen, 'Copyrighting Couture or Counterfeit Chic? Fashion Design: A Comparative EU – US Perspective' (2012) 7(10) *Journal of Intellectual Property Law & Practice* 728 (arguing that fashion has been transformed from a craft to produce clothes 'to cover and keep the body warm' to a form of creative expression').
2 Nancy J Troy, 'Art' in Malcom Barnard (ed), *Fashion Teory: A Reader* (2nd edn, Routledge, 2020) 66; Heidi Härkönen, *Fashion and Copyright: Protection as a Tool to Foster Sustainable Development* (Unpublished PhD Thesis, University of Lapland, 2021) 17.
3 Larry Shiner, *The Invention of Art: A Cultural History* (The University of Chicago Press, 2001) 5.
4 Malcolm Barnard, *Art, Design and Visual Culture: An Introduction* (Palgrave Macmillan, 1998) 61.
5 Shiner (n 3) 94–97.

DOI: 10.4324/9781003355922-4

were commissioned by patrons and not intended for sale. They were no longer creating for particular purposes, which allowed them to enjoy relatively greater freedom. The individuality of the artists earned prominence as art objects could be sold and resold in the commercial art market.[6] The image of genius and imaginative artistry dominated the aesthetic discourse in 19th century.[7] Artwork once created for utilitarian purposes – such as painting portraits, designing tapestries or decorating houses – was now becoming the aesthetic creation of sovereign artists, working independently and creating their own personal expressions. Accordingly, art and *aesthetics* emerged as distinct from craft and *functional*.

In the contemporary discourse, craft is still seen different from art. It is generally connected to the *function* that it achieves, whereas art is associated with expressions of genius and *aesthetics*.[8] One must also remember that the legacy of this distinction between art (aesthetics) and craft (function) has been highly blurred. Various movements in modern art and design, such as the Arts and Crafts Movement, the Art Nouveau, the Minimalism, the Bauhaus, the Art Deco, and the AI Art, have created a sense of *déjà vu* and significantly rendered this sharp distinction debatable in 20th century. And few artists can change the course of art history in the way that Marcel Duchamp did. By challenging the very notion of what is art, the submission of his most notorious of the 'readymades,' *Fountain*, to the 1917 Society of Independent Artists sent shock waves across the art world that can still be felt today. After the Society had rejected the work on the grounds that it was immoral and inappropriate, critics argued that an artist gave a new significance to an object when selected for display. Testing the limits of what constitutes a work of art, *Fountain* opened new grounds for the craft.

One of the mottos embraced by Germany's *Die Neue Sammlung*, the largest design museum in Europe, is 'Design ist Kunst, die sich nützlich macht' ('Design is art that makes itself useful'). This phrase is quite helpful to situate the discipline of fashion within a contemporary understanding of art. From this perspective, the value of art is not decreased when it also serves a function. If no object is endowed with artistic significance until one assigns it such a meaning, then art is truly in the eye of the beholder, regardless of the medium, whether it falls under the heading of fine, performing, decorative, or applied arts. As Kal Raustiala and Christopher Sprigman write, 'If fashion is speech, it is the wearer who speaks far more than the designer. And if fashion is art, it is still the wearer, as much as the designer, who makes it so.'[9]

Perhaps, it is more accurate to ask *when* fashion is art rather than *whether* fashion is art. Some designers easily embrace the label of artist. Cristóbal Balenciaga

---

6 Ibid 103, 126–127.
7 Elizabeth Prettejohn, *Beauty and Art 1750–2000* (Oxford University Press, 2005) 56–63.
8 Shiner (n 3) 5–6.
9 Kal Raustiala and Christopher Jon Sprigman, 'Faster Fashion: The Piracy Paradox and its Perils' (2021) 39(2) *Cardozo Arts & Entertainment Law Journal* 554.

Artificial intelligence and EU copyright protection 75

once said that 'a couturier must be an architect for design, a sculptor for shape, a painter for colour, a musician for harmony, and a philosopher for temperance.' While others, even those whose work might seem most aligned with conceptual art practices, make a clear distinction.

Perhaps for that reason, the Court of Justice of European Union (CJEU) in the *Cofemel* case abstained from navigating in these uncharted territories between art and design but said a conditional yes to the question of whether fashion designs can be protected by copyright (section 3.3.2.2.5).[10]

EU copyright law protects a wide range of creations in the literary, scientific and artistic domains. This includes cultural creations, such as works of literature, music, drama, film, photography and art. Functional types of subject matter, such as computer programs, databases, industrial design and works of applied art, also fall into the scope of protection.

Fashion designs often combine utility and aesthetics. This requires deciding whether to protect the design only by design law, only by copyright law or by both. These works may be mainly protected under design law. Whether they will be cumulatively protected under copyright law is a complicated matter.[11] The EU law touched quite minimally on this interface, as it only required the Member States to cumulate copyright and design laws without specifying rules to regulate the overlap.[12] Subsequently, Member States mainly followed their own traditions. This means that the law of Member States ranged from full cumulation to partial cumulation to no rules at all.[13]

The CJEU opened the door to the cumulative protection for designs in the *Flos* case in 2011.[14] The case concerned the design of the Arco lamp that was developed by Flos in 1962. Semeraro imported the Fludida lamp, which aesthetically and stylistically imitated the Arco lamp. The term of protection for the lamp design was expired. Despite this, the CJEU in *Flos* stated that the lamp design may qualify as a work under the Information Society Directive, if it meets the relevant conditions. The CJEU *Flos* judgment seemingly imposed the author's own intellectual creation level of originality for unregistered designs but left the determination level of originality to Member States. The ruling created even more uncertainty.[15]

---

10 Case C-683/17 *Cofemel – Sociedade de Vestuário SA v. G-Star Raw CV* ECLI:EU:C:2019:721 (12 September 2019) (Hereinafter 'Cofemel').
11 Estelle Derclaye, 'Introduction' in Estelle Derclaye (ed), *The Copyright/Design Interface: Past, Present and Future* (CUP, 2018) 1–2.
12 Design Directive Art 17, CDR Art 96; Directive 2001/29/EC of the European Parliament and of the Council of 22 May 2001 on the harmonisation of certain aspects of copyright and related rights in the information society Art 9 (Information Society Directive).
13 See contributions in Derclaye (n 11).
14 Case C-168/09 *Flos SpA v. Semeraro Casa & Famiglia SpA* (2011) ECDR 161.
15 Lionel Bently criticised the ruling by arguing that it literally repealed Article 17 of Design Directive and went against the spirit of the Information Society Directive. See; Lionel Bently, 'The Return of Industrial Copyright?' (2012) 34(10) *EIPR* 660–662.

The *Cofemel* case, as will be discussed later, has been another step in the CJEU's unfinished project of harmonising the cumulative protection and expanding copyright protection to cover fashion items.

This chapter focuses on the copyright issues related to the use of AI in fashion designs. Post-*Cofemel*, fashion designs have become protectable as a work by copyright law in addition to design law in the EU. Copyright in fashion designs arises on underlying two-dimensional works, such as drawings or patterns, or on the object itself or the photo of that object. For fashion creations to be protected under copyright law, they must meet the general requirements that apply to any type of work. This means that EU copyright law does not make any distinction between the protection standards of fashion designs (applied arts) and other types of works. Thus, this chapter explains the general framework of what copyright's protected subject matter is and what the meaning of authorship is in the EU. This analysis starts with explaining international norms that – according to the case law of the CJEU – affect EU copyright law (section 3.2). After explaining the general features of EU copyright law (section 3.3.1), it then continues to analyse the relevant standards of protection of any subject matter (section 3.3.2) and authorship of and entitlement to copyright on them (section 3.3.3). This investigation will enable us to understand whether AI-generated fashion designs can be protected under EU copyright law. The chapter then describes the general framework of exclusive rights (section 3.3.4) and exceptions (section 3.3.5). Later, it carries on by exploring two other main issues: liability deriving from infringement caused by AI-generated fashion designs and possible exceptions that can apply to it (section 3.3.6).

3.2. International legal framework

There are three main international conventions relevant to the EU copyright law, namely the Berne Convention for the Protection of Literary and Artistic Works,[16] the World Intellectual Property Organization Copyright Treaty (WCT),[17] and the Agreement on Trade-Related Aspects of Intellectual Property Rights (TRIPs Agreement).[18] How do these instruments define the concept of work? Are fashion

---

16 The Berne Convention is the first international convention that includes arrangements regarding literary and artistic works. It was signed by Germany, Belgium, France, Haiti, the UK, Spain, Switzerland, Liberia and Tunisia on 9 September 1886. Entering into force on 5 December 1987, the Convention has been amended for several times. It was amended on 4 May 1896 in Paris; on 13 November 1908 in Berlin, on 20 March 1914 in Berne; revised on 2 June 1928 in Rome, on 26 May 1948 in Brussels, on 4 July 1967 in Stockholm and on 24 July 1971 in Paris. The Convention was amended on 28 September 1979 in Paris. Berne Convention for the Protection of Literary and Artistic Works as amended on 28 September 1979, https://wipolex.wipo.int/en/text/283693.
17 WIPO Copyright Treaty (WCT) 1996. https://wipolex.wipo.int/en/text/295157.
18 Agreement on Trade-Related Aspects of Intellectual Property Rights (Marrakesh, Morocco, 15 April 1994), Marrakesh Agreement Establishing the World Trade Organization, Annex 1C, The Legal Texts: The Results of The Uruguay Round of Multilateral Trade Negotiations 321 (1999), 1869 U.N.T.S. 299, 33 I.L.M. 1197 (1994) (Hereinafter 'TRIPs Agreement').

3.2.1 Criteria for protection

The Berne Convention defines the expression 'literary and artistic works' in a very comprehensive manner to include 'every production in the literary, scientific and artistic domain, whatever may be the mode or form of its expression.'[19] It exemplifies the following subject matter that can be considered as works:

> Books, pamphlets and other writings; lectures, addresses, sermons and other works of the same nature; dramatic or dramatico-musical works; choreographic works and entertainments in dumb show; musical compositions with or without words; cinematographic works to which are assimilated works expressed by a process analogous to cinematography; works of drawing, painting, architecture, sculpture, engraving and lithography; photographic works to which are assimilated works expressed by a process analogous to photography; works of applied art; illustrations, maps, plans, sketches and three-dimensional works relative to geography, topography, architecture or science.[20]

The Convention thereby sets minimum standards for the concept of work and allows Member States to add subject matter to this long list of intellectual creations.[21] The Convention provides protection for these works as well: translations, adaptations, arrangements of music and other alterations[22] and collections such as encyclopaedias and anthologies.[23]

The WCT and the TRIPs Agreement do not contain the definition of work. These two conventions refer to the definition of work in the Berne Convention. Pursuant to the WCT, Contracting Parties shall apply Articles 2 to 6 of the Berne Convention in order to ensure the protection laid down under the Treaty.[24] The TRIPs Agreement states that the provisions concerning copyright law mentioned in Part II of the Agreement do not rule out the obligations of Member States arising from the Berne Convention.[25] In addition, both agreements envisage that Member States will comply with Articles 1 to 21 of the Berne Convention.[26]

---

19 Berne Convention Art 2(1). See; Paul Goldstein and P Bernt Hugenholtz, *International Copyright: Principles, Law, and Practice* (OUP, 2019) 35.
20 Berne Convention, Art 2/1.
21 Goldstein and Hugenholtz (n 19) 175.
22 Berne Convention Art 2/3.
23 Berne Convention Art 2/5 See; Goldstein and Hugenholtz (n 19) 35, 175.
24 WCT Art 3.
25 TRIPs Agreement Art 2(11).
26 WCT Art 1(4); TRIPs Agreement Art 9/1.

Hence, the definition of work under the Berne Convention will be applied with respect to the WCT and the TRIPs Agreement.

Computer programs are not included in the Berne Convention. However, the WCT[27] and the TRIPs Agreement[28] separately provide that computer programs shall be protected as literary works within the meaning of the Berne Convention. These two agreements also included databases in the list of subject matters that deserve copyright protection.[29]

Another issue that stands out with respect to these three conventions are subject matters that fall outside the realm of protection. As per WCT, 'Copyright protection extends to expressions and not to ideas, procedures, methods of operation or mathematical concepts as such.'[30] Similarly, the TRIPs Agreement provides that copyright protection encompasses 'expressions and not . . . ideas, procedures, methods of operation or mathematical concepts.'[31] It is also mentioned in the WCT and the TRIPs Agreement that the copyright protection provided for databases does not extend to the data and material itself.[32] The Berne Convention contains a provision that excludes certain subjects from protection: 'The protection of this Convention shall not apply to news of the day or to miscellaneous facts having the character of mere items of press information.'[33] The Berne Convention does not directly preclude the protection of ideas.[34] However, the requirement of originality sought for a work in the Conventions naturally requires that ideas cannot be protected.[35]

The Berne Convention grants discretionary power to member states in defining the criteria of eligibility for copyright protection. For instance, for the Convention, 'prescribing that works in general or any specified categories of works shall not be protected unless they have been fixed in some material form' shall be a matter for legislation in Member States.[36] With this provision, the Convention allows Member States to adopt the requirement of fixation for the protection of works.[37] It is also up to the Member States to determine the scope of protection in relation to official texts (legislative administrative and judicial),[38] *works of applied art, industrial designs* and *models*,[39] and political speeches and speeches delivered in the course of legal proceedings.[40]

---

27 WCT Art 4.
28 TRIPs Agreement Art 10(1).
29 WCT Art 5; TRIPs Agreement Art 10(2).
30 WCT Art 2.
31 TRIPs Agreement Art 9(2).
32 WCT Art 5; TRIPs Agreement Art 10(2).
33 Berne Convention Art 2(8).
34 Goldstein and Hugenholtz (n 19) 204.
35 Ibid.
36 Berne Convention Art 2(2).
37 Goldstein and Hugenholtz (n 19) 35; Justine Pila, 'The Authorial Works Protectable by Copyright' in Eleonora Rosati (ed), *The Routledge Handbook of EU Copyright Law* (Routledge, 2021) 66.
38 Berne Convention Art 2(4).
39 Berne Convention Art 2(7).
40 Berne Convention Art 2bis(1).

The Berne Convention several times mentions protection of 'original works.'[41] However, the Convention does not define the originality.[42] This is because originality was already a criterion in the national copyright laws of Member States for the recognition of copyright at the time when the Convention was adopted.[43] It is assumed that the definition of work in the Convention implies a human intellectual effort and creativity.[44] As Sam Ricketson notes, originality should be construed as a requirement that inherently exists in the expression 'literary and artistic works' identified in Art 2.[45] When it is said that a literary and artistic work should be sufficiently original, this points to the 'necessity that the author of the work is a person and has an intellectual contribution above and beyond a simple effort (sweat of the brow).'[46] However, this does not mean that works created by means of machines are left outside the realm of protection. For instance, photographs and cinematographic works are protected within the scope of the Berne Convention.

The Berne Convention gives permission to Member States for the registration of works.[47] However, this is not an obligation but a matter left to the discretion of Member States.

Regarding criteria for protection and originality, the provisions of the Berne Convention are also applied with respect to the WCT and the TRIPs Agreement.

In short, the Berne Convention (and accordingly the WCT and the TRIPs Agreement) mentions 'works of drawing' and 'photographic works' as protected subject matter. It further grants discretion to Member States to provide copyright protection for works of applied arts, industrial designs and models. This means that fashion designs can be considered as copyright work under the Berne Convention. It can also be deduced from its originality requirement that AI-generated fashion designs can be protected if there is any human contribution in the creation process.

3.2.2 Authorship and ownership

The Berne Convention is mostly built on the author's rights (*droit d'auteur*) system of continental Europe. This is inferred from the provision 'this protection shall operate for the benefit of the author and his successors in title.'[48] Although

---

41 Berne Convention Arts 2(3) (adaptations), 8 (right of translation), 11(2) (right of translation in dramatic or dramatico-musical works), 14(2) and 14 bis(4) (cinematographic works), 14ter(1) (resale right-*droit de suite*).
42 Daniel J Gervais, 'The Protection of Databases' (2007) 82(3) *Chicago-Kent Law Review* 1113.
43 Sam Ricketson, 'People or Machines? The Berne Convention and the Changing Concept of Authorship' (1991–1992) 16 *Columbia-VLA Journal of Law & the Arts* 10.
44 Goldstein and Hugenholtz (n 19) 177.
45 Ricketson (n 43) 10.
46 Ibid.
47 Berne Convention Art 2(2).
48 Berne Convention Art 2(6).

the concept of author is many times used in the text of the Berne Convention, a clear definition is not provided.[49]

The Berne Convention establishes two presumptions regarding authorship and ownership of copyright. First, the person whose name appears on the work is regarded as the author of a literary or artistic work.[50] Second, the person or legal entity whose name appears on a cinematographic work in the usual manner is presumed to be the maker of the work.[51] These two presumptions are refutable. Also, the publisher can legally represent the author in the case of anonymous and pseudonymous works until the author reveals their identity and establishes their claim to authorship of the work.[52] These rules do not define the author but offer some certainty and reduce the burden of proof for right holders. At first glance, it seems reasonable to argue that the author could then be a natural or legal person because both can exhibit their names on a work. In fact, some scholars state that the copyright protection in the Berne Convention does not necessarily stipulate human authorship. For them, the Convention does not exclude legal persons from copyright protection and acknowledges their authorship as an exemption to human authorship.[53]

However, the text and the historical context of the Convention indicates that the concept of author refers to 'the natural person who created the work.'[54] From this perspective, copyright protection belongs to the human author in the first place.[55] The reference in the Convention to the author as the person from whom the work originates and who is the right holder also support this.[56] The provisions of the Convention that explicitly grant moral rights to the author[57] also underline that a work and thus copyright protection emerge from human creativity.[58] Thus, the Convention does not impose any obligations in terms

---

49 Sam Ricketson, *The Berne Convention for the Protection of Literary and Artistic Works 1886–1986* (Kluwer, 1987) para 6.4; Jane C Ginsburg, 'The Concept of Authorship in Comparative Copyright Law' (2003) 52(4) *DePaul Law Review* 1069.
50 Berne Convention Art 15(1).
51 Berne Convention Art 15(2).
52 Berne Convention Art 15(3).
53 See; Enrico Bonadio and Nicola Lucchi, 'Introduction: Setting the Scene for Non-Conventional Copyright' in Enrico Bonadio and Nicola Lucchi (eds), *Non-Conventional Copyright. Do New and Non-Traditional Works Deserve Protection?* (Edward Elgar Publishing, 2018) 11–12; Anniina Huttunen and Anna Ronkainen, 'Translation Technology and Copyright' (2012) *Nordic Intellectual Property Review* 330–344.
54 Goldstein and Hugenholtz (n 19) 228–229; Ricketson (n 43) 11; Ginsburg (n 49) 1069.
55 Bernt Hugenholtz, João Pedro Quintais and Daniel Gervais, 'Legal Analysis' in European Commission, Directorate-General for Communications Networks, Content and Technology, C Hartmann, J Allan, P Hugenholtz et al (eds), *Trends and Developments in Artificial Intelligence: Challenges to the Intellectual Property Rights Framework: Final Report* (Publications Office, 2020) 68, https://data.europa.eu/doi/10.2759/683128.
56 Ibid.
57 Berne Convention Art 6*bis*.
58 Hugenholtz, Quintais and Gervais (n 55) 68.

of granting copyright protection to AI-generated works or more specifically fashion designs.[59]

The Berne Convention recognises joint authorship.[60] With the 1967 amendment to the Convention in Stockholm, special provisions were introduced in the relation to authorship and subsistence of cinematographic works.[61]

Regarding authorship, the WCT and the TRIPs Agreement resolve the issue by stating that the Berne Convention should be applied.[62]

3.3 EU law

3.3.1 General features of EU copyright law

Copyright law has been subject to a comprehensive harmonisation across the EU. Despite these harmonisation efforts, copyright is still protected by national legal systems. EU copyright law offers protection to all original works. This extends to computer programs, photographs and databases.

Copyright protection is governed as a sub-category of human rights under the right of property enshrined in Article 17(2) of Charter of Fundamental Rights of the EU. This also conforms to Article 1 of Additional Protocol 1 of the European Convention of Human Rights.

EU Member States are free to regulate copyright issues within the specified framework. But the efforts of the CJEU to harmonise EU copyright law through the preliminary rulings in accordance with Article 267 of the Treaty on the Functioning of the European Union[63] have raised doubts about the competence of Member States to legislate their national laws.[64]

EU copyright law operates within the framework of the international law. The EU adopted the TRIPs Agreement and the WIPO Treaty. All Member States acceded to the Berne and Rome Conventions. Therefore, both these latter conventions have a binding effect on the regulations and practices of Member States in relation to copyright, although they are not directly approved by the EU. The CJEU has deemed the Berne and Rome Conventions as sources of EU law in interpreting the EU legislation in its several decisions. Thus, the freedom and

---

59 Jane C Ginsburg, 'People Not Machines: Authorship and What It Means in the Berne Convention' (2018) 49(2) *International Review of Intellectual Property and Competition Law* 135.
60 Berne Convention Art 7*bis*.
61 Berne Convention Art 14*bis*.
62 TRIPs Agreement Art 9(1) and WCT Art 3.
63 For consolidated versions of the Treaty on European Union and the Treaty on the functioning of the European Union (OJ C115, 9.5.2008) see: Treaty of Lisbon Amending the Treaty on European Union and Treaty Establishing the European Community, O.J. 2007 C-306/1. Consolidated versions of the Treaty on European Union and the Treaty on the functioning of the European Union (OJ C115, 9.5.2008).
64 Lionel Bently describes this phenomenon as 'harmonization by stealth.' See; Lionel Bently, 'Harmonization by Stealth: Copyright and the ECJ' (20th Annual IP Law and Policy Conference, Fordham Law School, April 2012).

82 *Artificial intelligence and EU copyright protection*

competence to legislate in the national law is restricted by these international conventions.

Currently, there are 14 directives at the EU level that include provisions concerning copyright law:

- Council Directive 93/83/EEC of 27 September 1993 on the Coordination of Certain Rules Concerning Copyright and Rights Related to Copyright Applicable to Satellite Broadcasting and Cable Retransmission (Satellite and Cable Directive);[65]
- Directive 96/9/EC of the European Parliament and of the Council of 11 March 1996 on the legal protection of databases (Database Directive);[66]
- Directive 2000/31/EC of the European Parliament and of the Council of 8 June 2000 on Certain Legal Aspects of Information Society Services, in Particular Electronic Commerce, in the Internal Market (Directive on Electronic Commerce Directive);[67]
- Directive 2001/29/EC of the European Parliament and of the Council of 22 May 2001 on the harmonisation of certain aspects of copyright and related rights in the information society (Information Society Directive);[68]
- Directive 2001/84/EC of the European Parliament and of the Council of 27 September 2001 on the resale right for the benefit of the author of an original work of art (Resale Right Directive);[69]
- Directive 2004/48/EC of the European Parliament and of the Council of 29 April 2004 on the Enforcement of Intellectual Property Rights;[70]
- Directive 2006/115/EC of the European Parliament and of the Council of 12 December 2006 on rental right and lending right and on certain rights related to copyright in the field of intellectual property (Rental and Lending Rights Directive);[71]
- Directive 2006/116/EC of the European Parliament and of the Council of 12 December 2006 on the term of protection of copyright and certain related rights (Term Directive);[72]

---

65 See; Jan Rosén, 'The Satellite and Cable Directive' in Irini Stamatoudi and Paul Torremans (eds), *EU Copyright Law: A Commentary* (2nd edn, Edward Elgar Publishing, 2021) 151–179.
66 See; Estelle Derclaye, 'The Database Directive' in Stamatoudi and Torremans (n 65) 216–255.
67 2000/31/EC of the European Parliament and of the Council of 8 June 2000 on certain legal aspects of information society services, in particular electronic commerce, in the Internal Market.
68 See; Christophe *Geiger et al*, 'The Information Society Directive' in Stamatoudi and Torremans (n 65) 279–380.
69 See; Jens Gaster and Irini Stamatoudi, 'The Resale Right Directive' in Stamatoudi and Torremans (n 65) 255–278.
70 See; Irini Stamatoudi and Olivier Vrins, 'The Enforcement Directive' in Stamatoudi and Torremans (n 65) 381–478.
71 See; Sylvie Nérisson, 'The Rental and Lending Rights Directive' in Stamatoudi and Torremans (n 65) 118–150.
72 See; Gemma Minero, 'The Term Directive' in Stamatoudi and Torremans (n 65) 180–215.

- Directive 2009/24/EC of the European Parliament and of the Council of 23 April 2009 on the Legal Protection of Computer Programs (Software Directive);[73]
- Directive 2011/77/EU of the European Parliament and of the Council of 27 September 2011 amending Directive 2006/116/EC on the term of protection of copyright and certain related rights;
- Directive 2012/28/EU of the European Parliament and of the Council of 25 October 2012 on certain permitted uses of orphan works (Orphan Works Directive);[74]
- Directive 2013/37/EU of the European Parliament and of the Council of 26 June 2013 amending Directive 2003/98/EC on the Re-Use of Public Sector Information;
- Directive 2014/26/EU of the European Parliament and of the Council of 26 February 2014 on collective management of copyright and related rights and multi-territorial licensing of rights in musical works for online use in the internal market;[75]
- Directive 2019/790 of the European Parliament and of the Council of 17 April 2019 on copyright and related rights in the Digital Single Market and amending Directives 96/9/EC and 2001/29/EC (Digital Single Market Directive).[76]

Among these, the Computer Programs, Term, Database, Electronic Commerce, Information Society and Digital Single Market Directives are of particular importance. The Computer Programs Directive acknowledges that computer programs, which are original, should be protected. The Term Directive governs the term of protection of copyright or related rights and photographs, whether original or not. The Database Directive envisages a system in which databases, which are original, are protected as works, and databases that are not original are protected by the *sui generis* database right. The Electronic Commerce Directive establishes a legal framework regarding Electronic Commerce and regulates the liability regime in case of infringements by intermediary internet providers. The Information Society Directive governs the fundamental obligations of member states in relation to copyright and related rights prescribed by the Berne and Rome Conventions, the WIPO Copyright Treaty and the WIPO Performances and Phonograms Treaty. Finally, the Directive on Copyright and Related Rights in the Digital Single Market

---

73 See; Marie-Christine Janssens, 'The Software Directive' in Stamatoudi and Torremans (n 65) 75–117.
74 See; Uma Suthersanen and Maria Mercedes Frabboni, 'The Orphan Works Directive' in Stamatoudi and Torremans (n 65) 479–514.
75 See; Lucie Guibault and Sabine Jacques, 'The Collective Rights Management Directive' in Stamatoudi and Torremans (n 65) 515–574.
76 See; Irini Stamatoudi and Paul Torremans, 'The Digital Single Market Directive' in Stamatoudi and Torremans (n 65) 651–761; Eleonora Rosati, *Copyright in the Digital Single Market: Article-by-Article Commentary to the Provisions of Directive 2019/790* (OUP, 2021).

introduced new types of liability in the context of intermediaries for combatting more effectively against piracy on the internet environment, granted related rights to press publishers and provided an exception for data mining.[77]

3.3.2 Criteria for protection

Despite these comprehensive harmonisation efforts, EU copyright directives do not provide a general definition regarding the concept of work. Nor do they mention fashion designs. The Term Directive[78] is the instrument that comes closest to providing a general definition by stating that a copyright work is 'an intellectual and artistic work within the meaning of the Berne Convention.'[79]

The EU is a party to the WCT and the TRIPs Agreement. Considering this, the CJEU takes the concept of work in the Berne Convention as a benchmark in its rulings owing to the references made in these two agreements.[80] Hence, the concept of work in the Berne Convention has become a key instrument in the EU copyright law.[81]

EU copyright law has harmonised only four types of works: namely, computer programs,[82] databases,[83] photographs[84] and possibly visual works of art.[85] In addition, Justine Pila and Paul Torremans suggest that cinematographic works and audio-visual works are also protected across the EU.[86] In effect, the Rental and Lending Directive defines such works although it does not include an imperative provision for their protection.[87] It also states that the author of such works shall be considered as the director.[88] Likewise, the Term Directive includes the same provision as to the authorship of such works[89] and provides that such works shall be subject to copyright protection for 70 years.[90] Finally, the Berne Convention

---

77 For information on the general framework of EU copyright law: Annette Kur, Thomas Dreier and Stefan Luginbuehl, *European Intellectual Property Law: Text, Cases and Materials* (2nd edn, Edward Elgar Publishing, 2019) 287–405.
78 Term Directive Art 1.
79 Term Directive preamble para 16: 'A photographic work within the meaning of the Berne Convention is to be considered original if it is the author's own intellectual creation reflecting his personality, no other criteria such as merit or purpose being taken into account.'
80 For example see; Case C-277/10 *Martin Luksan v. Petrus van der Let* ECLI:EU:C:2012:65 para 59 (Hereinafter 'Luksan'); C-510/10 *DR and TV2 Danmark A/S v. NCB – Nordisk Copyright Bureau* EU:C:2012:244 para 29; C-135/10 *Società Consortile Fonografici (SCF) v. Marco Del Corso* EU:C:2012:140 paras 39–40; Case C-310/17 *Levola Hengelo BV v. Smilde Foods BV* ECLI:EU:C:2018:899 para 39 (Hereinafter 'Levola Hengelo'); *Cofemel* (n 10) para 41–42.
81 Hugenholtz, Quintais and Gervais (n 55) 68.
82 Software Directive Art 1.
83 Database Directive Art 3.
84 Term Directive Art 6.
85 Digital Single Market Directive Art 14 (Works of visual art in the public domain).
86 Justine Pila and Paul Torremans, *European Intellectual Property Law* (2nd edn, OUP, 2019) 256.
87 Rental and Lending Directive Art 2(1)(c).
88 Rental and Lending Directive Art 2(2).
89 Term Directive Art 2(1).
90 Term Directive Art 2(2).

defines cinematographic works[91] and states that these works shall be subject to copyright protection.[92]

EU copyright law has prescribed a two-tiered system of protection for films, photographs and databases.[93] Such works can enjoy copyright protection if they are the author's own intellectual creation. Databases that are not original could be protected as *sui generis* databases,[94] and the first fixation of a film and photographs that are not original could be protected in the framework of related rights.[95]

Apart from the aforementioned types of work, what are the criteria for an intellectual creation (and fashion design) to qualify as a work? It is fair to say that the concept of work in the context of EU law is harmonised as a result of a series of the CJEU rulings. For the first time in 2009, the CJEU in the *Infopaq* case set an originality standard applicable across the EU and began to accept this standard as a principal condition for copyright protection.[96] Later case law has elaborated the other criteria for copyright subsistence.

Justine Pila and Paul Torremans argue that a two-staged assessment needs to be performed for copyright protection under EU law, considering the *Infopaq* and following cases. In the first stage, one must determine whether the work in question is a creation that leaves room for making free and creative choices. In the second stage, if it leaves room to exercise free and creative choices, then one must assess whether that room was used by the author in a way that reflects the author's personality during the creation of the work.[97] In contrast, Bernt Hugenholtz, João Pedro Quintais and Daniel Gervais – by relying on the judgments of the CJEU – point out that the following criteria need to meet in order for a work to be protected by copyright:

1. The work must be in the literary, scientific or artistic domain.
2. The work must be original.
3. The work should be the product of human intellectual effort.
4. The work should be expressed 'in a manner which makes it identifiable (perceivable) with sufficient precision and objectivity, even though that expression is not necessarily in permanent form.'

In *Cofemel*, the CJEU indicated that fashion designs are not treated differently from other types of the works. For that reason, the following sections will elaborate these four criteria that apply to all protected subject matter, including fashion designs.

---

91 Berne Convention Art 2(1).
92 Berne Convention Art 14*bis*.
93 Pila and Torremans (n 86) 256, 260–261.
94 Database Directive Art 7.
95 Term Directive Art 6.
96 Case C-5/08 *Infopaq International A/S v. Danske Dagblades Forening* ECLI:EU:C:2009:465 (16 July 2009) (Hereinafter 'Infopaq').
97 Pila and Torremans (n 86) 252.

3.3.2.1 Literary, scientific or artistic domain

The definition of work in the Berne Convention[98] indicates that a subject matter should be created 'in the literary, scientific and artistic domain' to be considered as a copyright work. The CJEU seeks this requirement in some of its judgments, although it does not adopt it as a general and separate criterion. In the *Levola* case, which will be explained later, the CJEU indirectly employed this requirement when deciding that the taste of food is not a work protected under copyright law. The Court underscored that Articles 1 to 21 of the Berne Convention and the definition of work therein are binding for the EU because of the references made by the WCT,[99] although it is not a party to the Convention. The 'identifiable expression' criterion led the Court to devise the criterion of 'production in the literary, scientific or artistic domain.'

The CJEU does not explicitly apply this criterion in every case. Nevertheless, some leading academics attribute a normative weight to this criterion and require it in the consideration of copyright subsistence.[100] Most national legal systems require that an intellectual creation must fall into one of the work categories in their legislation as a condition for copyright protection.[101] Relying on this, it can be said that this criterion must equally be required at the EU level.

However, there are differing views about this requirement. Eleonora Rosati, for example, argues that when specifying the content of the originality standard, the CJEU has also harmonised an open-ended list of subject matter, comprising all conceivable intellectual creations, across the EU. For Rosati, the Court has not confined copyright protection to certain types of work even to those that exist in the Berne Convention.[102]

As mentioned in section 3.2.1, fashion designs are not excluded from the scope of the Berne Convention. Thus, AI-generated fashion designs would not have difficulty meeting this criterion.

3.3.2.2 Originality

Perhaps the most important requirement that must be met for copyright protection to arise is that the work must be original. Only the Software Directive, the Database Directive and the Term Directive require originality as a condition for copyright protection. The Software and Database Directives require that a

---

98 Berne Convention Art 2(1).
99 WCT Art 1(4).
100 Hugenholtz, Quintais and Gervais (n 55) 69; Goldstein and Hugenholtz (n 19) 176; Pila (n 37) 71.
101 Goldstein and Hugenholtz (n 19) 176.
102 Eleonora Rosati, *Originality in EU Copyright: Full Harmonization through Case Law* (Edward Elgar Publishing, 2013) 127 (Rosati, 2013); Eleonora Rosati, 'Closed Subject Matter Systems are No Longer Compatible with EU Copyright' (2014) 12 *GRUR International* 1112–1118; Eleonora Rosati, *Copyright and the Court of Justice of the European Union* (OUP, 2019) 92–93 (Rosati, 2019). For a similar opinion see; Marianne Levin, 'The Cofemel Revolution – Originality, Equality and Neutrality' in Rosati (n 37) 95.

computer program or database can be protected by copyright only where the program or database is original in the sense that it is the 'author's own intellectual creation.'[103] A similar requirement was also introduced for photographs in the Term Directive.[104]

What does the requirement that a work be its 'author's own intellectual creation' involve? The legislation offers very little explanation. The requirement has two dimensions. First, the work must be 'the author's own.' This means that the work originates from the author and is not copied from someone else. Second, and more importantly, the work must be an 'intellectual creation.' This two-dimensional standard is generally referred to as 'originality.'[105]

Originality in copyright law is different from individual character and novelty tests in design law. The 'design approach' on which current EU design law is built consciously chose a middle path between both legal models existing in pre-harmonised Europe. These were 'patent approach' and the 'copyright approach.'[106] The primary goal was neither to promote individual creativity nor technical progress but rather to strengthen the capacity of industrial design to serve as 'marketing tool'.[107] EU design law placed emphasis on the communication relationship between the design and the public. In contrast, the personal relationship between the author and the work is at the centre in EU copyright law. Thus, different from copyright, capability of a design to establish that relationship is assessed for design protection. The market (informed user's) perspective and prior art matters in this assessment.[108] In copyright, however, the work constitutes the personal expression of an individual author. Originality is the signifier that sets up the link between the author and the work by evidencing the author's 'contributions and choices that are directly relevant to the structuring of the expression of the work.'[109]

With the *Infopaq* case, the CJEU has held that the originality standard (namely, 'author's own intellectual creation') is applicable to all works of authorship in

---

103 Software Directive Art 1 (3); Database Directive Art 3(1).
104 Term Directive Art 6.
105 Objective originality means that the work originates from the author; it is not copied. In contrast, subjective originality means that the work bears the personal stamp of the author. For more information on the distinction between objective and subjective originality, see; Mireille Van Eechoud, 'Along the Road to Uniformity – Diverse Readings of the Court of Justice Judgments on Copyright Work' (2012) 3(1) *JIPITEC* 70; Tatiana-Eleni Synodinou, 'The Foundations of the Concept of Work in European Copyright Law' in Tatiana-Eleni Synodinou (ed), *Codification of European Copyright Law. Challenges and Perspectives* (Wolters Kluwer, 2012) 94.
106 Annette Kur and Marianne Levin, 'The Design Approach Revisited: Background and Meaning' in Annette Kur, Marianne Levin and Jens Schovsbo (eds), *The EU Design Approach: A Global Appraisal* (Edward Elgar Publishing, 2018) 5–7.
107 Annette Kur, '*Unité de l'art* is Here to Stay – *Cofemel* and its Consequences' (2020) 15(4) *Journal of Intellectual Property Law & Practice* 294.
108 Ibid 295.
109 Lionel Bently, Brad Sherman, Dev Gangjee and Phillip Johnson, *Intellectual Property Law* (5th edn, OUP, 2018) 106.

addition to computer programs, databases and photographs.[110] No common originality threshold existed across EU before *Infopaq*. In the UK, which terminated its membership, the work must originate from the author and must not be copied, and the author must exhibit 'labour, skill and judgement' for the work to be original.[111] In Continental European countries sometimes a higher, sometimes a more flexible standard was sought,[112] such as 'personal intellectual creation' (*'persönliche geistige Schöpfungen'*),[113] 'intellectual production with creative character'[114] or 'intellectual work' (*'oeuvre de l'esprit'*).[115] The originality standard of the 'author's own intellectual creation' has reconciled the 'labour, skill and judgement' concept in the UK law and the certain level of creativity (*'Gestaltungshohe'*) concept in the German law.[116]

Post *Infopaq*, subsequent cases have further elaborated the inherent features of the originality.[117] The following section will discuss these features.

3.3.2.2.1 *INFOPAQ*

The *Infopaq* case concerned the question of whether an electronic news-clippings service infringed copyright when it reproduced an 11-word fragment comprising the five words on either side of a search term. The service of Infopaq included drawing up these fragments of news and articles that it obtained by scanning original texts from newspapers through a data-capture technique and sending these fragments to its customers by e-mail.[118] The publications that were scanned were deleted afterward.[119]

A Danish court referred the case to the CJEU by asking whether this comprised a 'part' of an article protected by copyright. The Court took the view that to decide whether the reproduction of an 11-word news extract was infringement required an assessment of the conditions of copyright protection for that 'part.' Reviewing the Berne Convention and the Community *acquis* on copyright (the Software,

---

110 Rosati 2013 (n 102) 111; Levin (n 102) 89; For an opinion suspicious about this; Thomas Höppner, 'Reproduction in Part of Online Articles in the Aftermath of Infopaq (C-5/08): *Newspaper Licensing Agency Ltd v. Meltwater Holding BV*' (2011) 33 *EIPR* 331.
111 Bently *et al* (n 109) 96–97.
112 Rosati 2013 (n 102) 69–80.
113 Urheberrechsgestetz Art 2(2).
114 Legge 22 April 1941 No 633 – *Protezione del diritto d'autore e di altri diritti connessi al suo esercizio* Art 1(1) ve Codice Civile Art 2575.
115 Code de la propriété intellectuelle Art L111–1(1).
116 Agnès Lucas-Schloetter, 'Is There a Concept of European Copyright Law? History, Evolution, Policies and Politics and the *Acquis Communautaire*' in Stamatoudi and Torremans (n 65) 10; Levin (n 102) 89.
117 For academic commentaries on the originality requirement see; Rosati 2019 (n 102) 88–93; Synodinou (n 105) 99; Tito Rendas, 'Copyright Protection of Designs in the EU: How Many Originality Standards Is Too Many?' (2018) 13 *Journal of Intellectual Property Law & Practice* 442.
118 *Infopaq* (n 96) para 13.
119 Ibid paras 16–20.

Database and Term Directives), the CJEU accepted a generalised standard of originality for all authorial works: namely, the 'author's own intellectual creation.'[120]

The CJEU then emphasised a few points on the assessment of when parts of a work, instead of the work as a whole, shall be considered original and therefore protected by the reproduction right.[121] The originality in newspaper articles clearly derives from the form of the text. The form of a literary work manifests itself through the presentation of the subject and the 'linguistic expression.'[122] Words considered in isolation cannot constitute an original work and therefore cannot enjoy copyright protection. The author may express their creativity only 'through the choice, sequence and combination of those words' and 'achieve a result which is an intellectual creation.'[123] Sentences or parts of sentences taken from the article, which is the author's own intellectual creation, can be protected as a work in accordance with the Information Society Directive.

The Court indicated that whether the 11 words were a 'partial reproduction' depended on whether they were themselves intellectual creations and that this was a matter to be assessed by the national court.[124]

Consequently, a work must be 'the author's own intellectual creation' to be considered original.[125] This applies to all categories of work prescribed in the Berne Convention.[126]

The Court of Justice has thus felt it necessary to give further content to the concept, referring to the need for the exercise of 'creative choices.'

3.3.2.2.2 EXTERNAL CONSTRAINTS AND CREATIVE FREEDOM

According to EU copyright law, the author must have a creative freedom without being exposed to some external constraints during the creation process. External constraints can be rule-based, technical, functional or informational.[127] The meaning of these constraints will be elaborated in the text that follows.

3.3.2.2.2.1 Rule-based constraints The genre or style rules related to literature, cinema, arts, music and fashion design is one of the prominent rule-based constraints. For instance, creating a painting in suprematism style requires specific

---

120 Ibid paras 34–37.
121 Parts of sentences taken from the news article comprising eleven words.
122 *Infopaq* (n 96) para 44.
123 Ibid para 45.
124 Ibid para 48.
125 Ibid para 51.
126 Ibid paras 34, 48. See; Noam Shemtov, 'Software and Graphical User Interfaces' in Tanya Aplin (ed), *Research Handbook on Intellectual Property and Digital Technologies* (Edward Elgar Publishing, 2020) 6 (arguing that the creativity threshold of the traditional UK standard of originality – skill, labour and judgement – is lower and easier to meet compared to the 'author's own intellectual creation' standard).
127 Hugenholtz, Quintais and Gervais (n 55) 72.

standard features of expression such as drawing simple geometric shapes.[128] Composing a Blues song requires including specific standard harmony and rhythms.[129] Inspired by the 1960s hippie aesthetic and festival culture, the hallmarks of bohemian fashion style are flowing maxi dresses, long skirts, bell-bottom pants, large-brimmed hats and slouchy handbags. Clothing must incorporate earth tones, natural fabrics and dyes, and prints to be considered 'boho chic.' EU copyright laws have found a solution to the style constraints by excluding style from the subject matter of production.[130] Such an exclusion from copyright protection is a result of idea/expression dichotomy. This outcome stems from the principle that copyright protection 'extends to expressions and not to ideas, procedures, methods of operation or mathematical concepts as such.'[131]

Creative freedom can falter when it meets game rules. One of the cases that dealt with the constraining effect of game rules was *Football Association Premier League (FAPL)*.[132] The claimant in the *FAPL* case was the Football Association Premier League Ltd, which runs the English Premier League. This company films the English Premier League football matches. The company also concludes the licensing agreements on television broadcasts and makes the audio-visual content of sporting events available to the public by means of television broadcasting.[133] FAPL transmits the signals of Premier League football matches to the broadcasters it has an agreement with (which have won the tender by auction).[134]

The live broadcasting rights of Premier League football matches in the UK at the date of the case belonged to BSkyB Ltd. Entities in the UK wishing to make these broadcasts available to the public at places like hotels and restaurants had to sign a commercial subscription agreement with BSkyB Ltd.[135] However, some businesses in the UK transmitted the Premier League broadcasts of Greek televisions by using decoders they bought from foreign countries rather than the broadcasts offered by BSkyB Ltd. The businesses therefore avoided paying higher fees to BSkyB Ltd and made the matches available for more affordable fees.[136]

The dispute inevitably arose in the context of whether the (unauthorised) acts of transmission of football matches could amount to an infringement of the reproduction right under the Information Society Directive. This question again required the assessment of whether football matches are original works under EU

---

128 See; Susie Hodge, *50 Art Ideas (50 Ideas You Really Need to Know)* (Quercus Publishing, 2011).
129 For instance, for 12-bar Blues pattern, see; Joachim-Ernst Berendt and Günther Huesmann, *The Jazz Book: From Ragtime to the 21st Century* (7th edn, Lawrence Hill Books, 2009) 208.
130 Stef van Gompel, 'Creativity, Autonomy and Personal Touch. A Critical Appraisal of the CJEU's Originality Test for Copyright' in Mireille van Eechoud (ed), *The Work of Authorship* (Amsterdam University Press, 2014) 112.
131 TRIPs Agreement Art 9(2); WCT Art 2.
132 Joined Case C-403/08 and C-429/08 *Football Association Premier League Ltd v. QC Leisure and Karen Murphy v. Media Protection Services Ltd* [2011] ECR I-09083 (4 October 2011) (Hereinafter 'FAPL').
133 *FAPL* (n 132) paras 30–35.
134 Ibid para 36.
135 Ibid para 41.
136 Ibid para 42.

copyright law. Recalling the originality criterion in the *Infopaq* case,[137] the CJEU indicated that sporting events could not be classified as original (authorial) works in the context of the Information Society Directive.[138] The Court further stated that this principle applied particularly to football matches 'which are subject to rules of the game, leaving no room for creative freedom for the purposes of copyright.'[139] Accordingly, the CJEU held that football matches were not classifiable as works because they are not original due to constraining effects of the game rules.[140]

The second ruling related to the impact of game (and perhaps business-centred operational) rules on creative freedom was delivered in *Football Dataco*.[141] In this case, the claimants alleged that the four defendants that operated as media and betting companies infringed their copyright by using the football fixture lists without paying any licence fee.[142] The CJEU was asked to advise on whether the creation of football fixture lists in the form a database was an act of 'intellectual creation.'

The Court once more underlined that the phrase 'author's own intellectual creation' denoted originality for databases as well. For the setting up of the database, the originality requirement is satisfied when the author expresses their creative ability by making free and creative choices through 'the selection or arrangement of the data' the database contains. This meant that any creativity that went into the *generation* of data (the dates and times of the football fixtures) was irrelevant to the originality of the database. In contrast, this criterion would not be satisfied when there are technical considerations, rules or constraints in the setting of databases that leave no room for creative freedom.[143]

The Court also indicated that 'significant amount of labour and skill' was not itself sufficient to render a work original in the European sense. Adding 'a significant meaning to' the data by choosing and arranging the data did not give rise to an author's own intellectual creation either. What is required is an 'original expression of the creative freedom of its author.'[144]

Thus, the CJEU held that football fixture lists could not benefit from copyright protection because they could not be considered original when they were prepared in line with rules, parameters, organisational constraints and the demands of clubs that leave no room for creative freedom.

3.3.2.2.2.2 Functional and technical constraints
3.3.2.2.2.2.1 Computer programs
Under EU copyright law, where expression is 'dictated by function' or technical considerations, originality will not be present. Functional and technical

---

137 Ibid para 97.
138 Ibid para 98.
139 Ibid.
140 Ibid para 99.
141 Case C-604/10 *Football Dataco Ltd v. Yahoo! UK Ltd* ECLI:EU:C:2012:115 (1 March 2012) (Hereinafter 'Football Dataco').
142 Ibid paras 20–21.
143 Ibid paras 32–39.
144 Ibid paras 41–42.

constraints generally arise in connection to technological products and products of applied arts. The first type of work that springs to mind in relation to functional intellectual creations is computer programs.[145]

As mentioned previously, EU copyright protection does not cover ideas, methods, application principles, mathematical formulas or scientific theories.[146] The Software Directive provides that algorithms cannot be protected to the extent that they comprise ideas and principles. For that reason, they are not protected under the Directive.[147] This is because extending protection to the ideas and principles underlying algorithms would create a monopoly on such information that everybody could use to contribute to technological progress.[148] David Bainbridge states that because algorithms are significant parts of the development and design of computer programs,[149] they should be made available for others to use.[150] In contrast, Marie-Christine Janssens suggests that algorithms could be protected by copyright law under certain circumstances. According to Janssens, this is so where algorithms go beyond abstract definition of the solution method and simple instructions and generate structured solutions.[151] Leaving algorithms outside the scope of the copyright protection seems a more appropriate approach because this will prevent monopolising ideas and creating any constraints on the freedom to create.

In *BSA*[152], the CJEU considered the question of whether 'graphical user interfaces' are non-functional and whether technical considerations necessary for their development affect the creative freedom of their author. This inquiry also required the assessment of when a 'graphical user interface' would be protected as an ordinary authorial work in comparison to a computer program.

According to the CJEU, computer programs in laws language refer to codes in any form of expression such as 'source code and object code' that could be reproduced in computer (data processing) languages.[153] Graphical user interfaces are interactive interfaces that allow for communication between the user and the software.[154] Emphasising this distinction, the CJEU held that graphical user interfaces cannot be regarded as computer programs and therefore cannot benefit from the protection afforded for computer programs under the Software Directive. This

---

145 Pila (n 37) 69.
146 TRIPs Agreement Art 9(2); WCT Art 2.
147 Software Directive preamble 11.
148 David Bainbridge, *Intellectual Property* (10th edn, Pearson, 2018) 313.
149 Ibid 313.
150 David Bainbridge, *Information Technology and Intellectual Property Law* (7th edn, Bloomsbury Professional, 2019) 99.
151 Janssens (n 73) 83. For a similar argument see; Michel Walter and Walter Blocher, 'Computer Program Directive' in Michel Walter and Silke von Lewinski (eds), *European Copyright Law: A Commentary* (OUP, 2010) 104.
152 Case C-393/09 *Bezpečnostní softwarová asociace – Svaz softwarové ochrany v. Ministerstvo kultury v. Minister- stvo kultury* ECLI:EU:C:2010:816 (22 December 2010) (Hereinafter 'BSA').
153 *BSA* (n 152) paras 34–35.
154 Ibid para 40.

derives from the fact that they do not enable 'the reproduction of a computer program.'[155]

The CJEU, however, indicated that graphical user interfaces can be protected under Information Society Directive if they meet relevant requirements. For copyright protection to arise, graphical user interfaces must be original as stated in *Infopaq*. The originality of such works is deemed present, where the author could demonstrate their creative choices through 'the specific arrangement or configuration of all the components forming graphical user interfaces.'[156]

The originality criterion is not met in such cases where the components that form the user interface 'differ only by their *technical functions*.'[157] To support this, the CJEU employed the idea/expression dichotomy: because applying an idea with different methods becomes so limited that the idea and the expression become inseparable.[158] In this case, there would be only a very limited space where the author could exercise their creativity, and therefore the final product would lack originality.[159] This means that where the components are *dictated by their function*, they are associated with the concept of 'idea' rather than 'expression.'[160]

Graphical user interface, in a broader sense, encompasses both textual and graphical elements of the configurations on user screens. Accordingly, there are three types of graphical user interface: (i) desktop (full screen area); (ii) static elements displayed on the full screen area such as pointers, icons and menus and (iii) animated effects and motion features such as the genie effects in MAC operating systems.[161]

A graphical user interface must be distinguished from the elements that serve its technical function, and its originality must be determined in line with its special arrangement and format.[162] Hence, when there is only one or limited number of ways to express an idea, the idea and the expression merge, in which case copyright protection would not arise. Is the intention of the author in the design of the subject matter decisive in determining this issue? Or should it be assessed whether there are alternative ways of expressing an idea as a work? Noam Shemtov thinks that the CJEU considered the merger doctrine and adopted the latter interpretation by looking at the existence of alternative ways of expressing an idea.[163] However, later in the *Brompton Bicycle* case, the existence of alternative ways of expression was deemed inconsequential in this respect.

---

155 Ibid paras 41–42.
156 Ibid para 48.
157 Ibid para 48.
158 Ibid para 49.
159 Ibid para 50.
160 Irini Stamatoudi, 'Originality under EU Copyright Law' in Paul Torremans (ed), *Research Handbook on Copyright Law* (2nd edn, Edward Elgar, 2017) 78.
161 Shemtov (n 126) 3.
162 *BSA* (n 152) para 48.
163 Shemtov (n 126) 5.

Shemtov further argues that an icon can benefit from copyright protection since the functional considerations do not exclusively shape its configuration and design. Shemtov also suggests that the same can be said with respect to pointers but thinks that it is not very likely that they could be qualified for the copyright protection. According to Shemtov, the selection and arrangement of the sub-elements of menus is just like compilations: thus, menus could be protected by copyright, provided they reflect the free and creative choices of the author. The fact that a sub-menu element is primarily designed for a functional and pragmatic purpose does not preclude it from copyright protection.[164] Indeed, the icons made by Susan Kare for Macintosh Computer programs can be attached to fashion design and protected under copyright law.[165]

The CJEU has set out an important 'mechanical' principle stating that where creative choice is highly constrained by rules or functional considerations, the resulting 'work' is unlikely to be original. This principle was reiterated by the Court in the *SAS* case concerning program functionality, data file formats, programming languages and user manuals.[166]

In the case, the defendant developed a program using the same programming language and file format with the same functionality without access to the source codes of the computer program belonging to the plaintiff. The CJEU thus took the opportunity to examine the conceptual nature of these subject matters. The Software Directive excludes program functionality and programming languages from protection.[167] Yet, the question of whether the said elements could be protected by copyright was examined in the case.

The idea/expression dichotomy and exclusion of functionality was invoked once again in *SAS*. Examining the Software Directive,[168] international instruments[169] and its assessments in the *BSA* case,[170] the CJEU held that program functionality cannot be protected by copyright law because it is an idea, not a form of expression.[171] According to the CJEU, extending copyright protection to program functionality would lead to the monopolisation of ideas, which would be detrimental to technological progress and industrial development.[172] The purpose of extending protection to computer programs under the Directive is to leave other authors the 'desired latitude' to create other computer programs.[173] Accordingly,

---

164 Ibid 8.
165 Alexandra Lange, 'The Woman Who Gave the Macintosh a Smile' (*New Yorker*, 19 April 2018) www.newyorker.com/culture/cultural-comment/the-woman-who-gave-the-macintosh-a-smile.
166 Case C-406/10 *SAS Institute Inc v. World Programming Ltd* ECLI:EU:C:2012:259 (2 May 2012) (Hereinafter 'SAS Institute').
167 Software Directive preamble 7.
168 *SAS Institute* (n 166) paras 29–32.
169 WCT and TRIPs agreement. See; *SAS Institute* (n 166) paras 33–34.
170 *SAS Institute* (n 166) paras 35–38.
171 Ibid para 39.
172 Ibid para 40.
173 Ibid para 41.

it is free to write a program that overlaps with, and even completely bears the identical function of, another computer program.

According to the CJEU, just like program functionality, programming languages and file formats are not considered as forms of expression under the Software Directive. Thus, these elements are not protected under the Directive.[174] Notwithstanding this, the situation does not represent an obstacle to the protection of programming languages or file formats under the Information Society Directive if they are the author's own intellectual creation.[175]

Justine Pila and Paul Torremans note that the CJEU judgment in *SAS* seems to be justified regarding these three subject matters and is consistent with the principle discussed earlier that copyright may subsist in a subject matter (computer program) as well as its description (program functionality, data file formats and programming languages). However, these two authors find it difficult to understand how the subject matter excluded from the legal definition of a computer program to limit copyright protection could somehow be regarded as an authorial work protected by copyright on another basis.[176]

When considering whether and when a user manual might be an original literary work, the CJEU explicitly stated that 'keywords, syntax, commands and combinations of commands, options, defaults and iterations' used in creating software are unprotected because they consist of 'words, figures or mathematical concepts' that are not intellectual creations of the author of the computer program.[177] However, the Court accepted that the 'choice, sequence and combination' of these elements might be such that the author expresses their creativity and creates an 'intellectual creation.'[178] Although it is not stated in long lines, it seems clear that for the Court originality can arise only from the 'choice, sequence and combination' of these elements; their functional and ideational aspects are not considered in the assessment of copyright subsistence.

Another technology-related subject matter worth mentioning is video games. The legal status of video games in the EU law was analysed in the *Nintendo* case.[179] The case essentially concerned the legality of a software bearing a 'modchip,' which could be used to circumvent the authentication systems in video games. However, the question also involved the assessment of the legal nature of a videogame. In *Nintendo*, the CJEU stated that a video game is a hybrid product 'comprising not only a computer program but also graphic and sound elements.'

---

174 Ibid paras 43–44.
175 Ibid paras 45–46.
176 Pila and Torremans (n 86) 259. See also; Richard Arnold, 'Copyright in Software: Functionality' in Aplin (n 126) 41 (suggesting that considering the CJEU decision in *SAS Institute* on file formats, application programming interfaces cannot be protected as computer programs since they mostly ensure interoperability).
177 *SAS Institute* (n 166) para 66.
178 Ibid para 67.
179 Case C-355/12 *Nintendo Co Ltd and others v. PC Box Srl* ECLI:EU:C:2014:25 (Hereinafter 'Nintendo').

According to the CJEU, graphic and sound elements, although created in computer language, have a unique creative value. The Court opined that these elements cannot be reduced to that language and form the parts of the originality of the video game. Accordingly, it was ruled that a computer program, graphic and sound elements are protected together with the entire work (video game) by copyright regime under the Information Society Directive (not under the Software Directive).[180] The CJEU seems to adopt the 'unitary approach' rather than the 'distributive approach.' Under this approach, video games are treated as an integrated work bigger than the components forming them.[181]

The CJEU's *Nintendo* judgment gave rise to various interpretations and criticism. Daithí Mac Síthigh states that graphics and sounds are protected by copyright together with the entire work 'when they are part of the originality of the game.'[182] In a similar vein, Justine Pila and Paul Torremans suggest that the protection granted to video games by the Information Society Directive is supplementary to the protection granted to the computer programs underlying the games by the Software Directive.[183] Likewise, James Russell maintains that the expression 'together with the entire work' used in the *Nintendo* judgment implies both that the video game could be protected in its entirety and that the components thereof could be protected separately as works. Russell goes on to state that the judgment was handed down specific to the technological protection measures in the Nintendo game consoles and recalls that the potential impact of the judgment would remain limited.[184] If there is one thing certain in *Nintendo*, it is that a video game cannot be described solely as a computer program. It is obvious that the judgment led to several controversies.[185]

3.3.2.2.2.2.2 Works of applied arts
Many products we use in our daily lives, like fashion designs, stand out with their aesthetic design in addition to their technical functions. Like computer programs, whether the functional elements of such products surpass their creative design is an important factor in determining copyright subsistence over them. In this way, it becomes possible to establish whether the author was left with sufficient space for their creative choices in the creation of the subject matter. One such product is the Brompton Bicycle that has a special design. What makes the bicycle special

---

180 *Nintendo* (n 179) para 23.
181 James Russell, *Pawnership: Is Copyright Appropriately Equipped to Handle Videogames* (Uppsala Universitet Master Thesis, 2018) 13.
182 Daithí Mac Síthigh, 'The Game's the Thing: Property, Priorities and Perceptions in the Video Game Industries' in Megan Richardson and Sam Ricketson (eds), *Research Handbook on Intellectual Property in Media and Entertainment* (Edward Elgar Publishing, 2017) 348.
183 Pila and Torremans (n 86) 260.
184 Russell (n 181) 14.
185 For another critical view see; Marcella Favale, 'A Wii Too Stretched? The ECJ Extends to Game Consoles the Protection of DRM – on Tough Conditions' (2015) 37 *European Intellectual Property Review* 105.

is that it can have three different positions: 'folded position,' 'unfolded position' and a 'stand-by position enabling the bicycle to stay balanced on the ground.' In *Brompton Bicycle*,[186] whether the design of this bicycle constituted an authorial work was brought before the CJEU.[187] A Belgian court particularly asked whether a subject matter, the appearance of which is even partially dictated by its technical function, could be protected as a work under EU copyright law and particularly under the Information Society Directive.[188]

The CJEU admitted that the bicycle's design – being folded into three positions, one of which allows it to be kept balanced on the ground – shows that its shape is necessary to achieve a certain technical result.[189] Nevertheless, as the CJEU warned, the fact that the shape of the bicycle is the result of a technical function does not mean that it will automatically be excluded from copyright. Under these circumstances, the national court must ascertain whether the author has reflected their personality, free and creative choices on the bicycle, and whether the shape of the bicycle is 'solely' a result of its technical function and therefore whether the work is original.[190]

The *Brompton Bicycle* case means that although technical considerations have impact on the creation of a subject matter, the work will still be protected under copyright law. This depends on the condition that the author manages to put their personal stamp on that subject matter.[191] However, if the shape of the subject matter is entirely dictated by a technical consideration, protection will not subsist.[192]

In the Court's assessment of whether the shape of the product is relevant in achieving a technical result, these four considerations are taken as reference points: the existence of alternative shapes is not a decisive factor for the purposes of this assessment; the effectiveness of the shape in achieving the technical result is also irrelevant;[193] the intention of the author in achieving this technical result is examined; and the existence of (then expired) patent can be considered in such assessment to the extent that they reveal what is considered in the selection of shape of the product.[194]

3.3.2.2.2.3 Informational constraints Another external constraint affecting the creative freedom is the information content of the subject matter. The *Funke Medien* case[195] is an example where this kind of informational constraint

---

186 Case C-833/18 *Brompton Bicycle Ltd v. Chedech/Get2Get* ECLI:EU:C:2020:461 (11 June 2020) (Hereinafter 'Brompton Bicycle').
187 For a practical analysis of the case, see; Eleonora Rosati, 'Round-up of CJEU Copyright Decisions in 2020' (2021) 16(6) *Journal of Intellectual Property Law & Practice* 527–529.
188 *Brompton Bicycle* (n 186) paras 18–19.
189 Ibid para 29.
190 Ibid paras 30–34.
191 Ibid para 26.
192 Ibid para 33.
193 Ibid para 35.
194 Ibid para 36.
195 Case C–469/17 *Funke Medien NRW GmbH v. Bundesrepublik Deutschland* ECLI:EU:C:2019:623 (29 July 2019) (Herein after 'Funke Medien').

emerges.[196] The dispute in *Funke Medien* was not to do with informational constraints but concerned the legality of the unauthorised publication of the government's military status reports by a German media company. However, the CJEU also felt obliged to make observations on the possibility of copyright protection of such subject matter.

The CJEU once again explained that for a subject matter to be regarded as a 'work,' it must be original and clearly expressed. For the Court, the originality criterion required assessing the impact of informative content of the reports over the author's ability to make free and creative choices in drawing them up. The Court then made the following observations: if the weekly military reports are solely factual, and the content of the reports are essentially composed of facts, the expressions and facts in the reports have become inseparable. Under these circumstances, the reports are characterised only by their informative content, which eliminates originality. Because the writers of the reports have to adhere to the technical facts presented to them and the form in which such facts are conveyed, and it is not possible for them to express their creativity in such a way to create an original work.[197] Therefore, if they do not have the possibility to add their creativity to the reports, then the reports will not qualify as a work.

The CJEU's ruling on military status reports mirrors the general principle under copyright law that protection cannot be extended to information and facts (just like ideas and functions) per se. It seems clear that the Court views the input into the creation of basic facts, ideas and functions as irrelevant to the assessment of whether the ultimate production based upon those facts, ideas, and function is an 'intellectual creation.' However, it raises a significant question in the context of consistency of judicial decisions: 11-word text in *Infopaq* (though meaningless and pretty much informational) can qualify as a work under EU copyright law, whereas a complete report in *Funke Medien* (including so many meaningful words and sentences) cannot. This is difficult to reconcile for the sake of legal clarity.

---

196 For academic commentaries on this case, see; Caterina Sganga, 'A Decade of Fair Balance Doctrine, and How to Fix It: Copyright Versus Fundamental Rights before the CJEU from Promusicae to Funke Medien, Pelham and Spiegel Online' (2019) 41(11) *European Intellectual Property Review* 683–696; Thom Snijders and Stijn van Deursen, 'The Road Not Taken – the CJEU Sheds Light on the Role of Fundamental Rights in the European Copyright Framework – a Case Note on the Pelham, Spiegel Online and Funke Medien Decisions' (2019) 50 *International Review of Intellectual Property and Competition Law* 1176–1190; Jonathan Griffiths, 'European Union Copyright Law and the Charter of Fundamental Rights – Advocate General Szpunar's Opinions in (C-469/17) Funke Medien, (C-476/17) Pelham GmbH and (C-516/17) Spiegel Online' (2019) 20 *ERA Forum* 35–50; Christophe Geiger and Elena Izyumenko, 'The Constitutionalization of Intellectual Property Law in the EU and the Funke Medien, Pelham and Spiegel Online Decisions of the CJEU: Progress, but Still Some Way to Go!' (2020) 51 *International Review of Intellectual Property and Competition Law* 282–306.

197 *Funke Medien* (n 195) para 24.

3.3.2.2.3 PERSONALITY AND CREATIVE CHOICES

As the CJEU's case law suggests, where sufficient 'creative space' is available for the creator, this is a strong indicator for originality. But is this enough to qualify as a work? Or should this 'creative space' be used? Under EU copyright law 'if the author expresses their creative skill in the production of the work by making free and creative choices,'[198] then another aspect of originality standard is met.[199] The CJEU first developed this *metaphysical* principle in *Painer*[200] and recently adopted in *Funke Medien*[201] and *Cofemel*.[202] After setting out mechanical standards of creating of a work, the Court perhaps is now searching for 'the first causes of things.'

The CJEU has in several cases mentioned 'creative choices.'[203] This language precisely indicates that using the creative space 'non-creatively' (such as rather mundane choices) would be likely to lead not to qualify as a protected work. However, as will be discussed in the next section, the criterion of originality does not require artistic superiority or aesthetic quality and does not require the work to be new.[204]

In *Painer*, a photographer brought an action against newspapers, claiming that they infringed her copyright by using the photographs taken by her without authorisation.[205] One of the questions that was referred to the CJEU was whether 'portrait photos . . . are afforded "weaker" copyright protection or no copyright protection at all against adaptations because, in view of their "realistic image," the degree of formative freedom is too minor?'[206] Thus, the question was related to whether a portrait photograph of a schoolgirl taken in an ordinary way could be considered as a work.

The CJEU started its evaluations as regards this question by referring to the originality standard it set in the *Infopaq* case: copyright protection arises in relation to a photograph, 'which is original in the sense that it is its author's own intellectual creation.'[207] The Court then added another dimension to originality in stating that to talk about the author's own intellectual creation, 'the work must reflect the author's personality.' This is the case 'if the author was able to express his creative abilities in the production of the work by making free and creative choices'[208] and if there is 'creative freedom' to exhibit this.[209]

---

198 See; Case C-145/10 *Eva-Maria Painer v. Standard Verlags GmbH* (2011) ECR I-2533 (1 December 2011) paras 87–88 (Hereinafter 'Painer'); *Funke Medien* (n 195) para 19.
199 Hugenholtz, Quintais and Gervais (n 55) 70.
200 *Painer* (n 198).
201 *Funke Medien* (n 195) para 19.
202 *Cofemel* (n 10) para 30.
203 *Painer* (n 198) para 93.
204 Hugenholtz, Quintais and Gervais (n 55) 74.
205 *Painer* (n 198) paras 37–39.
206 Ibid para 43.
207 Ibid para 87.
208 Ibid paras 88–89.
209 Ibid para 93.

What are the relevant parameters of making free and creative choices? In other words, which choices are regarded as creativity? In *Infopaq*, the creativity (originality) emerged by the selection, arrangement and combination of words in the context of literary works.[210] The same was sought for military status reports in *Funke Medien*.[211] It was 'the selection or arrangement of the data' for databases in *Football Dataco*.[212]

In *Painer*, the CJEU listed the parameters concerning the creative choices that would give rise to originality when elements not protected in isolation are combined. According to the CJEU, a photography artist can make creative choices in three stages:

> In the preparation phase, the photographer can choose the background, the subject's pose and the lighting. When taking a portrait photograph, he can choose the framing, the angle of view and the atmosphere created. Finally, when selecting the snapshot, the photographer may choose from a variety of developing techniques the one he wishes to adopt or, where appropriate, use computer software.[213]

Painer judgment is illuminating in terms of subject matter created with the aid of machines and portrait photographs. According to the CJEU:

> The photographer can make free and creative choices in several ways and at various points in the production of a work. . . . By making those various choices, the author of a portrait photograph can stamp the work created with his 'personal touch.' Consequently, as regards a portrait photograph, the freedom available to the author to exercise his creative abilities will not necessarily be minor or even non-existent.[214]

The concept of personal touch acknowledged in the judgment is a useful tool to distinguish carefully structured photographic works from plain snapshots.[215] Therefore, *Painer* demonstrated that the creative choices can be made at different stages of creation of work, namely conception, execution and redaction phases, and at various degrees.[216] Creativity even in the preparation stage could be sufficient for originality.

---

210 Ibid para 45.
211 *Funke Medien* (n 195) para 23.
212 *Football Dataco* (n 141) paras 38–39.
213 *Painer* (n 198) para 91.
214 Ibid paras 92–93.
215 See; Yin Harn Lee, 'Photographs and the Standard of Originality in Europe: *Eva-Maria Painer v. Standard VerlagsGmbH, Axel Springer AG, Süddeutsche Zeitung GmbH, SPIEGEL-Verlag Rudolf AUGSTEIN GmbH & Co KG and Verlag M. DuMont Schauberg Expedition der Kölnischen Zeitung GmbH & Co KG* (C-145/10)' (2012) 34(4) *European Intellectual Property Review* 290–293.
216 Hugenholtz, Quintais and Gervais (n 55) 73; Ana Ramalho, 'Originality Redux: An Analysis of the Originality Requirement in AI-generated Works' (2019) *AIDA* 7.

The EU law focuses on doing creative acts by making free and creative choices. This means that economic investments are not relevant for protection. Indeed, in *Football Dataco*, The 'significant labour and skill' exerted in making the football fixture lists was not counted as a factor in determining originality.[217] Also, in *Funke Medien*, the mere intellectual effort and skill of creating military status reports were viewed irrelevant in that regard.[218] It is highly difficult to reconcile the treatment of informational works in *Funke Medien* and portrait photographs considered in *Painer*. However, it would be fair to say that the requirement for originality highlights 'its dependence on an act of intellectual (literary or artistic) creation by an author to subsist.'[219]

3.3.2.2.4 MINIMUM CREATIVITY

What level of creativity is sufficient? Early CJEU judgments suggest that the level of creativity required for originality is rather low if the external constraints grant the author sufficient freedom to create.[220] In *Infopaq*, the 11-word news clipping was considered as a work.[221] In *Painer*, the originality of a photograph was almost taken for granted. Stef van Gompel critiques this approach and proposes that:

> While the existence of creative space is a *prerequisite* for an author to make an 'original' creation, this does not of itself lead to the conclusion that the creation must therefore also *be* original. Instead, ... courts should distinguish the *presence* of creative space from how it is used. An individual assessment of the use of space in expressive form should thus be the ultimate test for establishing originality.[222]

In his opinion on the *Renckhoff* case, Advocate General Campos Sanchez-Bordona stated that it is problematic that even simple photograph shots meet the criteria laid down in *Painer*.[223] This might lead to overprotection, as *Renckhoff* illustrates. The subject matter in *Renchoff* was the photo showing the Roman bridge, a view of the Mosque-Cathedral and the Alcaraz on the other side of the Guadalquivir. The photographer initially published it on a travel page. A student at the secondary school from Germany used this photograph in their presentation by citing the travel page. Afterwards, the school published the presentation, including the photograph, on its website. The photographer sued the government claiming that this breached his right of communication to the public. According to

---

217 *Football Dataco* (n 141) para 42.
218 *Funke Medien* (n 195) para 23.
219 Pila (n 37) 74.
220 Van Gompel (n 130) 100.
221 See; *Infopaq* (n 96).
222 Van Gompel (n 130) 121 (Emphasis original).
223 Case C-161/17 *Land Nordrhein-Westfalen v. Dirk Renckhoff* [2018] Opinion of AG Campos Sánchez-Bordona ECLI:EU:C:2018:279 para 54.

the CJEU, the use of a photograph found on the internet by another person on their web page was an unauthorised communication to the public.[224] Normally, this is a 'standard view' of well-known attractions combining the different historical times of the city. The same view is photographed every day by tourists all over the world countless times. Nevertheless, this did not change the fact that the ordinary photo of Cordoba was considered as an original work.

In contrast, in *Funke Medien*, the CJEU said that military status reports were not considered a work, since their purely informative nature and the standard formats in which they were drafted left little room for creativity.[225]

3.3.2.2.5 AESTHETIC QUALITY

Post-*Infopaq*, all authors and their works are treated equally and subject to the same requirement under EU law. This is originality. The *Cofemel* case,[226] as Marianne Levin suggests, created an 'revolutionary' effect and confirmed the neutral originality requirement when customising an EU cumulation on this basis.[227] In *Cofemel*, the CJEU has also provided some insights regarding under which conditions fashion designs (and accordingly works of applied art) shall be considered a work.

In the case, the famous fashion company G-Star filed a lawsuit against Cofemel in Portugal. G-Star claimed that Cofemel used its designs of jeans, sweatshirts and T-shirts without its permission and infringed its copyright. Cofemel objected to this claim by stating that the designs were not original works. The court of first instance reached the conclusion that copyright subsisted in the apparel and ruled that Cofemel had infringed G-Star's copyright. The Court of Appeal upheld this decision.[228] Cofemel appealed the judgment. The Supreme Court of Portugal submitted the following two questions through the preliminary ruling of the CJEU: (i) What are the application conditions for designs of the Article 2 of the Information Society Directive? and (ii) Does the requirement for a design to be considered a work of art (artistic creation) by creating an aesthetically significant visual effect beyond its intended use comply with the EU law?[229]

The CJEU emphasised that copyright protection of works of applied art (fashion designs) must be assessed exclusively under the criteria developed in *Infopaq* and subsequent case law. The Court thus rejected the implementation of beyond 'their practical purpose, a specific and aesthetically significant visual effect' as a requirement of copyright protection. In *Cofemel*, the 'aesthetic effect' was viewed subjective, being dependent on the 'sensation of beauty experienced by each individual who may look at that design.' Thus, for the Court, the subjectivity would

---

224 Case C-161/17 *Land Nordrhein-Westfalen v. Dirk Renckhoff* [2018] EU:C:2018:634.
225 *Funke Medien* (n 195) para 23.
226 *Cofemel* (n 10).
227 Levin (n 102) 82.
228 *Cofemel* (n 10) paras 16–22.
229 Ibid para 25.

hinder the expression of a subject matter from being 'identifiable with sufficient precision and objectivity.'[230] It was also declared incompatible with the criterion of 'intellectual creation reflecting the freedom of choice and personality of its author' established by the case law of the CJEU.[231]

The CJEU's rejection of aesthetics in *Cofemel* seems to be grounded on two fundamental tenets. First, the EU originality criterion represents a *benchmark*, preventing any additional condition. Further requirements that are not reconcilable with the EU originality must be excluded. The harmonised EU originality criterion excluding additional requirements was also echoed in *Brompton*, dealing with the applied arts within the context of functionality, as previously mentioned. Second, the 'aesthetics effect' denotes subjectivity and thus impairs the identifiability of the author's creative choices.

According to the CJEU, the cumulative protection of designs in accordance with the copyright and design laws does not undermine the purposes and effects of these two different protection systems and does not affect the protection conditions. The EU cumulative protection of designs that the Court envisaged was grounded on the condition 'that the respective objectives and effectiveness of those two forms of protection are (not) undermined.' This was limited to 'only in certain situations.'[232]

The decision has been interpreted as a breaking point, which marks a potential shift in many jurisdictions that lay down aesthetic quality as an additional requirement. Whether the elimination of aesthetics signals a dramatic impact on national copyright laws is questionable.[233] The CJEU did not offer sufficiently concrete guidelines for the application of the EU copyright protection standards for works of applied art (fashion designs). The ways an author (designer) of a fashion design can demonstrate their creative choices are not explicitly specified in the judgment.[234] Annette Kur, for example, distinguishes between the two possible meanings of 'aesthetics.' For Kur, *aesthetics* refers to beauty or eye-pleasing character of an object, the evaluation of which would depend on personal taste and is unacceptable in copyright. However, as Kur argues:

> 'Aesthetic' rather appears to represent the opposite of '(merely) functional.' In that sense, the term comes very close in its meaning to what the CJEU

---

230 *Cofemel* (n 10) para 53.
231 Ibid para 54.
232 Ibid paras 50–52.
233 Kur (n 107) 294; Koray Güven, 'Eliminating 'Aesthetics' from Copyright Law: The Aftermath of Cofemel' (2022) 71(3) *GRUR International* 214.
234 AG Szpunar thought that *haute couture* fashion products can be protected by copyright and suggested that rather banal aspects of the fashion designs, such as 'specific composition by shapes, colors, words and numbers, color combination, position of the bags in hip height or manufacture by sewing together . . . three parts' should be viewed as ideas or functional solutions and thus excluded from copyright protection. See; Case C-683/17 *Cofemel – Sociedade de Vestuário SA v. G-Star Raw CV* EU:C:2019:363 Opinion of AG Szpunar paras 3–4, 60.

regards as constituting the result of free creative choices made by the author of a work. And whether that standard is met or not cannot be measured in objective scales, but must be assessed by judges who, as human beings, inevitably include their own personal impression and mindset in the evaluation, thus rendering it 'subjective' at least to some extent.[235]

Annette Kur further suggests that the Court's ruling confining the cumulation to certain cases gives a subliminal message that it will be applied only in exceptional cases.[236] However, Marianne Levin argues that the principle of *l'unité de l'art*,[237] which means full cumulative protection, was not adopted in the *Cofemel* decision. According to Levin, the *Cofemel* decision does not mean that every creation protected in design law will also be protected under the copyright law. Instead, cumulative protection should only be available 'in certain cases' when all EU standards for copyright subsistence are met for designs.[238]

It is true that the CJEU in *Cofemel* dealt with the vexed question of cumulative protection in the EU. It only accepted the possibility of a cumulative protection without a clear and thorough guidance on the matter. The nature and conditions of the cumulation needs further elaboration. The Court also did not consider these diverse and long-standing standards of the Member States on cumulative protection. As Annette Kur reminds:

> Whether it is the intention of the artist, the manner of production ('industrial' versus 'artisan'), the number of copies, the separability of creative elements from those that are functional, or the requirement of an 'artistic character' or 'elevated degree of originality': one or the other mode of keeping copyright protection restricted to a fraction of design creations has been employed by legislatures and courts through the times and in most countries of the world.[239]

In conclusion, the EU originality does not require artistic quality/superiority or aesthetic characteristics.[240] In other words, the aesthetic beauty of a work (fashion design) is not a prerequisite for it to be considered a protected work under the EU copyright law. Due to the subjectivity in human's choices, aesthetic effects do not help determine originality of expression. Fashion designs can cumulatively

---

235 Kur (n 107) 294.
236 Ibid 293.
237 Article L511–1 *Code de la propriété intellectuelle*.
238 Levin (n 102) 97–98. Levin also suggests that spare part designs can also be protected when one considers the outcomes of the *Infopaq* and *Cofemel* cases. Levin (n 102) 95–96.
239 Kur (n 107) 296 (Internal notes omitted). For these different approaches of Member States see contributions in Estelle Derclaye (ed), *The Copyright/Design Interface: Past, Present and Future* (Cambridge University Press, 2018).
240 For example, the preamble 8 of the Software Directive states that qualitative or aesthetic quality is not considered in determining the originality of computer programs. Also see, Van Gompel (n 130) 99; Ramalho (n 216) 7.

be protected by design and copyright laws when they fulfil the requirements of copyright protection standards.[241]

3.3.2.2.6 PRELIMINARY CONCLUSION ON ORIGINALITY OF AI-GENERATED FASHION DESIGNS

It follows from *Cofemel* and *Brompton* that functional creations including fashion designs can be protected by copyright. However, in the EU law context, the question of whether a fashion design can be considered a work protected by copyright is predominantly related to originality.

In the light of the CJEU judgment in *Brompton*, it seems that the mere existence of functionality in fashion designs has limited effect on their originality. What is important here is whether the fashion designer has, regardless of technicalities of fashion designing, somehow managed to make free and creative choices and hence reflected their personality in the final output. Thus, a fashion design can be original even in cases where the creative freedom of the designer is limited by factors such as certain style or production standards (i.e. retro style) or product shapes (i.e. a handbag) or how a garment fits to a person's body (i.e. skinny jeans).

Another aspect of originality is the level of creativity that must be shown in the fashion design by the contribution of the designer. *Cofemel* clarified that the level of creativity for fashion designs is not different from other types of works (that is, minimum level of creativity), and artistic quality is not needed to justify protection. *Haute couture* designs would not have difficulty in representing the creative and free choices of their designer because they are generally unique and go beyond what exists in the creative environment of the field. In contrast, commonplace and mundane garments (such as classic-cut white shirt, standard sleeves or collars) or accessories (such as plain black handbag) would falter in showing creativity. Thus, creativity in fashion designs can be manifested by not copying previous designs and, as *Infoqaq* and *Painer* suggest, slightly contributing to its expressive value of the fashion design by reflecting creative and free choices.

Where there is a human contribution in any part of the creation process, AI-generated fashion designs can be original.

3.3.2.3 *Expression*

The third condition for copyright protection is that 'human' creativity is 'expressed' in the subject matter. The author's use of creative freedom must be perceptible. Works without a shape or form may not be considered as a work. In many of its

---

241 Estelle Derclaye, 'Doceram, Cofemel and Brompton: How Does the Current and Future CJEU Case Law Affect Digital Designs?' in Barbara Pasa E (ed), *Il design, l'innovazione tecnologica e digitale, Un dialogo interdisciplinare per un ripensamento delle tutele – Design, Technological and Digital Innovation. Interdisciplinary Proposals for Reshaping Legal Protections* (ESI Press, 2021) Available at SSRN: https://ssrn.com/abstract=3507802 (arguing that Cofemel 'may reduce the incentive for designers to register their designs' as copyright has 'more attractive features').

decisions, the CJEU ruled that this is an essential requirement for the copyright protection. In *Infopaq* and *BSA*, the CJEU stated that the author must '*express* his creativity in an original manner.'[242] In *Painer*, it is emphasised that in order for a work to be original, 'the author must express . . . [their] creative abilities in the creation of the work by making free and creative choices.'[243] Similarly, in *Funke Medien*, it is stated that 'only works that express the intellectual creations of the author may be accepted as a work within the meaning of the [Information Society Directive].'[244]

The Berne Convention provides that 'the exercise and implementation of copyright are not subject to any *formality*.'[245] However, Member States may stipulate that 'any specified categories of works shall not be protected unless they have been fixed in some material form.'[246] Thus, as a principle, under the Berne Convention copyright emerges automatically with the creation of the work and can be used by anyone.[247] This fundamental principle has also been adopted in the EU law, with one exception, and no formality has been imposed for the subsistence and exercise of copyright.[248] Works with unknown authors, works with pseudonyms in fact (works leading to uncertainty regarding the identity of the author), joint works and works whose authors are anticipated as legal persons must be communicated to the public in accordance with the law for them to be protected in the context of copyright.[249]

The requirement for expression denotes the causal link between the creative act of the author (using their freedom of creativity) and the form of the work created.[250] Does the requirement for fixation, which exists in relation to literary, musical and dramatic works[251] under the UK law,[252] also represent a requirement under the EU copyright law? To what extent is the protection of sensory copyright[253] in relation to taste and smells accepted in the EU law? What is required

---

242 *Infopaq* (n 96) para 45; *BSA* (n 152) para 50.
243 *Painer* (n 198) para 89.
244 *Funke Medien* (n 195) para 20.
245 Berne Convention Art 5(2).
246 Berne Convention Art 2(2).
247 Pila and Torremans (n 86) 271.
248 Ibid.
249 Term Directive Art 1(3)-(4).
250 Hugenholtz, Quintais and Gervais (n 55) 75; Pila (n 37) 74.
251 In French Law, the fixation of choreographic works is also sought. See; Code de la propriété intellectuelle Art L112–2.
252 CDPA Art 3(2). For explanations on this requirement, see; Bently *et al* (n 109) 91–92; Paul Torremans, *Holyoak and Torremans Intellectual Property Law* (9th edn, OUP, 2019) 176, 185; Stavroula Karapapa and Luke Mcdonagh, *Intellectual Property Law* (OUP, 2019) 55–56; Abbe Brown, Smita Kheria, Jane Cornwell and Marta Iljadica, *Contemporary Intellectual Property: Law and Policy* (5th edn, OUP, 2019) 57–59.
253 For information regarding the inconveniences that may arise, if taste and smells are subject to the copyright protection, see; Caterina Sganga, 'Say Nay to a Tastier Copyright: Why the CJEU should Deny Copyright Protection for Taste (and smells)' (2019) 14(3) *Journal of Intellectual Property Law & Practice* 187–196.

in the case law of the CJEU is that the creative choices of the author must clearly be expressed. The underpinning requirements of this principle were substantially established in the *Levola* case.[254] *Levola* concerned a Dutch company's copyright infringement claim on the taste of 'herbed cream cheese.'[255]

The CJEU again retreated two cumulative conditions of copyright subsistence that autonomously apply to any work in the EU: first, the subject matter must be original;[256] and second, only works that are the expression of the author's own intellectual creation may be classified as a work.[257]

At this point, the CJEU emphasised that the provisions concerning the concept of the work under international agreements should be considered when making such assessment. The Court further noted that although the EU is not a party, as per the reference made by the WCT,[258] it is obliged to comply with Articles 1 to 21 of the Berne Convention.[259]

According to the CJEU, 'the subject matter protected by copyright must be expressed in a manner which makes it identifiable with sufficient precision and objectivity.' It is not necessary for the expression in question to be permanently recorded a material form.[260] Conventional copyright works are expressed in the objectively identifiable languages of musical notes, written or spoken words, and represented images. Variations in perception is minimal for conventional works. They all at least originate from a single objectively verifiable object.[261] The Court might think that it can never be possible to achieve the same uniformity with taste.

The principle that the subject matter should be clearly and objectively expressed ensures that it is identified as a copyright-protected work by the authorities, businesses and commercial competitors. This is important for the sake of legal certainty.[262] The CJEU found that it is not possible to determine the taste of food products clearly and objectively. The requirement of objectivity in the identification of a work means the subjective and variable taste sensations generated by food product clearly are in contradiction with its categorisation as work.[263] The main rationale behind the Court's denial of copyright protection for taste is related to the fact that science does not currently provide a means of precisely and objectively identifying the taste of food such that it can be distinguished from other tastes.[264]

---

254 *Levola Hengelo* (n 80).
255 Ibid para 17.
256 Ibid para 36.
257 Ibid para 37.
258 WCT Art 1(4).
259 *Levola Hengelo* (n 80) para 38.
260 Ibid para 40.
261 Jani McCutcheon, '*Levola Hengelo BV v. Smilde Foods BV*: The Hard Work of Defining a Copyright Work' (2019) 82(5) *Modern Law Review* 948.
262 *Levola Hengelo* (n 80) para 41.
263 Ibid para 42.
264 Ibid para 43.

The *Levola* case has four important results. First, the judgment delivered in this case provides a strong legal basis that smells as well as tastes are not deemed as a work.[265] Second, although the CJEU has referred to the Berne Convention in many cases until this case, it accepted the binding effect of this agreement for determining the conditions of a work under the EU law and made it an EU law norm. Third, the ECJ focuses on the concept of 'creative choice' as the defining feature of an intellectual creation. It is accepted that this could be achieved by unleashing the link between expression and the creation process. This shows that the choices in the creation process are accepted as the determining factor for the availability of copyright protection.[266] This is also supported by the fact that artistic and qualitative superiority or characteristic is not *required* under the EU law.[267] Lastly, the fact that a work is sufficiently clear and perceivable by humans does not mean that the work must be fixed (recorded in a material form), and the phenomenon of fixation is not recognised as a requirement for qualification as a work.[268] However, it is a fact that there is a *de facto fixation* requirement in practice in order to prove the case.[269]

The principle of an 'author's own intellectual creation' does not only require that a human is the protagonist, driving the creation process. But it also necessitates that the author has a certain level of will and intention to create. The logical outcome of this proposition then points to the fact that the work is conceptually created by a human author and expressed by them afterward. Therefore, natural events that occur randomly are excluded from the scope of copyright protection. So, should the author's will and intention to create cover all the steps in the creation process? Or is a general (rather than specific) will and intention to create enough? Expecting that the author could anticipate every possible output in the entire creation process is almost impossible. Instead, it can be sufficient for the work to be designed in general without being expressed and to provide space for unexpected expressive outcomes and features.[270]

In short, the question of being expressed should not be a problem for AI-generated fashion designs. This derives from the fact that the final product is visibly embodied and the human designer involved in the creative process has a clear intention to produce such fashion design.

---

265 Leon Dijkman, 'CJEU Rules that Taste of a Food Product Is Not Protectable by Copyright: *Levola Hengelo BV v. Smilde Foods BV*, C-310/17 [2018] Court of Justice of the European Union, ECLI: EU:C:2018:899' (2019) 14(2) *Journal of Intellectual Property Law & Practice* 86.
266 See; Martin Senftleben and Laurens Buijtelaar, 'Robot Creativity: An Incentive-Based Neighboring Rights Approach' (2020) 42(12) *European Intellectual Property Review* 717 ff.
267 Hugenholtz, Quintais and Gervais (n 55) 75.
268 Pila (n 37) 66–67; Eleonora Rosati, 'Round-up of CJEU Copyright Decisions in 2019' (2020) 15 *Journal of Intellectual Property Law & Practice* 274–275.
269 Caterina Sganga, 'The Notion of "Work" in EU Copyright Law After Levola Hengelo: One Answer Given, Three Question Marks Ahead' (2019) 41(7) *European Intellectual Property Review* 415–424.
270 Hugenholtz, Quintais and Gervais (n 55) 75.

3.3.2.4 Intellectual effort

Is an intellectual effort prerequisite for copyright protection under EU law? Under EU copyright law, there is no provision that expressly states that copyright requires a human creator.[271] However, an 'anthropocentric' understanding of human authorship has pervaded its every corner.[272] The CJEU's case law on originality draws attention to the existence of a human being who shows creative choices and performs creative acts. For example, as specified in the opinion of Advocate General Trstenjak delivered in *Painer* based on the Art 6 of the Term Directive, and as accepted later by the CJEU, 'only human creations can be protected,' and this covers situations in which technical devices such as cameras are used.[273]

Once more, as stated by the CJEU in *Painer*, 'by making various (creative) choices, the author of the portrait photograph can leave his/her mark on the work he/she has created with his/her "personal touch." '[274] Similarly, in *Cofemel*, the CJEU stated that

> if a subject matter is to be capable of being regarded as original, it is both necessary and sufficient that the subject matter reflects the personality of its author, as an expression of . . . free and creative choices.[275]

The cases of *Painer*, *BSA* and *Renckhoff* clearly suggest that a medium can be used in creating a work if the fashion design is an 'author's own intellectual creation' and reflects the personality of its creator. In this sense, AI is not different from cameras or computer programs. Thus, if an AI-generated design meets these four criteria, who would be the author? The next section will seek answers to this question.

3.3.3 *Authorship and ownership*

The work and the author are two complementary concepts in copyright law. If there is a work, it must belong to an author. Authorship arises only if there is a work that can be credited to its creator.

The concept of authorship is not clearly defined under EU copyright law.[276] The law gets inspiration largely from the concept of authorship in the Berne Convention.[277]

---

271 Ibid 69.
272 See; Ramalho (n 216) 11.
273 Opinion of Advocate General Trstenjak on *Painer* case, para 121.
274 *Painer* (n 198) para 92.
275 *Cofemel* (n 10) para 30.
276 Lucas-Schloetter (n 116) 10.
277 Hugenholtz, Quintais and Gervais (n 55) 76.

The Information Society Directive recognises the rights of reproduction, distribution and communication to the public for 'authors, in respect of their works.'[278] It is also harmony with the Berne Convention providing that '[t]he protection of this Convention shall apply to ... authors.'[279] The Term Directive also determines the copyright term of protection depending on the life span of natural persons. The concept of authorship is not defined in these Directives and the Convention.

Saying that authors own copyrights adds little to understanding the legal relations around the work without defining who an author is. Despite the lack of a general definition of 'author' in the EU directives and international instruments, it is a well-established principle that the author of a work is the person whose *expression originates from the intellectual creation*. To use the language of the CJEU, this is the person who has made free and creative choices in creating the work and whose personal stamp is attached to the work in consequence of act of creation.[280] The Court in its many decisions attributes authorship to a 'human author,' not to legal persons such as film producers or broadcasters.[281] It can, therefore, be said that initial ownership of the copyright should vest in who creates the work.

The EU copyright directive contains three exceptions to this general principle. The first concerns computer programs. According to the Software Directive, the copyright holder of a computer program is essentially the natural person(s) who have created the work. In cases where the legislation of the Member State identifies a legal person as the author, this legal person may act as the initial owner of the copyright.[282]

The second concerns databases. The Database Directive follows the Software Directive's approach: the creator(s) of the database or (if recognised) the designated legal person is the owner of the copyright.[283]

The third concerns cinematographic or audio-visual works. In the Satellite and Cable Directive[284] and the Rental and Lending Directive,[285] it is provided that the principal director of a cinematographic or audio-visual work shall be considered as its author or one of its authors, and that Member States shall be free to designate other co-authors.

The impact of these last provisions has been explored by the CJEU in the *Luksan* case.[286] In 2008, Martin Luksan, as scriptwriter and principal director, and Petrus van der Let, as producer, concluded a directing and authorship agreement.

---

278 Information Society Directive Arts 2–4.
279 Berne Convention Art 3(1).
280 Pila and Torremans (n 86) 272.
281 See; *Luksan* (n 80); Case C-572/13, *Hewlett-Packard Belgium SPRL v. Reprobel SCR*, ECLI:EU:C:2015:750.
282 Software Directive Art 2(1).
283 Database Directive Art 4(1).
284 Satellite and Cable Directive Art 1(5).
285 Rental and Lending Directive Art 2(2).
286 *Luksan* (n 80). See also; Stefano Barazza, 'Authorship of Cinematographic Works and Ownership of Related Rights: Who Holds the Stage?' (2012) 7(6) *Journal of Intellectual Property Law & Practice* 394–396.

The subject matter of the agreement was a documentary regarding German photography art during the World War II. In the agreement, the right to distribute the documentary on digital networks, closed-circuit and pay television channels was preserved to Luksan. Other financial rights have been assigned to the producer. However, once the film was shot, the producer made it available on the internet and assigned pay TV rights to a TV network. Luksan sued the producer, contending that these forms of exploitation violated rights that were reserved to him in the contract and claiming that half of the statutory rights to remuneration were vested in him. The producer responded by arguing that a statutory assignment of those rights is provided to him by virtue of Article 38(1) of the Austrian Copyright Act and that the provision in the agreement regarding the transfer of some financial rights to the director was invalid.[287]

The following two questions were referred to the CJEU: (i) should the author of a cinematographic or audio-visual work be deemed as the director under the EU law? (ii) is the Austrian Act granting the financial rights on these works to the producer in accordance with the EU law?[288]

After clarifying that, within EU law, the principal director is always considered an author of such works,[289] this interpretative path followed by the CJEU made its way to Article 14*bis* of the Berne Convention. Article 14*bis* allows Member States to grant the rights of reproduction and communication to the public to the producer instead of the director, denying the principal director certain exploitation rights. These rights were at issue in the main proceedings. At this point, the CJEU stated that EU is subject to Article 14*bis* of the Berne Convention because of the reference contained in the WCT.[290] On this account, the CJEU noted that the international agreement allows, but does not require, such a provision. According to the CJEU, Member States are expected to refrain from adopting an optional measure that is contrary to EU law, and 'accordingly, they can no longer rely on the power granted by Article 14*bis* of the Berne Convention.'[291] Thus, it has been accepted that the Austrian law, which entitles the producer instead of the director, conflicts with the Term Directive and the purpose of the Information Society Directive. In addition, the law was also found to be in breach of the human right to intellectual property under Article 17 of the Charter of Fundamental Rights of the EU.[292]

In the EU, copyright exists from the creation of a work and does not require formal registration. The Enforcement Directive introduces a refutable presumption of authorship in order not to leave a loophole in legal proceedings concerning copyright claims. The Directive prefers to adopt the rule laid down in the Berne Convention. This presumption gives the fictional authorship of a literary or

---

287 *Luksan* (n 80) paras 23–31.
288 Ibid paras 32–36.
289 Ibid paras 37–53.
290 Ibid paras 55–63.
291 Ibid para 64.
292 Ibid paras 78–72.

artistic work to the person whose name appears on the work in the usual manner. It can only be used in 'applying the measures, procedures and remedies' under the Directive.[293]

In EU copyright law, there are special norms regarding the ownership of the work. The Computer Directive recognises the employer's ownership of economic rights on computer programs created by their employees. This can be the case where computer program is created when the employee performs their duties or follows the instructions given by their employer. Employee and employer may agree otherwise by a contract.[294] Apart from this provision, there is no general provision on the assignment of copyright ownership of the works created by the employees to others. Justine Pila and Paul Torremans state that domestic law arrangements can be made to ensure that persons (especially employers) other than the author shall be entitled to copyright if they are in accordance with the purpose and rules of EU copyright law and if the reasons behind them are well presented.[295]

According to the Computer Directive, authors jointly own the rights on the computer program in relation to the works they have created together as a group.[296] However, the Directive does not elaborate on how to exercise these rights. Since the Directive is a framework regulation, it can be stated that the Member States can freely employ the detailed provisions on how to exercise the rights in joint authorship in their domestic laws. A similar provision is also included in the Database Directive.[297]

Several issues related to authorship are regulated under the domestic laws of Member States.[298] If two or more authors cooperate in creating a subject matter and their personal creative contributions cannot be separated from each other, this subject matter will be considered a work of joint authorship. Persons providing these creative contributions to a work will be considered joint authors.[299] Most national laws require that the joint authors work according to a common design, making the joint work a 'concerted creative effort.'[300] In a similar vein, there are national rules that directly vest authorship in persons other than the author, though in rare circumstance. Assignment of copyright ownership to non-authors is quite common in the EU as well.[301]

In most Member States, there are also refutable presumptions in relation to the authorship or ownership.[302] Thus, under EU copyright law there is no clear answer

---

293 Enforcement Directive Article 5(a).
294 Software Directive Art 2(3).
295 Pila and Torremans (n 86) 273.
296 Software Directive Art 2(2).
297 Database Directive Art 4(3).
298 Hugenholtz, Quintais and Gervais (n 55) 76.
299 Goldstein and Hugenholtz (n 19) 233.
300 Hugenholtz, Quintais and Gervais (n 55) 76.
301 Ibid 77.
302 Ibid 77.

as to who the author of AI-generated fashion designs should be. The possible suggestions in this sense will be explained in Chapters 4 and 5.

3.3.4 Exclusive rights

EU copyright law views exclusive economic rights as 'the core component of copyright legislation.'[303] For that reason, the rights of reproduction, distribution, communication to the public – including the right to making protected subject matter available to the public – and the rental and lending right have been harmonised for authors.[304] These rights are to a large extent also conferred to owners of neighbouring rights.[305] A special set of rights has been granted to owners of the *sui generis* protection of databases: the exclusive rights to extraction and re-utilisation of the whole or of a substantial part of the contents of a database.[306]

There are four notable exceptions to harmonisation of economic rights. First, the right of communication to the public under the Information Society Directive only refers to communication to a public that is not present at the place where the communication originates.[307] Thus, the right to perform the work in public does not fall under the Information Society Directive and remains unharmonised within the EU. Second, no exclusive right of communication to the public exists regarding computer programs.[308] Third, the Rental and Lending Directive explicitly empowers Member States to also introduce an exclusive public lending right, provided that at least authors obtain a remuneration for such lending.[309] Fourth, there still is a lack of harmonisation in relation to the adaptation right, except computer programs and databases.

Despite all the harmonising efforts concerning economic rights, moral rights remain unregulated in the EU.[310] The portrayal of Lionel Bently et al in the following lines over the harmonisation of exclusive rights is a telling one:

> For the most part, the rights have developed in a piecemeal way in response to external pressures, most obviously to technological change. As well as

---

303 Kur, Dreier and Luginbuehl (n 77) 347.
304 Information Society Directive Arts 2, 3 and 4; Software Directive Art 4; Database Directive Art 5; Rental and Lending Directive Art 3(1)(a).
305 Information Society Directive Arts 2 (b) and 3 (2); Rental and Lending Directive Art 3 (1) (b)–(d) (not mentioning, however, broadcasting organisations).
306 Database Directive Art 7(1).
307 Information Society Directive Art 3(1). See; Case C-283/10 *Circul Globus București v. Uniunea Compozitorilor și Muzicologilor din România* (2011) *ECR* I–12031.
308 See Software Directive Art 4, which only contains the reproduction, adaptation and distribution rights.
309 Rental and Lending Directive Art 6(1).
310 Term Directive Art 9 and Recital 20; Database Directive Recital 28; Information Society Directive Recital 19 ('moral rights remain outside the scope of this Directive').

producing a complicated regime, the cumulative way in which the rights have developed has also led to a degree of overlap between them.[311]

It is envisaged that the financial rights shall be protected for 70 years after the death of the author.[312]

3.3.5 Exceptions

Exceptions to economic rights represent a more complex picture. The Information Society Directive provides one mandatory exception to the right of reproduction, namely the exception for transient or incidental copies.[313] In addition to the mandatory exception for temporary copies, the Directive offers Member States an exhaustive list of 20 exceptions they can choose to implement.

Article 5(2) lists five optional exceptions to the reproduction right: reprographic copying; private copying; non-profit copying by public libraries, educational establishments or museums; temporary copying by broadcasters; and copying of broadcasts by social institutions.

Article 5(3) then provides for 15 optional exceptions to the rights of reproduction and communication to the public: use for teaching and scientific research; uses for people with disabilities; use for reporting current events; quotations; uses for public security; use of political speeches; use during religious celebrations; use of works of architecture; incidental inclusion of a work or other subject-matter; use for advertising public exhibitions; use for caricature, parody or pastiche; use concerning the demonstration or repair of equipment; use for the reconstruction of buildings; use for research or private study; and use in other cases of minor importance.[314]

In addition to these exceptions, other Directives have introduced further exceptions to the rights of reproduction and communication to the public under the Information Society Directive. More recently, for example, the Orphan Works Directive and the Marrakesh Directive have complemented the long list with two mandatory exceptions. These respectively cover uses for the purpose of allowing the digitisation of works with no known author by cultural heritage institutions[315] and the production of works in accessible format for visually disabled individuals.[316] In addition, the Digital Single Market Directive has brought three new mandatory exceptions to the right of reproduction. These are text and data mining

---

311 Bently *et al* (n 109) 141 (Internal notes omitted).
312 Pila and Torremans (n 86) 222.
313 Information Society Directive Art 5(1). Conditions of applicability of Article 5(1) will be explained in more detail later.
314 The Digital Single Market Directive and the Directive implementing the Marrakesh Treaty in the EU has amended the language of some of these exceptions.
315 Orphan Works Directive Art 6(1)(b).
316 Marrakesh Directive Art 3(1).

for scientific and general purposes,[317] online teaching activities[318] and digitisation directed to the preservation of collections.[319]

The exception listed in the Directives are also subject to the 'three-step test.' This requires that exceptions must be applied only to certain special cases. They must not also interfere with the normal exploitation of the work/subject matter and must not prejudice the 'legitimate interests' of authors/right holders.[320]

3.3.6 Infringement

Under EU copyright law, three requirements must be met for (primary) infringement to occur: (i) the alleged infringer must carry out one of the activities that falls within the copyright holder's control (existence of a protected right); (ii) the infringing work must be derived from the copyright work (a causal connection); (iii) the restricted act must have been carried out in relation to the *work* or a *part* thereof.

As *Cofemel* demonstrates, fashion designs have long struggled to pass the originality threshold. Some fashion designs are unable to meet the criterion of originality. If the source data is comprised of fashion designs that do not pass the originality threshold, will there be an infringement? Where the considerable amount of data (Use 1) is used to feed the AI and this AI by machine learning (Use 2) generates a fashion design that is very similar to another designer's work (Use 3), these acts would not necessarily constitute a copyright infringement.[321] However, there are admittedly fashion designs that do pass the originality threshold. In these cases, the possibility of AI using original fashion designs as its source data and producing designs identical and similar to others' design should be considered.

3.3.6.1 Right of reproduction

The three acts (Uses 1, 2 and 3) defined in Chapter 2 concerning use of third-party designs (or copyright material) in AI-generated fashion designs (works) concern the right of production amongst others. The right has been harmonised at an EU level specifically with respect to computer programs[322] and databases,[323] and more generally with respect to other authorial works. Article 2 of the Information Society Directive requires Member States to confer on authors, film producers,

---

317 Digital Single Market Directive Arts 3 and 4.
318 Digital Single Market Directive Art 5.
319 Digital Single Market Directive Art 6.
320 Information Society Directive Art 5(5); Marrakesh Directive Art 3(1); Rental and Lending Rights Directive Art 10; Database Directive Art 6(3); Digital Single Market Directive Art 7(2).
321 Heidi Härkönen, 'Fashion Piracy and Artificial Intelligence – Does the New Creative Environment Come with New Copyright Issues?' (2020) 15(3) *Journal of Intellectual Property Law & Practice* 169.
322 Software Directive Art 4(a).
323 Database Directive Art 5(a).

phonogram producers and broadcasters 'the exclusive right to authorise or prohibit direct or indirect, temporary or permanent reproduction by any means and in any form, in whole or in part.'

The precise contours of what counts as a 'reproduction' varies according to the type of the work in question. One factor that is common to all works is that infringement takes place whether the copy is direct or indirect, temporary or permanent.[324] This right covers reproductions by 'any means and in any form.'[325] Thus reproduction is not limited to replicating a work in the same manner as it was originally produced, such as redrawing a design. The conversion of a work from analogue into digital form (or vice versa) is likewise treated as a reproduction.[326] In defining the notion of 'reproduction,' the EU law has extended the remit of copyright into just about every dimension of the digital world. This means that storing a work on a USB,[327] taking a material from one website and placing it on another,[328] creating transient sequential fragments of the work within the memory of a satellite decoder and on a television screen,[329] uploading or downloading content through peer-to-peer systems (such as The Pirate Bay) would all give rise to infringement (absent a defence). Interestingly, a material is reproduced when a person accesses it from a computer (at which point, a temporary copy is made in the memory of a computer) or when they access an internet stream. Temporary reproductions made by the end users on multimedia players with pre-installed links to unlicensed content is equally an infringement.[330] Moreover, the image created on a computer screen, or television screen, is also regarded as a reproduction, although it is a temporary one.[331]

Under EU law, the right to make an adaptation of a work – except databases[332] and computer programs –[333] has not been harmonised. Thus, where a person transforms a protected work such that it is no longer a reproduction, national law applies to the question of liability.[334] In this sense, multiplication of work is a classical way of reproduction. However, the CJEU has held that reproduction can

---

324 Bently *et al* (n 109) 140.
325 Information Society Directive Art 2; Software Directive Art 4(a); Database Directive Art 5(a).
326 Mikko Antikainen and Daniël Jongsma, 'The Art of CAD: Copyrightability of Digital Designs Files' in Rosa Maria Ballardini, Marcus Norrgård and Jouni Partanen (eds), *3D Printing, Intellectual Property and Innovation – Insights from Law and Technology* (Wolters Kluwer, 2017) 269; Geiger *et al* (n 68) 285. Case C-117/13 *Technische Universität Darmstadt v. Eugen Ulmer KG* EU:C:2014:2196 para 37 (digitisation is an act of reproduction).
327 Case C-117/13 *Technische Universität Darmstadt v. Eugen Ulmer KG* EU:C:2014:2196 para 52 (copy on USB drive).
328 Renckhoff (n 224) para 46.
329 *FAPL* (n 132) para 159.
330 Case C-527/15 *Stichting Brein (Filmspeller) v. Jack Frederik Wullems* EU:C:2017:300 para 72 (Hereinafter 'Filmspeller').
331 Bently *et al* (n 109) 145.
332 Database Directive Art 5(b).
333 Software Directive Art 4(b).
334 Caterina Sganga, 'The Right of Reproduction' in Rosati (n 37) 141.

also occur where material from one object is replaced on a different object. For instance, removing an image from a poster and reapplying it to canvas involves reproduction.[335]

While the three acts that can been seen in AI's design production touch upon right of reproduction, the question of whether its designs are derived from previous ones is controversial. To make sense of whether there is a causal link between the work used (that is, reproduced by AI) and the copyright work, Edward Lee defines a tripartite taxonomy. According to Lee's taxonomy, there are three types of uses (reproductions) of copyright works in technologies: *operational, creational* and *output* uses. Operational uses refer to uses that 'occur during the operation of the technology once it has already been created.'[336] In this type of use, copies are generated by AI systems in order for the AI software to function as designed.[337] By contrast, a creational use means use of a copyright work 'to create a technology.'[338] Finally, output uses involve relocating some portion of the copyright work directly to the output.[339] For Lee, operational and creational uses are inherently non-infringing, while output uses are inherently infringing.[340]

Amanda Levendowski argues that training an AI program with copyright works is a 'quintessential example of a "purely operational" use under Lee's framework.'[341] She notes that:

> When humans experience (copyright) works, we call them 'works.' When AI systems do it, these works are transformed into 'data.' A best-selling novel becomes data about how humans use language; a selfie becomes data about the features of the human face; a conversation from a film becomes data about human voices.[342]

The kinds of uses that are based on digitisation of and processing the works during the training process (Uses 1 and 2) do not aim at appropriating their content. In such cases, the works are not valued for their expressive nature. Rather, the factual nature of the works (for fashion designs such as physical placement and contextual relationship of parts of garments depicted, their geometries, sizes, colourings, etc.) are used in a computational manner, as Maurizio Borghi and Statroula Karapapa have described, 'as data.'[343]

---

335 Case C-419/13 *Art & Allposters v. Pictoright* EU:C:2015;27 paras 43–46.
336 Edward Lee, 'Technological Fair Use' (2010) 83 *Southern California Law Review* 843.
337 Ibid 843.
338 Ibid 842.
339 Ibid 844.
340 Ibid 842–847.
341 Amanda Levendowski, 'How Copyright Law Can Fix Artificial Intelligence's Implicit Bias Problem' (2018) 93(2) *Washington Law Review* 624, fn 221.
342 Ibid 625 (Brackets added).
343 Maurizio Borghi and Statroula Karapapa, 'Non-Display Uses of Copyright Works' (2011) 1 *QMJIP* 21.

In a similar vein, Abraham Drassinower suggests that 'because a work is a communicative act, to reproduce it is to recommunicate it. To copy is to repeat an author's speech as such. Uses of the work as a mere pattern of ink, so to speak, in the absence of recommunication, are not uses of the work as a work.'[344] The technical reproductions used in training AI constitute non-communicative uses. They are tools for a technical process or for achieving a function. Thus, they are merely needed to train AI. For Drassinower, when a work is not used for a communicative use, it should not be qualified as a 'fair use'[345] but simply a 'non-use of the work.'[346] For that reason, as Alain Strowel argues, '(t)hose intermediate copies should not fall within the copyright realm properly conceived. Reconstructing the reproduction right by taking into account the fundamental communicative aspect of a copyright work automatically limits its scope to cases where a work is used as an expressive work.'[347]

Is the purpose of use of copyright work in training AI systems relevant for interpreting the concept of 'reproduction' under EU law? The EU right of reproduction relies on a technology-neutral notion. Under the current approach, reproduction occurs irrespective of whether the user values the work for its expressive or communicative content.[348] The non-expressive uses, as well as expressive ones (such as Use 3), are currently caught by the reproduction right, and their legality therefore requires the availability of an exception.

But do Uses 1 and 2 really count as a *use* whether the purpose is expressive or not? Under EU law, a work is a literary, scientific or artistic *expression*. Expressions are legible, visual, audible or perceptible embodiments of ideas. While expressions exist in our world in concrete forms, ideas are mere abstractions. For that reason, expressions are protected by copyright if they meet requirements of copyright protection, whereas ideas are in public domain. The use of a work in training AI means using 'idea' content of an expression, not the expression itself. It is true that it is not conveying the message of the expression to others even in digital world. But it is a non-use not because it is non-communicative or non-expressive. It is a non-use because perceptible embodiments of a work, that is the expression itself, is not used. Expression is not only 'datafied' but also deduced to its unprotected core content, that is the idea on which it is built. Given that under the conventional approach of the CJEU even very mundane and minimally

---

344 Abraham Drassinower, *What's Wrong with Copying?* (Harvard University Press, 2015) 87.
345 Jessica L. Gillotte Claims that 'Using Copyrighted Works to Train AI is Fair Use'. See; Jessica L. Gillotte, 'Copyright Infringement in AI-Generated Artworks' (2020) 53 *University of California Davis Law Review* 2679–2690.
346 Drassinower (n 344) 13 and 87.
347 See; Alain Strowel, 'Reconstructing the Reproduction and Communication to the Public Rights: How to Align Copyright with Its Fundamentals' in P Bernt Hugenholtz (ed), *Copyright Reconstructed: Rethinking Copyright's Economic Rights in a Time of Highly Dynamic Technological and Economic Change* (Kluwer Law International, 2018).
348 Bently *et al* (n 109) 145.

creative works are protected against digital uses, Uses 1 and 2 might be considered infringement of the right of reproduction as well.

3.3.6.2 Partial reproduction

The Software Directive,[349] the Database Directive[350] and the Information Society Directive[351] all give the owners of copyright a right to control the reproduction of the work in 'whole' or 'in part' in computer programs, databases and authorial works. The EU law has extended protection from identical copying to copying of 'any part' of a work. In so doing, it enables a copyright owner to control situations of *taking part of a work*[352] and *changing the form of the work*.[353] The CJEU views the question of what counts as a 'part' as a matter of European law.

In *Infopaq*,[354] one of the questions referred to the CJEU was whether the news clippings comprising of 11 words amounted to reproduction 'in part' under the Information Society Directive. The Court noted that there was nothing in the EU law that suggested that 'parts are to be treated any differently from the work as a whole' and concluded from this that parts 'are protected by copyright since, as such, they share the originality of the whole work.'[355] The Court added that 'the various parts of a work . . . enjoy protection . . . provided that they contain elements which are the expression of the intellectual creation of the author of the work.'[356] The judgment indicates that a fragment of a work will be a protected 'part' only if that fragment itself is original.[357] The originality of the part taken is only requirement for a finding of infringement under EU law. This means that copyright infringement can occur where 'any part,' as opposed to any 'substantial part,' of a work is reproduced.[358]

The partial uses of copyright work in the final output of AI (Use 3) can amount to infringement of the reproduction right. Again, exceptions come into play.

3.3.6.3 Temporary technology-dictated copies

There are three potentially relevant defences to these uses: temporary technology-dictated uses, uses for research, and text and data mining. Digital tools generally work by the generation of temporary copies. Such copies are positively desirable

---

349 Software Directive Art 4(1)(a) ('in part or in whole').
350 Database Directive Art 5(a) ('in whole or in part').
351 Information Society Directive Art 2.
352 For example, where a part of fashion design is copied.
353 For example, where a fashion design (two-dimensional works, such as drawings or patterns) is converted into a garment accepted as a protected work itself.
354 *Infopaq* (n 96).
355 Ibid para 38.
356 Ibid para 39.
357 Ibid para 49.
358 For the test of substantial part under UK law see; Bently *et al* (n 109) 203 ff.

since they enable these technologies to function speedily and efficiently. They do not harm the economic interests of copyright holders either. Recognising this, the EU laws exclude from copyright liability certain temporary copies that are transient or incidental to other activities.[359] The Information Society Directive exempts a person making temporary copies only if: (i) the copies are temporary; (ii) the copies are transient or incidental; (iii) the copies are an integral and essential part of a technological process; (iv) their sole purpose is to enable a transmission in a network between third parties or a lawful use; (v) they have no independent economic significance.[360]

The rationale behind the temporary copying exception is providing a leeway for transmission through computer networks or browsing the internet. The CJEU has considered the meaning of this exception on a few occasions. The first two cases were *Infopaq I* and *Infopaq II*.[361] These cases concerned temporary copies made at various stages in the data capture process for a news-clippings service. The data capture process contained four stages: creating TIFF files by scanning, converting them into searchable text files, storing data and printing out text files. The CJEU noted that the temporary copying exception does not cover the printing of the text files.[362] According to the Court, however, the other three stages of the data-capturing process fulfil the requirements of the exception.[363]

In the later cases, 'the transient fragments of the works within the memory of a satellite decoder and on a television screen'[364] and 'temporary screen and cache copies'[365] that facilitate web browsing are added to list of the acts exempted from copyright infringement under Article 5(1) of the Information Society Directive.[366]

The CJEU seemed to embrace a flexible purposive interpretation of this exception. If reproduction does not have independent economic significance and enables a lawful end use, it does not infringe copyright. Relying on this, it is possible to argue that scanning and conversion of previous designs into an AI (software) readable format (Use 1) are just like acts of scanning and conversion of format

---

359 Information Society Directive Recital 33.
360 Information Society Directive Art 5(1).
361 Case C-302/10 *Infopaq International A/S v. Danske Dagblades Forening* EU:C:2012:16 (Hereinafter '*Infopaq II*').
362 *Infopaq* (n 96) para 74.
363 *Infopaq II* (n 361) para 58.
364 *FAPL* (n 132) para 180.
365 Case C-360/13 *Newspaper Licensing Agency (NLA) v. Public Relations Consultants Association* EU:C:2014:1195 *para 63 ('Meltwater')*.
366 All these cases were related to copies created by technology providers. The CJEU has also answered the question of the availability of temporary copy exception to an end user with a categorical 'no.' In *Stichting Brein (Filmspeller)*, the dispute was over the sale of a multimedia player that was pre-programmed with add-ons that enable users to access to unlawful streaming of broadcasts. If the user operated the player, inevitably, they would produce a transient copy of the stream. The CJEU made it clear that this type of temporary copies would fall outside the temporary copy exception. See; *Filmspeller* (n 330) paras 69–72.

Artificial intelligence and EU copyright protection 121

of text files in *Infopaq I* and *II*. The exception applies, even though the process is initiated by a human being, such as the scanning of the newspapers. Generation of intermediate copies in AI's training process (Use 2) is also like acts of transmission of data in *FAPL* and *Meltwater*. However, the temporary copying exception does not apply to copies stored permanently either by AI or by AI operators before its feeding phase (Uses 1 and 2). For example, some neural networks can also store copyright works in their internal memories, which might not be temporary. Even though these networks store works in an abstract form, if they reproduce the creative elements of a work (Use 2), it will amount to making a copy. Where these copies are temporary, they could fall into the scope of this exception.

3.3.6.4 Text and data mining

The Information Society Directive additionally contains a scientific research exception. According to this exception, a person does not infringe copyright in a work if the 'sole purpose' of the use is for the 'illustration for teaching or scientific research.' This is on the condition that the source and the author's name are acknowledged, and the use is for non-commercial purpose.[367] The DSM Copyright Directive has further provided an additional mandatory exception to allow the digital reproduction of works for the very same purpose.[368]

More importantly, the DSM Copyright Directive has introduced two different text and data mining exceptions that might concern AI's use of copyright work. The first one concerns text and data mining for scientific research.[369] This exception covers two rights. The first right is the right of reproduction of copyright works,[370] databases[371] and on-demand press publications.[372] The second right is the right of extraction of whole or a substantial part of databases covered by the *sui generis* database right.[373] Only research organisations and cultural heritage institutions can benefit from this exception for pursuing non-commercial uses, if they have lawful access to the resources to be mined. Once all these conditions are fulfilled, a person can mine text and data for scientific research.[374] The miner can also retain the copies of the works for the purposes of scientific research, including the verification of research results.[375] The right holders cannot use contractual terms[376] or security or protection measures to prevent the exercise of this exception.[377]

---

367 Information Society Directive Art 5(3)(a).
368 Digital Single Market Directive Art 5(1).
369 Digital Single Market Directive Art 3.
370 Information Society Directive Art 2.
371 Database Directive Art 5(a).
372 Digital Single Market Directive Art 15.
373 Database Directive Art 7(1).
374 Digital Single Market Directive Art 3(1).
375 Digital Single Market Directive Art 3(2).
376 Digital Single Market Directive Art 7(1).
377 Digital Single Market Directive Art 3(3). See; Alain Strowel and Rossana Ducato, 'Artificial Intelligence and Text and Data Mining: A Copyright Carol' in Rosati (n 37) 299–316.

The second text and data mining exception that the DSM Copyright Directive provides is broader than the first one.[378] Not only research organisations and cultural heritage institutions but anyone with lawful access to the resource can resort to this exception. Text and data mining is not only limited to the purposes of scientific research. It can also be performed for any purpose whether non-profit or for profit. This exception covers the rights to reproduction[379] and adaptation[380] of computer programs in addition to the rights mentioned earlier. However, unlike the text and data mining for scientific research, the right holder can restrict this exception through contractual terms.[381]

The two exceptions are narrowly drafted and are subject to several limitations. Notably, the text and data mining exception for scientific research is available only for two categories of beneficiaries (research organisations and cultural heritage institutions) and for a specific objective (research purposes).[382] The right holder has the power to reserve the right of reproduction and stay out of the text and data mining exception for general purposes (Article 4). As Rossana Ducato and Alain Strowel have demonstrated, 'many online platforms are already prohibiting text and data mining in their online terms of use.'[383] Eleonora Rosati suggests that because the reach of both exceptions is quite limited, they might not have a positive impact on the development of AI creativity.[384]

As previously mentioned, fashion brands frequently use text and data mining for fashion designing with the aid of AI. If they mine data for contributing to fashion designing from a scientific angle, they must be research organisations to take shelter in exception of the text and data mining for scientific research. This is a rare situation, because their main objective in fashion designing is almost always for commercial purposes. To utilise the text and data mining exception for general purposes, however, they need to meet two conditions. First, they need to have lawful access to the images to be reproduced. Second, they need to make sure that the relevant right holders have not reserved the right to make reproductions.[385] Otherwise, text and data mining would not be of use to escape from liability in any of AI's uses of copyright work.

Where a database is used for text and data mining, the Database Directive leaves some room for such use. For the CJEU, the *sui generis* right of extraction[386] of databases protects its maker from unauthorised 'reconstitution by a user

---

378 Digital Single Market Directive Art 4.
379 Software Directive Art 4(1)(a).
380 Software Directive Art 4(1)(b).
381 Since Article 7(1) of the Digital Single Market Directive does not refer to Article 4.
382 Strowel and Ducato (n 377) 303.
383 Rossana Ducato and Alain Strowel, 'Limitations to Text and Data Mining and Consumer Empowerment: Making the Case for a Right to Machine Legibility' (2019) 50 *International Review of Intellectual Property and Competition Law* 649.
384 Eleonora Rosati, 'Copyright as an Obstacle or an Enabler? A European Perspective on Text and Data Mining and its Role in the Development of AI Creativity' (2019) 2 *Asia Pacific Law Review* 215.
385 Ibid 216.
386 Database Directive Art 7(1).

or a competitor of that database or a substantial part of it at a fraction of the cost needed to design it.'[387] This *sui generis* right does not cover acts of 'consulting that database for information purposes.'[388] In addition, text and data mining could fall among the lawful uses recognised by the Database Directive for copyright protected databases.[389] Article 6(1) of the Database Directive allows the lawful users to make a copy of the database to access the contents or to allow a 'normal use' of the same. Performing text and data mining would in this sense be considered as a normal use of the database.[390]

3.4 Conclusion

International copyright norms have played a significant role in the CJEU's judgments. In almost all cases the Court has referred to them. These references make it clear that the concepts of work and authorship stated in the Berne Convention, WCT and TRIPs Agreement become reference points in determining whether a subject matter is an original work in the European sense.

No EU copyright directive has a provision regarding AI-generated works or more specifically fashion designs. The CJEU's seemingly elaborate analysis setting the parameters of copyright subsistence has revealed two cumulative conditions. First, the subject matter must be original. Second, the subject matter must be expressed with sufficient clarity and in an objectively perceptible manner. This chapter has assessed whether these two conditions are met according to the four-stage test specified by Bernt Hugenholtz, João Pedro Quintais and Daniel Gervais. Thus, in order for an AI-generated subject matter to be considered as a work (and a fashion design) under the EU law, it must be: (i) a production in the literary, scientific or artistic domain; (ii) a product of human intellectual effort; (iii) a result of creative choices that (iv) are expressed in the output.[391] The case law of the CJEU has, however, revealed a more complex test for copyright subsistence.

The main tenet of this test is originality. To emphasise this point, the CJEU has frequently stated that 'the author must express . . . [their] creativity in an original manner' so that they can achieve 'the author's own intellectual creation.'[392] 'The author's own intellectual creation' thus constitutes the core of the originality analysis. The level of creativity manifested in a work is considered as the most vital factor for benefiting from copyright protection.[393] In the EU, originality is an autonomous concept that requires uniform interpretation.

---

387 Case 3C. 04/07 *Directmedia Publishing GmbH v. Albert-Ludwigs-Universität Freiburg* (2008) ECLI:EU:C:2008:552 para 33.
388 Ibid para 53 (noting that this is so where 'the contents of that database (is) accessible to third parties, even . . . on a paid basis').
389 Database Directive Art 6(1) and 8.
390 Strowel and Ducato (n 377) 311.
391 Hugenholtz, Quintais and Gervais (n 55) 117.
392 *Infopaq* (n 96) para 45; *BSA* (n 152) para. 50.
393 Van Gompel (n 130) 99.

The standard of originality applies to all categories of works, even to applied art such as fashion designs.[394] The EU originality emphasises the personhood of the author.[395]

If the word *original* is understood in the meaning of daily language, it can be concluded that copyright would include new, innovative or extraordinary intellectual creations that differ from traditional forms of expression.[396] However, when analysed closely, to identify creativity in a subject matter other features are added to the construction of 'the author's own intellectual creation.' In this sense, all these features justifying the European autonomous originality can be summarised as follows:

1 *Availability of the creative space:* when there is only one way of expressing an idea (when the form and content of the work are combined) or when an expression is determined by a purpose or dictated by restrictive rules, leaving no room for free and creative choices, in brief, when it comes to a subject matter that does not provide the author with an opportunity to create, that work is not original. Rule-based, technical, functional or informational constraints do not prevent an intellectual creation from protection if they leave enough room for making creative choices. However, if the space left for the author is too small or absent due to these external constraints, the subject matter cannot be considered as the author's own intellectual creation.
2 *Using the creative space:* where there is free creative space to create, it must be used by the author.
3 *Author's own intellectual creation:* the subject matter created by the author within their free creative space must be 'the author's own intellectual creation.' To achieve this, the subject matter must originate from its author. This applies to all subject matter covered by the EU copyright regime.
4 *Intellectual effort*: the author must exercise an 'intellectual effort' by using their free creative space; the requirement of intellectual effort by a person precludes productions created without the human contribution from copyright protection.
5 *Personal stamp:* intellectual effort must include a minimum level of creativity. For minimal creativity to arise, the author must make creative and free choices and reflect their personality to the work accordingly when creating a subject matter. This work is considered original when it bears its author's personal mark.
6 *No aesthetics:* the artistic quality and aesthetic characteristics of the work are not relevant (and must not be required) in determining the originality.

---

394 See; Cofemel (n 10).
395 *Painer* (n 198) paras 88, 89 and 92.
396 Van Gompel (n 130) 99.

Artificial intelligence and EU copyright protection 125

The second part of the test of copyright subsistence for any subject matter is that it must be expressed. In the CJEU's case law, the following two points are evaluated for a subject matter to be deemed as expressed:

1 *Objectively conceivable expression:* the subject matter must be expressed with sufficient clarity and in an objectively perceivable manner.
2 *Literary, scientific or artistic expression:* the subject matter expressed in this way must be in 'a production in the literary, scientific or artistic domain.'

Thus, in light of these criteria, the CJEU has ruled that a 11-word news fragment (*Infopaq*), graphical user interfaces, object and source codes in computer programs (*BSA*), a portrait photograph (*Painer*), a simple panoramic photograph of a city (*Renchoff*), user manuals and programming languages (*SAS*), video games (*Nintendo*), a lamp (*Flos*), bicycle (*Brompton*) or clothing designs (*Cofemel*) can be protected as a work under EU copyright law, provided that these are the author's own intellectual creations. However, ideas that are not expressed (*Cofemel*), single words (*Infopaq*), algorithms and software functionality (*SAS Institute*), match fixture lists (*Football Dataco*), match broadcasts (*FAPL*), military status reports (*Funke Medien*) and the taste of food products (*Levola*) are excluded from the scope of protection.[397]

The CJEU cases analysed in this chapter point to human nature as the originality requirement in the EU law.[398] As Christian Handig emphasised, '[t]he expression "author's own intellectual creation" clarifies that a *human author* is necessary for a copyright work.'[399] Similarly, Justine Pila points out that 'an author is a natural person; someone who exploits the scope for free and creative choices afforded by a certain type of expressive object to produce a work that reflects her personality.'[400]

Thus, under EU copyright law, it inevitably becomes necessary to conclude that the author can be a human and that the work must reflect their personality.[401] Considering this, it is possible to argue that AI cannot be an author in the legal sense. AI authors will not likely be considered the owners of their creations. This derives from the fact that EU laws place human intellectual effort at the centre of protection. However, human authors can still have copyright on AI-generated subject matter by proving that the conditions of the protection are satisfied.[402]

---

397 Pila and Torremans argue that perfumes can also be considered a work. See; Pila and Torremans (n 86) 257–259.
398 Andres Guadamuz, 'Do Androids Dream of Electric Copyright? Comparative Analysis of Originality in Artificial Intelligence Generated Works' (2017) 2 *Intellectual Property Quarterly* 178.
399 Christian Handig, 'The Copyright Term "Work" – European Harmonisation at an Unknown Level' (2009) 40(6) *International Review of Intellectual Property and Competition Law* 668 (Emphasis added).
400 Pila (n 37) 77.
401 Guadamuz (n 398) 178.
402 Ginsburg (n 49) 1074.

The rules on the authorship and ownership under the EU law are not completely harmonised. This leaves a leeway to Member States to adopt legal arrangements regarding AI-generated creations.

As a result, under the EU copyright law, protection is granted for AI-generated fashion designs, which are also shaped by human creative choices. Creating a work with the help of computers or machines is always welcome with human intellectual effort. This conclusion can be drawn even if AI systems have a dominant role in the creation process.

The question of whether copies made during the AI training process (Uses 1 and 2) or AI-generated subject matter that reproduces any part of copyright work (Use 3) infringe will likely emerge soon. Courts can adopt the rationale of 'datafied and ideational' uses of third-party copyright material and continue to take machine learning questions on a case-by-case basis. Alternatively, they can use the question as an opportunity to draw clearer contours around the exceptions that exist in the EU copyright law. This second approach would enlighten the qualitative questions of whether a work is created automatically in a machine's operation and deleted automatically after use. If an infringement is identified, the question of to whom the law can attribute liability arises. This is closely related to the question of to which human actors the authorship on AI-generated fashion designs can be granted. The following sections will try to find out answers to these questions.

4 Authorship of artificial intelligence

Global solutions and disjunctions

4.1 Introduction

The law provides intellectual property rights for certain intangible creations of humans, such as designs for product appearances and copyright for books and music. The law, however, remains disinterested when it comes to AI involved in creating 'products of the mind.'

As previously mentioned, the existence of design rights and copyright in most cases requires that a designer or an author be a natural person and the initial owner of that right. Designers and authors can transfer their rights to others; this can happen automatically when employees create something within the scope of employment. As a matter of fact, 'artificial' persons in the form of companies own most designs.

The relevant EU laws were not designed with AI in mind, and there is no norm specifically about AI-generated fashion designs in the EU. AI-generated fashion designs are left in the twilight zone of law. As a result, it is unclear who the owner of such a design could be, who could be considered a designer and who could be liable in case of infringement.

These questions require a framework that offers practical solutions. The current debate about the regulation of AI is divided into two extremes: 'those who view AI as a path towards "superintelligence" that transcends humanity, and those who think AI is merely a glorified version of data analysis and statistical inference.'[1]

Realistic estimates show that soon machines will be able to perform more tasks in more efficient and autonomous ways than humanity can currently envision. These machines will be more central to production of intellectual creations. Normally, these AI machines do not need intellectual property rights. But the people who use AI do. Because of the economic value of these innovations, the interest in benefiting from these intellectual creations through intellectual property rights

---

1 Rosa Maria Ballardini, Kan He and Teemu Roos, 'AI-Generated Content: Authorship and Inventorship in the Age of Artificial Intelligence' in Taina Pihlajarinne, Juha Vesala and Olli Honkkila (eds), *Online Distribution of Content in the EU* (Edward Elgar Publishing, 2019) 117.

DOI: 10.4324/9781003355922-5

will be more prominent. In this context, a key question relates to how to regulate creations generated by AI systems.

Allowing intellectual property rights for AI-generated intellectual creations (including fashion designs) would make creative AI more valuable. This would also incentivise AI development, which would ultimately result in more innovation. In the opposite scenario, failing to do so would discourage businesses from using AI to generate new intellectual property, even in cases where it would be more effective than a person. The prospect of intellectual property rights thus provides an additional financial motivation for designers.

Making a case for a regulatory framework for the future technologies is extremely difficult. But international legal scholars have put forward diverging suggestions on the subject. Considering the classification of Rosa Maria Ballardini *et al*, it is possible to categorise them into three groups: romantic (section 4.2), revolutionary (section 4.3) and modernist (section 4.4) schools.[2] In this chapter, these schools (and their followers) will be explained. UK and US copyright systems will also be discussed to exemplify these schools. However, a caveat must be put here: many of the thoughts discussed in this chapter mostly concern copyright law. But these discussions still have significance for AI-generated fashion designs for two reasons. First, these kinds of creations can be copyright work as discussed in Chapter 3. Second, although their ideologies and justification are different, suggestions and discussions made under copyright law are still valid in other fields of intellectual property – including design law – in factually identifying the authors and infringers.

4.2 Romantic school

4.2.1 Public domain

The romantic school[3] suggests that the existing intellectual property frameworks should be construed to allow only natural persons to be authors and designers.[4] This approach would categorically deny intellectual property entitlement for AI-generated creations, so that such works would simply fall into *public domain*. According to this school, AI does not have the human attributes set out in judicial decisions in relation to producing a work that is 'original' in copyright sense.[5] The same logic applies to designs (the designer doctrine). Since there are not any human authors participating in the making of such products, nobody can benefit from protection for such productions under intellectual property law.[6]

---

2 Ibid 129–134.
3 Ibid 132–133.
4 Maria Iglesias, Sharon Shamuilia and Amanda Anderberg, *Intellectual Property and Artificial Intelligence – A Literature Review EUR 30017 EN* (Publications Office of the European Union 2019) 14.
5 Ibid 14.
6 Ibid 14. See also; Daniel J Gervais, 'The Machine as Author' (2020) 105 *Iowa Law Review* 2099 (arguing that 'machines that make decisions and cross the autonomy threshold produce public domain material to which no copyright rights attach').

AI-generated outputs are comparable to things that cannot be monopolised under intellectual property right, such as music that the wind generates, or the sounds of a waterfall, or birds singing at dawn.[7] In this case, they are considered as works in public domain and open to the use of everybody.

Authors like Mark Perry and Thomas Margoni,[8] Daniel Schönberger[9] and Victor M Palace[10] adopt the idea that AI-generated subject matter should be precluded from intellectual property protection. Heidi Härkönen,[11] Bingbin Lu[12] and Haochen Sun[13] diverge from these authors and in their separate studies argue that AI works (and fashion designs) generated solely by *autonomous* AI systems should be placed in the public domain without copyright protection.

A more powerful critique to grating copyright ownership to AI-generated works comes from Carys Craig and Ian Kerr's *The Death of the AI Author*.[14] The classical copyright understanding uses a construction of 'romantic authorship' to justify and to articulate when and how to confer upon certain people exclusive rights over certain productions. Under this conception, an author is an autonomous and independent agent who creates *ex nihilo*. Craig and Kerr – by combining copyright theory and literary theory – question this description of human creativity that bears little relation to how actual humans create. In normal life, authors build on each other's work. They constantly create dialogue with audiences and with other authors. Their works emerge under this densely dialogical and relational atmosphere. Craig and Kerr take this idea in a new direction: the same critique applies to AI authorship. For them, 'human communication is the very point of authorship as a social practice,' and this cannot be found in AI productions that 'merely identify existing patterns, reinforce them, and replicate them.'[15] Craig and

---

7 Amir H Khoury, 'Intellectual Property Rights for Hubots: On the Legal Implications of Human-like Robots as Innovators and Creators' (2016–2017) 35 *Cardozo Arts & Entertainment Law Journal* 668; Daryl Lim, 'AI & IP: Innovation & Creativity in an Age of Accelerated Change' (2019) 52(3) *Akron Law Review* 840.
8 Mark Perry and Thomas Margoni, 'From Music Tracks to Google Maps: Who Owns Computer-generated Works?' (2010) 26(6) *Computer Law & Security Review* 621–629.
9 Daniel Schönberger, 'Deep Copyright: Up – And Downstream Questions Related to Artificial Intelligence (AI) and Machine Learning (ML)' in Jacques De Werra (ed), *Droit d'auteur 4.0/ Copyright 4.0* (Schulthess Editions Romandes, 2018) 145–173.
10 Victor M Palace, 'What If Artificial Intelligence Wrote This? Artificial Intelligence and Copyright Law' (2019) 71 *Florida Law Review* 217–242.
11 Heidi Härkönen, 'Fashion Piracy and Artificial Intelligence – Does the New Creative Environment Come with New Copyright Issues?' (2020) 15(3) *Journal of Intellectual Property Law & Practice* 169.
12 Bingbin Lu, 'A Theory of "Authorship Transfer" and Its Application to the Context of Artificial Intelligence Creations' (2021) 11(1) *Queen Mary Journal of Intellectual Property* 22.
13 Haochen Sun, 'Redesigning Copyright Protection in the Era of Artificial Intelligence' (2022) 107 *Iowa Law Review* 1248–1251.
14 Carys Craig and Ian Kerr, 'The Death of the AI Author' (2021) 52(1) *Ottawa Law Review* 31.
15 Ibid 86.

Kerr believe that 'the death of the romantic author therefore entails the death of the AI author.'[16]

4.2.2 US law

The public domain argument is not essentially a theoretical argument. This approach is an accepted norm under US law where AI-generated works are not entitled to protection.[17]

Under US copyright law, to be eligible for copyright, the work must be *original* and *fixed* in a material form.[18] The Supreme Court evaluated the originality requirement in the context of a telephone directory in the *Feist* case.[19] The court went beyond the 'sweat of the brow' doctrine, which had dominated US law by the time of the case, and held that mere intellectual contribution was not sufficient to demonstrate originality. Under the sweat of the brow doctrine, a certain amount of effort in the creation of a work was considered adequate for that work to be original. In the *Feist* case, it was held that for the originality requirement to be met, the work must not be copied from another work (must be created independently) and possess a 'modicum of creativity.'[20] Thus, the phone directory at issue in the proceedings was not considered as an original work.

For a work to be considered original under US law, absolute novelty is not required;[21] however, it must reflect the unique thought, skill or labour of the author.[22] Works based on pre-existing work are not precluded from copyright protection because they can be protected as derivative works, to the extent they show substantial but not trivial improvements.[23] In the US, a work must be 'fixed in a tangible medium of expression' in addition to being original to be protected.[24] For practical purposes, fixation involves recording or reducing works to writing.

In the *Burrow-Giles Lithographic Co v. Sarony* case, the famous photographer Sarony filed a lawsuit claiming that Burrow-Giles had infringed his copyright. Sarony argued that the portrait photograph of the famous writer Oscar Wilde,

---

16 Ibid.
17 Enrico Bonadio and Luke McDonagh, 'Artificial Intelligence as Producer and Consumer of Copyright Works: Evaluating the Consequences of Algorithmic Creativity' (2020) 2 *Intellectual Property Quarterly* 132.
18 The relevant article of the *"Copyright Act"* is as follows: "[c]opyright protection subsists, in accordance with this title, in *original* works of *authorship* fixed in any *tangible medium of expression*, now known or later developed, from which they can be perceived, reproduced, or otherwise communicated, either directly or with the aid of a machine or device." 17 USC § 102(a) (2000) (Italicised).
19 *Feist Publications Inc v. Rural Telephone Service Co* 499 US 340 (1991).
20 *Feist Publications Inc v Rural Telephone Service Co* 499 US 340, 345 (1991).
21 *Alfred v Bell & Co*, 191 F2d 99, 102 (1951).
22 *L Batlin & Son, Inc v Snyder*, 536 F2d 486, 491 (2d Cir 1976) (en banc).
23 For definition of derivative works, see; 17 USC § 101 (2000).
24 Copyright Act, 17 USC § 102(a) (2000).

which he had taken, was sold in the form of lithographs without his authorisation. Prior to the infringement claim, the Supreme Court considered whether the photograph qualified as a work. The Supreme Court held that a photograph would be considered as a work as long as it was 'the author's original intellectual conception.' As specified in the court's reasoning, whether a photograph is a mere mechanical reproduction or an original work of art is a question to be decided on a case-by-case basis, depending on the proof of the facts, originality, intellectual creativity, and conception on the part of the author. Thus, a mere mechanical creation was not considered adequate for copyright subsistence. It was acknowledged that the subject matter would be elevated to the level of work where the person standing behind the camera expresses their idea.[25]

Copyright vests initially in the author or authors of the work, and the authors of a joint work are co-owners of copyright in the work.[26] The author is defined as 'he to whom anything owes its origin; originator; maker.'[27]

Under US copyright law, authorship is not explicitly attributed to human beings. However, the US Copyright Office has recently made it clear that non-human authorship is not possible. The Copyright Office declares in its Compendium[28] on registration procedures that it only registers an original work created by a human being.[29] In fact, the Copyright Office takes a step further and states that it will not register 'works produced by a machine or mere mechanical process that operates randomly or automatically without any creative input or intervention from a human author.'[30] The Compendium is a non-binding document and can be amended any time. Nevertheless, it represents official viewpoint on AI-generated works under US law.[31]

Quite recently, the US Copyright Office once again maintained its trenchant position and said that it will not let AI-generated works enter the copyright's wonderland. Dr Stephen Thaler – the inventor of DABUS – made an application to register an AI-generated picture. The name of the artwork was *A Recent Entrance to Paradise*, and it was generated by an AI system called Creativity Machine. The Review Board of the Office rejected the application on two grounds. First, the Review Board explained that human authorship is a well-established principle

---

25 *Burrow-Giles Lithographic Co v. Sarony* 111 US 53, 58 (1884).
26 Copyright Act, 17 USC § 201(a) (2000).
27 *Burrow-Giles Lithographic Co v. Sarony* 111 US 53, 58 (1884).
28 US Copyright Office: Public Draft of Compendium of U.S. Copyright Office Practices, Third Edition (28 January 2021) www.copyright.gov/comp3/docs/compendium.pdf (Hereinafter 'Compendium').
29 Ibid para 306.
30 Ibid para 313.2.
31 In 1956, US Copyright Office rejected an application for registration of the computer-generated song *Push Button Bertha* created by mathematicians Martin Klein and Douglas Bolitho. See; Annemarie Bridy, 'The Evolution of Authorship: Work Made by Code' (2016) 39(3) *Columbia Journal of Law & the Arts* 395–397. In 1964, this time, the registration application for a floor tile design drawn by a machine using random shapes was rejected because it was not a product of an author. See; US Copyright Office, Register of Copyright, 67th Annual Report of the Register of Copyrights (1964) s. 7–8.

under US copyright law. Second, the Board underlined that AI-generated works cannot be protected under the work-made-for-hire doctrine, as a machine cannot enter a binding employment contract.[32]

Similar lines of reasoning can be also seen in the world's most famous (monkey) selfie case: the *Naruto* case.[33] The case was filed by the animal rights association People for the Ethical Treatment of Animals (PETA). The defendant was David Slater, a photographer who published a book comprised of selfies shot by Naruto the monkey using a camera Salter had left unattended. PETA claimed that Naruto owned the copyright on the photographs. The District Court of California underlined that the concepts of authorship and work are not clearly defined by the law. This is an intentional choice by the legislator to allow for flexibility in the interpretation of the concepts at stake. In conclusion, the court ruled that although animals had constitutional rights, they did not have the right of standing before a court to claim copyright infringement.

4.3 Revolutionary school

4.3.1 AI as a designer

The identification of authorship of AI-generated subject matter is a long continuum. The romantic and revolutionary schools stand at its opposite ends. The revolutionary school supports the idea that the law could (and should) include an explicit norm that recognises non-human authorship of a design.[34] Ryan Abbott elaborates this thought in terms of patent law as follows:

> The principle of *AI legal neutrality* suggests that the law should allow intellectual property protections for AI-generated inventions. Although the prospect of a patent would not directly motivate AI to invent, it will inspire the people who build, own, and use AI. Intellectual property protections for AI output will incentivize the development of inventive AI that will lead to innovations and scientific advances – the primary purpose of the patent system.[35]

The central thesis of Abbott's contention is that 'AI legal neutrality' should be a new guiding principle to AI regulation. This principle requires that the law should not discriminate between AI and human behaviour. For Abbott, the current legal systems are not neutral: for instance, 'AI may be better at generating certain types

---

32 Franklin Graves, 'Thaler Loses AI-Authorship Fight at U.S. Copyright Office' (*IP Watchdog*, 23 February 2022) www.ipwatchdog.com/2022/02/23/thaler-loses-ai-authorship-fight-u-s-copyright-office/id=146253/.
33 *Naruto v Slater* 2018 US App LEXIS 10129 (9th Cir Cal, 23 April 2018).
34 See; Ryan Abbott, 'I Think, Therefore I Invent: Creative Computers and the Future of Patent Law' (2016) 54(2) *College Law Review* 1079–1126; Ryan Abbott, *The Reasonable Robot* (CUP, 2020) 10 (Abbott 2020).
35 Abbott 2020 (n 34) 72 (emphasis added).

of innovation, but businesses may not want to use AI if this restricts ownership of intellectual property rights.'[36] In Abbott's understanding, the neutral legal treatment entails the recognition of AI inventorship without for AI's having rights or legal personhood.

Abbott maintains that acknowledging AI as inventors has some benefits: patenting AI-generated inventions and acknowledging AI as an inventor is compatible with the incentive theory.[37] Recognising AI as an inventor has substantial significance independent of the value of AI itself. Patenting will also encourage businesses and computer engineers to develop and use inventive AI. This in turn would result in more innovation for society.[38] Granting patents to the AI-generated inventions would also increase the public disclosure of trade secrets and commercialisation of new products. Moreover, the decline in investment in pharmaceutical and biotechnology industries will be prevented, which have costly and arduous research and development stages.[39] Acknowledging AI as an inventor will also ensure the smooth functioning of the patent system and safeguard the moral rights of the inventor. It would prevent people who do not play a role in the generation of AI inventions from receiving undeserved acknowledgment.[40]

Abbott states that AI does not need to have the ability to think to be registered as an inventor: as a matter of fact, the validity of the concept of a 'mental act,' which is sought as a patentability requirement particularly in US court decisions, has become irrelevant.[41]

But who would own the patent right? Abbott's answer to this question is the owner of the AI.[42] The owner of the right could be the computer's owner (who owns it like a chattel), the developer or user of the program.[43]

Abbot also has a prediction for the future: when general AI is invented, it will replace the hypothetical skilled person used in the determination of the inventive step; and when super-intelligent AI is invented, it will go beyond it and possess all the knowledge. In this case, the inventive step and skilled person requirements for receiving a patent will need to be redefined.[44]

Representing ideas from the revolutionary school, Colin R Davies argues that one of the ways of granting authorship to AI would entail attributing legal

---

36 Ibid 4.
37 Abbott points to the constitutional basis of this theory under US law. US Constitution, Article I, Section 8, Clause 8, of the United States Constitution grants Congress the power 'to promote the progress of science and useful arts, by securing for limited times to authors and inventors the exclusive right to their respective writings and discoveries.'
38 Abbott 2020 (n 34) 83.
39 Ibid.
40 Ibid 83–84.
41 Ibid 84–86.
42 Ibid 87–88.
43 Abbott 2016 (n 34) 1114.
44 Ibid 98–106.

personhood to AI.⁴⁵ The rationale behind this argument is rewarding the creativity of AI that exhibits a human attribute.⁴⁶ As Davies suggests, the personhood should not be regulated as a form of share holdership that exists in the corporations, but for acknowledging AI as a person that can cover both rights and liabilities. Especially, possible solutions to satisfy financial obligations imposed by a lawsuit would include the establishment of some form of deposit account or an insurance scheme for such liabilities.⁴⁷

In Davies's imagination of AI personhood, the rights arising from authorship could be transferred. If a programmer continues to use AI in creating copyright works without transferring the right of property on the machine, then the AI should be considered as the employee of the programmer. In this case, the authorship of the work must belong to the programmer as a *sui generis* right.⁴⁸

Moreover, Davies also proposes some solutions for cases where AI programs are the subject of a contract. If an AI program is the subject of a licensing agreement, the status of copyright ownership must be specified in the contract. However, if it is an assignment contract, all copyrights will be deemed transferred and the new owner of the program will be the copyright holder as an employer on AI-generated outputs. If AI generates a work within the scope of a commission by a third party, it will be presumed that a *joint venture* contract is concluded between the programmer and the commissioner.⁴⁹

Davies's model overlooks much of the historical and practical distinction between the copyright and author's rights (*droit d'auteur*) systems. The solution proposed by Davies is compatible with the fact that moral rights are not recognised for computer-generated works in the United Kingdom. However, for the countries embracing the author's rights system, which does not provide such an arrangement, the chances to implement this model in relation to moral rights seem implausible. Hence, in Davies's model the fate of protection of AI-generated outputs by moral rights is left uncertain. Davies contends that the 'person who would [be] identifiable from the outset could be required to make any necessary arrangements for protection.'⁵⁰ This means this person is given initial right of copyright on computer-generated subject matter. Although the impression is that this person could be the programmer, it has not been clearly evaluated whether the employer is entitled to copyright protection if the program is produced in the context of an employment relationship. But the most important question that can be posed

---

45 Colin R Davies, 'An Evolutionary Step in Intellectual Property Rights – Artificial Intelligence and Intellectual Property' (2011) 27(6) *Computer Law & Security Review* 617.
46 Simon Chesterman, 'Artificial Intelligence and the Limits of Legal Personality' (2020) 69(4) *International & Comparative Law Quarterly* 834–835; Eliza Mik, 'AI as a Legal Person?' in Jyh-An Lee, Reto Hilty and Kung-Chung Liu (eds), *Artificial Intelligence and Intellectual Property* (OUP, 2021) 419–420.
47 Davies (n 45) 618.
48 Ibid.
49 Ibid.
50 Ibid.

against Davies's model is: should AI be granted personhood solely for generating a work and exhibiting very limited mental faculties, if there is any?

4.3.2 AI and legal personality

The word *person* in English etymologically originates from the Latin word *persona*. The word *persona* means a 'mask worn by an actor portraying a character within the context of a stage play.' This word later came to be used to refer to the human being (the person) wearing such a mask.[51] Could AI put on a personality mask?

Legal personhood is a foundational concept in law. Being a person in law denotes the entitlement to one or more legal positions. The definition of legal personhood, however, is a highly debated topic. It is mainly constructed on the dichotomy of 'owning rights' and 'bearing duties.' A common understanding is that 'the question whether an entity should be considered a legal person is reducible to other questions about whether or not the entity can and should be made the subject of a set of legal rights and duties.'[52] In the orthodox view, 'to be a legal person is to be the subject of rights and duties.'[53]

In modern legal systems, two forms of legal persons are recognised: natural and juridical. It is almost universally accepted that *all humans* should have legal personhood. Legal personhood in this sense is essentially attributed to humans by virtue of the fact that they are human. For that reason, human beings are acknowledged as *natural* persons. Legal personhood is also extended to other artificial entities. One of the more basic and common examples of this recognition relates to corporations. A company is a person of legal fiction. Corporate structures, therefore, are known as *juridical* persons. Associations, foundations, corporations, states and international organisations can be cited as examples of juridical persons.[54] Arguments have been also put forward for the extension of legal personhood to other artificial entities that have been *physically made* by humans. This sentiment has been voiced for the extension of legal personhood to AI.

Legal personhood for AI has also been highly topical among lawyers, since Lawrence Solum published his seminal article in 1992.[55] The tension in these discussions relies on two tenets of AI that carry meaning in modern societies. The first relates to whether personhood should be granted for inherent reasons. Inherent reasons make us ask whether AI has some moral attributes worthy of receiving

---

51 David J Gunkel and Jordan Joseph Wales, 'Debate: What is Personhood in the Age of AI?' (2021) 36 *AI and Society* 473.
52 Lawrence B Solum, 'Legal Personhood for Artificial Intelligences' (1992) 70 *North Carolina Law Review* 1231.
53 Bryant Smith, 'Legal Personality' (1928) 37(3) *Yale Law Journal* 283.
54 John Zerilli, *A Citizen's Guide to Artificial Intelligence* (MIT Press, 2021) 77.
55 Solum (n 52) 1235–1237. Solum refers to Christopher Stone to discuss this idea two decades earlier: Christopher D Stone, 'Should Trees Have Standing? Towards Legal Rights for Natural Objects' (1972) 45 *Southern California Law Review* 450, 456 n 26.

legal protections that legal persons such as human beings enjoy.[56] The second relates to arguments for instrumental reasons that are framed with references to the most common artificial legal persons, namely the companies.[57] Instrumental reasons have to do with AI's defined role as commercial actors, such as buying, selling and being in other types of legal relations, etc.[58]

This speculative discussion around granting legal personhood for AI has gained a new dimension when Saudi Arabia granted citizenship to the humanoid robot Sophia[59] and when an online system animating the personality of a seven-year-old boy was granted 'residency' in Tokyo.[60]

Recently, the European Parliament joined this discussion on the legal status of AI in 2017. In its 'Report with Recommendations on Civil Law Rules on Robotics,' it proposed that robots should be granted 'electronic personality' rather than real or legal personality for setting out the rights and responsibilities of robots equipped with AI technology. Noting that AI could not have a human's legal status for the time being, the report stated that it would be suitable to assign special personality to robots, which would entitle them to both rights and liabilities, and also to sue and be sued when they give rise to any damage.[61] Another significant proposal included in the report is that it introduces tort liability for robots' wrongdoings.[62] However, the EU Parliament has apparently changed of tune from the creation of 'electronic persons' in 2017 to its 2020 'Resolution on Intellectual Property Rights for the Development of Artificial Intelligence Technologies.' The Parliament in that Resolution noted that:

> The autonomisation of the creative process of generating content of an artistic nature can raise issues relating to the ownership of IPRs covering that content; considers, in this connection, that it would not be appropriate to seek to impart legal personality to AI technologies and points out the negative impact of such a possibility on incentives for human creators.[63]

---

56 Visa Kurki describes this approach as 'ultimate-value context' (whether artificial intelligence has intrinsic moral value, not derived from its usefulness to other entities). See; Visa A J Kurki, *A Theory of Legal Personhood* (OUP, 2019) 176.
57 Chesterman (n 46) 820.
58 Kurki describes this approach as 'commercial context' (whether artificial intelligence can function as a commercial actor) See; Kurki (n 56) 176.
59 Olivia Cuthbert, 'Saudi Arabia Becomes First Country to Grant Citizenship to a Robot' (*Arab News*, 26 October 2017) www.arabnews.com/node/1183166/saudi-arabia.
60 Anthony Cuthbertson, 'Artificial Intelligence "Boy" Shibuya Mirai Becomes World's First AI Bot to Be Granted Residency' (*Newsweek*, 6 November 2017) www.newsweek.com/tokyo-residency-artificial-intelligence-boy-shibuya-mirai-702382.
61 European Parliament Resolution with Recommendations to the Commission on Civil Law Rules on Robotics (2015/2103(INL)) (European Parliament, 16 February 2017) para 59(f).
62 Ibid para 54.
63 European Parliament Resolution on Intellectual Property Rights for the Development of Artificial Intelligence Technologies (2020/2015(INI)) (European Parliament, 20 October 2020) para 13. See also; European Parliament, Resolution with Recommendations to the Commission on Civil Liability Regime for Artificial Intelligence (2020/2014(INL)) para 7.

This shows that whether AI systems could be afforded some form of legal personhood is 'a matter of decision rather than discovery.'[64]

4.3.2.1 Juridical personality

In practice, most legal systems recognise aggregations of human actors as juridical persons. In some legal systems, juridical personality is also granted to some entities that are truly non-human. For example, religious idols in India,[65] a river in New Zealand[66] and the whole ecosystem in Ecuador[67] are granted personality.[68]

Visa Kurki contends that when AI can perform similar tasks as human beings, this means that it can function as legal persons. This can be the case for strong AI. And if an AI can function as a legal person, it can be granted legal personhood on somewhat similar grounds as a human, regardless of whether such AIs are worthy of moral consideration.[69]

As previously mentioned, some legal scholars and law-making bodies have advocated for assigning juridical personality to AI particularly based on tort liability.[70] These suggestions are built on the instrumental approach to personality. In this approach, juridical personality is seen as a tool used to enable human beings to achieve certain goals.

There are three main distinguishable theories explaining the way the legal system regulates artificial entities through conferring juridical personhood on them. Corporations have been the first and foremost owner of this status, and so these theories of personhood often take corporations as their main point of reference.[71] The first theory is known as the 'aggregate theory,' sometimes referred to as the 'contractarian' or 'symbolist theory.' According to this theory, the law gives artificial entities to natural persons as instruments. This personhood is endowed to realise 'the (legal) relations between the natural persons (who are members of the artificial entity) and the entity itself, as well as relations between the entity and the world.'[72] The second theory is the 'fiction' or 'concession' theory. Accordingly, the legal personality of corporations exists because the legal system prefers them to do so. Legal personhood for artificial entities is a positive law construct that the

---

64 Samir Chopra and Laurence F White, *A Legal Theory for Autonomous Artificial Agents* (University of Michigan Press, 2011) 154.
65 For the judgment on the subject handed down by the Supreme Court of India, see; Shiromani Gurdwara Prabandhak Committee, Amritsar v Shri Somnath Dass AIR 2000 SC 1421 (Supreme Court of India).
66 Te Awa Tupua Law ('Whanganui River Claims Settlement') adopted in 2017 (New Zealand) Art 14(1).
67 2008 Ecuadorian Constitution Art 10.
68 Chesterman (n 46) 822; Zerilli (n 54) 77.
69 Kurki (n 56).
70 For explanations on the entities that could be assigned legal personality, see; Kurki (n 56) 127–152.
71 Nadia Banteka, 'Artificially Intelligent Persons' (2021) 58 *Houston Law Review* 553.
72 Ibid 555.

law attributes to certain fictional beings.[73] This positivist approach finds expression especially in case law and law texts. The third theory is the 'realist' theory. Under this theory artificial entities are neither a symbol nor fiction. They are real beings that exist beyond the law even before being granted personality. The law perceives them as objective entities and grants personality to that being by only recognising them.[74]

Simon Chesterman states that these three theories are applicable to AI in various degrees. However, Chesterman suggests that corporate personality is different from AI personality: 'a corporation is made up of human beings, through whom it operates, whereas an AI system is made *by* humans.'[75] According to Chesterman, juridical personality can be afforded to AI by using the instrumental approach, provided that the content of the juridical personality is structured particularly in terms of the capacity to sue and be sued, to enter into contracts, to incur debt, to own property. Tax obligations, piercing of the veil of corporate personality and criminal liability are other areas that should be regulated in such a construction of personality.[76]

4.3.2.2 Extension of natural personality

Many of the arguments in favour of AI personality implicitly or explicitly assume that AI systems exhibit some form of human qualities. These approximate attributes entitle them to comparable recognition before the law.[77] The idea here is that certain AI systems might have an entitlement to some legal positions conferred to natural personality because of their inherent qualities.[78] How and why can natural personhood be extended?

Human rights are the result of a cumulative historical process that takes on a life of its own, *sui generis*, beyond the orations and writings of progressive thinkers. These rights reflect the process of historical continuity and change that helped shape their present substance.[79] Eventually this helped form the Universal Declaration of Human Rights adopted by the General Assembly of the United Nations in 1948. Drawing on the battle cry of the French Revolution, René Cassin, one of the main drafters of the document, outlined the four pillars of the declaration as 'dignity, liberty, equality, and brotherhood.' The declaration embodied these pillars when it proclaimed that human beings were 'born free and equal in dignity and rights.' After various developments and movements, human rights

---

73 Ibid 554.
74 Ibid 555. See also; Chesterman (n 46) 830.
75 Chesterman (n 46) 830 (Emphasis original).
76 Ibid 824–830.
77 Ibid 831.
78 Ibid.
79 Micheline R. Ishay, *The History of Human Rights from Ancient Times to the Globalization Era* (2nd edn, University of California Press, 2008) 3.

have become more egalitarian and yet remain a site of contestation. Today human adults are recognised as persons before the law in almost all legal systems.[80]

Some arguments regarding the extension of natural personality to AI do not only rise on the progressive rhetoric of natural personhood but on 'the darker history of slavery.'[81] Joanna Bryson, in her book *Robots Should Be Slaves*, provocatively suggests that 'robots should be built, marketed and considered legally as slaves, not companion peers.'[82]

Similarly, Andrew Katz and Ugo Pagallo draw similarities with the *peculium* institution in the ancient Roman law.[83] A slave who is granted *peculium* acts as an authorised agent of his owner and does not possess a personality of on his own.[84] Here, the use of AI as a tool is associated with the instrumentality arising from the use of the slave as an authorised agent rather than his inherent qualities as a person.[85] With a degrading narrative concerning human dignity, these slavery-based proposals are premised on the theory of the instrumentality of technology and a tradition dating back to the ideas of Aristoteles,[86] who defined a slave as 'living tool.'[87] David Gunkel warns that the application of instrumental slave theories to AI is problematic because this would create a new instrumental servant or slave.[88] This would ultimately open the dangerous discussion and rewind the times to the darkest and most sorrowful ages of humanity where not everybody was granted rights and personality on an equal footing.

Another alternative approach regarding recognition of natural personality of AI focuses on the attribution of rights to animals. Several legal attempts initiated to realise this have not yielded much success, just like the *Naruto* case. For instance,

---

80 Chesterman (n 46) 832.
81 Ibid.
82 Joanna J Bryson, 'Robots Should be Slaves' in Yorick Wilks (ed), *Close Engagements with Artificial Companions: Key Social, Psychological, Ethical and Design Issues* (Natural Language Processing) (8th edn, John Benjamins Publishing, 2010) 63.
83 Adrew Katz, 'Intelligent Agents and Internet Commerce in Ancient Rome' (2008) 20 *Society for Computers and Law* 35; Ugo Pagallo, *The Laws of Robots: Crimes, Contracts, and Torts* (Springer, 2013) 103–106.
84 In Roman law, it was a common practice for the owner of the slave (generally the father, *paterfamilias*) to give the slave (or the son) some commodities called *peculium* to be used in the business of the slave (or son). *Peculium* and the profits obtained thereof officially belonged to the owner of the slave. The slave was not authorised to transfer the commodities contained in the *peculium*, and all the goods were completely returned to the owner upon the death of the slave. To encourage the slave, the owner would undertake to set the slave free depending on the increase in his wealth. For comprehensive information on *peculium* see; Henry Hansmann, Reinier Kraakman and Richard Squire, 'Incomplete Organizations: Legal Entities and Asset Partitioning' in Giuseppe Dari-Mattiacci and Dennis P Kehoe (eds), *Roman Commerce in Roman Law and Economics Volume I: Institutions and Organizations* (OUP, 2020) 216–221.
85 Chesterman (n 46) 833.
86 Aristotle, *Politics*, translated by H Rackham (Harvard University Press, 1944) 1253b26–40.
87 David J Gunkel, *How to Survive a Robot Invasion: Rights, Responsibility, and AI* (Routledge, 2020) 53.
88 Gunkel (n 87) 59–60.

in 2013, the non-governmental organisation called Nonhuman Rights Project filed lawsuits concerning the predicament of four chimpanzees that were taken captive. It was claimed in the case that chimpanzees had a personality by arguing that they had human-like cognitive skills, autonomy and self-consciousness. Rejecting the claims, the New York State Court Appellate Division ruled that chimpanzees are not entitled to personality rights despite having the attributes defined by the claimant.[89]

These anthropomorphic arguments have attracted criticism. Neil Richards and William Smart, for instance, describe these trends on the humanisation of AI as 'android fallacy,'[90] that is, a mistaken belief that AI has human-like attributes. John-Stewart Gordon also adopts a critical approach toward giving personality to robots particularly in the context of tort law as proposed by the European Parliament. Modern robots, as he argues, are not fully equipped with human-like skills such as rationality, autonomy, conception and having social relations.[91]

Joanna Bryson, Mihailis E Diamantis and Thomas D Grant do not welcome the idea of granting personhood to AI systems either. They argue that this solution will come with high social costs while its moral gains remain very limited.[92] Furthermore, if AI systems are granted personality, they can be used as a shield to cover up the wrongful acts of human beings.[93]

Jacob Turner, in his book *Robot Rules*, critiques the argument of Bryson *et al* and suggests that whether an artificial entity's ability to understand its own actions or whether they are alive or human are irrelevant in granting personhood to any potential entity.[94] Turner also founds the argument that giving personality to AI would allow humans to shield themselves from liability ill-founded. This derives from the fact that corporations have been holding a separate personality in modern economies for a long time and have played a significant role in commerce.[95] Turner thinks that rather than these questions, the law should be concerned with how the personality of AI will be shaped.[96] Adopting a more social perspective, David Gunkel states that the answer to the question of whether AI systems could be natural persons is negative because we cannot precisely define being conscious, if that is the requirement for acquiring natural personality.[97] Like Turner, Gunkel also contends that it is possible to tailor a legal personality to AI if social institutions and necessities require so, but this must be done in the right way.[98]

---

89 *People ex rel Nonhuman Rights Project, Inc v. Lavery*, 998 NYS 2d 248 (App Div, 2014).
90 Neil Richards and William Smart, 'How Should the Law Think About Robots?' in Ryan Calo, Michael Froomkin and Ian Kerr (eds), *Robot Law* (Edward Elgar Publishing, 2016) 18–21.
91 John-Stewart Gordon, 'Artificial Moral and Legal Personhood' (2021) 36 *AI & Society* 457–471.
92 Joanna J Bryson, Mihailis E Diamantis and Thomas D Grant, 'Of, for, and by the People: The Legal Lacuna of Synthetic Persons' (2017) 25 *Artificial Intelligence and Law* 273–291.
93 Ibid 286.
94 Jacob Turner, *Robot Rules: Regulating Artificial Intelligence* (Palgrave, 2019) 190–191.
95 Ibid 191.
96 Ibid 205.
97 Gunkel and Wales (n 51) 475.
98 Ibid 476.

A final approach as to the recognition of AI systems as persons, as Colin R Davies contends, is focusing on what they can do rather than whether they are like humans. As Eliza Mik recalls, autonomy is seen as the best technical and objective reference for creativity. If something is autonomous, then it is independent from human beings, acts without human influence and generates its own outputs by making its own decisions. Hence, when AI systems become autonomous, they must be distinguished from human beings who operate them and be recognised as persons on their own.[99] Mik argues that granting personality to AI based on autonomy is not a correct solution because autonomy technically is an advanced form of automation.[100]

Bryant Smith points to the two dimensions of the notion of legal personhood, noting that 'to confer legal rights or to impose legal duties, therefore, is to confer legal personality.'[101] According to Smith, entities with legal personality are parties to *legal relations*.[102] Drawing on this principle, non-human beings can also be given a personality inasmuch as the function of personality is to regulate behaviour.[103] Being a party to a legal relation establishes the essence of Smith's perception of personality. Here, the owner of the personality is not required to have free will, be autonomous, rational or intelligent. Legal personality arises where there is a certain legal relation.

Theoretically, establishing a legal personality based on solely generating an intellectual creation is possible. However, building a personhood of this kind on a very narrow legal relation (namely, creating a work only), which would have implications not only in intellectual property law but also in other fields of law, must carefully be thought of in terms of maintaining the internal consistency of the law itself.[104] For instance, who would represent AI in a case before courts or in an administrative procedure before relevant state bodies? Would AI be able to be a member of a collecting society? How would it, which does not have complete ability to act and choose which action to perform, be possible to assess mental fault of an AI in the context of tort and crime liabilities? How would this be proven and demonstrated before a court? Would AI be conferred to the human right to intellectual property? Would the royalties stemming from AI-generated works be taxed?

Granting a legal personality to AI would lead to such legal questions.[105] Moreover, do current AI technologies display a sufficient degree of creativity to merit legal personality? This question will be revisited in the following chapter. But in

---

99 Mik (n 46) 421.
100 Ibid 422–423.
101 Smith (n 53) 283.
102 Ibid 293–294.
103 Ibid 296.
104 Mik (n 46) 433.
105 Bert-Japp Koops, Mireille Hildebrandt and David-Oliver Jaquet-Chiffelle, 'Bridging the Accountability Gap: Rights for New Entities in the Information Society?' (2010) 1(2) *Minnesota Journal of Law, Science & Technology* 514; Mik (n 46) 433.

its 'Resolution on Intellectual Property Rights for the Development of Artificial Intelligence Technologies' the European Parliament considers that it would not be appropriate to give a personality to AI by just relying on the fact that it generates a work. It is accepted in the Resolution that this would have a negative impact on incentives for human creators, which is the aim of the EU in ensuring copyright protection.[106]

4.4 Modernist school

The modernist school holds that natural person(s) behind the arrangements necessary for the creation of the AI-generated works should be considered as the author or right holder. Just like the romantic school, these legal scholars claim that non-human entities should not be granted authorship.[107] There are various arguments about to whom authorship or ownership of copyright should be conferred. The following section will explain these opinions.

4.4.1 Programmer or user?

When identifying the actors who take part in a legal relation around a 'thing,' several actors emerge. Amongst them, the first that comes to mind is the creator of that thing. For AI, it is the programmer. By citing Harold Cohen's AI art, Dan Rosen suggests that the 'programmer' should be the author.[108] Rosen views AI as the representation of the programmer's 'original intellectual conception.'[109] The subject matter is created within the boundaries of the creative space designed by the programmer no matter who uses the AI technology.[110] The programmer writes the substantial algorithm; displays creative choices in model selection; performs data selection and allocation; sets parameters and checks the additional steps required to monitor and modify the algorithm once it is operational.[111]

---

106 European Parliament Resolution on Intellectual Property Rights for the Development of Artificial Intelligence Technologies (2020/2015(INI)) (European Parliament, 20 October 2020) para 13.
107 Ballardini, He and Roos (n 1) 133–134.
108 Dan Rosen, 'A Common Law for the Ages of Intellectual Property' (1984) 38(5) *University of Miami Law Review* 804.
109 Bonadio and McDonagh (n 17) 122.
110 Rosen (n 108) 804. See also; Palace (n 10) 234–238; Samantha Fink Hedrick, 'I 'Think', Therefore I Create: Claiming Copyright in the Outputs of Algorithms' (2019) 8(2) *NYU Journal of Intellectual Property & Entertainment Law* 346; Darin Glasser, 'Copyrights in Computer-Generated Works' (2001) 24(1) *Duke Law and Technology Review*; Kalin Hristov, 'Artificial Intelligence and the Copyright Dilemma' (2016) 57(3) *IDEA: The IP Law Review* 444; Tim W Dornis, 'Artificial Creativity: Emergent Works and the Void in Current IP Doctrine' (2020) 22 *Yale Journal of Law & Technology* 49–53.
111 Hedrick (n 110) 341.

Pamela Samuelson argues that the author of AI-generated subject matter should be the 'user of the program.'[112] Caen A Dennis, on the other hand, states that in AI-generated creation, users who have 'purchased the AI device,' that is to say, fashion houses or independent designers, should be considered as the author.[113] According to these scholars, programmers do not create a work through a machine[114] but rather generate 'a potential to create.'[115] AI machines are considered tools in the hands of users to create works.[116]

4.4.1.1 UK law: programmer

A typical reflection of the modernist school on legislation is section 9(3) of the CDPA of the UK. In UK law, the main law governing intellectual property rights is the Copyright, Designs and Patents Act 1998 – CDPA. According to CDPA, a subject matter must meet the following requirements to benefit from copyright protection:

1   *The subject matter must fall into one of the categories of works prescribed by the law.* These categories of works are: (i) literary works;[117] (ii) dramatic works;[118] (iii) musical works;[119] (iv) artistic works;[120] (v) films;[121] (vi) sound recordings;[122] (vii) broadcasts[123] and (viii) typographical arrangements of published editions.[124]

    UK law does not draw a distinction between the authorial and entrepreneurial works that exist in international instruments;[125] all subject matter is called 'work.'[126] Only performers' rights are regulated under a separate section.[127]

---

112 Pamela Samuelson, 'Allocating Ownership Rights in Computer-Generated Works' (1985–1986) 47 *University of Pittsburg Law Review* 1208.
113 Caen A Dennis, 'AI-Generated Fashion Designs: Who or What Owns the Goods?' (2020) 30(2) *Fordham Intellectual Property, Media and Entertainment Law Journal* 593–644.
114 Samuelson (n 112) 1209.
115 Glasser (n 110) 24.
116 Samuelson (n 112) 1220. Samantha Fink Hedrick suggests that both the programmer and the program user can be authors. See; Hedrick (n 110) 337–348.
117 CDPA s 3.
118 Ibid.
119 Ibid.
120 CDPA s 4.
121 CDPA s 5, 5B.
122 CDPA ss 5, 5A.
123 CDPA ss 6–7.
124 CDPA ss 8.
125 The Berne Convention (1886) lays down the rights of the author, while Rome Convention (1961) includes provisions on related rights.
126 Lionel Bently, Brad Sherman, Dev Gangjee and Phillip Johnson, *Intellectual Property Law* (5th edn, OUP, 2018) 58.
127 CDPA ss 180–205N.

144 *Authorship of artificial intelligence*

2   *The subject matter must be recorded, in writing or otherwise.* This requirement applies to literary works, dramatic works and musical works only.[128]
3   *The subject matter must be original.* This requirement also applies to literary works, dramatic works, musical works and works of art.[129] Before the *Infopaq* case, the traditional British originality standard contained four dimensions. First, the work is considered original if it comes from the creator and is not copied from another work.[130] Second, the work is considered original if it displays the 'labour, skill and judgement' of the person who created it.[131] Third, the 'labour, skill and judgement' performed to create the work should not be insignificant; it should reach to a substantial level.[132] Fourth, only performing the right kind of 'labour, skill and judgement' enables a work to qualify as original; that is, copying another work cannot give rise to copyright protection regardless of the intensity of effort spent to create a work.[133]
4   *The subject matter must be sufficiently related to U.K. law.* This requirement applies to all categories of works.[134]
5   *Subject matter must not be excluded from the scope of protection due to public order.*[135]

Under UK copyright law, the person who creates the subject matter is considered the author,[136] and copyright, as a rule, vests initially in this person.[137] There are four exceptions to this rule. These exceptions are copyright ownership of employers,[138] Crown,[139] Parliamentary[140] and certain international organisations.[141]

Special authorship rules apply to entrepreneurial works such as sound and film recordings, broadcasts and topographic arrangements. These authors are producers of musical works or films, the person making the broadcast and publishers of topographical arrangements.[142] Legal entities may be the author of the entrepreneurial work.

128   CDPA s 3(2).
129   CDPA ss 1(1)(a).
130   *University of London Press v. University Tutorial* [1916] 2 Ch 601.
131   By applying this criterion, football betting coupons were granted copyright protection. See; *Ladbroke (Football) v. William Hill (Football) Ltd* [1964] 1 All ER 465 HL at 466 and 469.
132   Face paint, for instance, is not protected by copyright. See; *Merchandising Corporation v. Harpbond* [1971] 2 All ER 657.
133   *Interlego AG v. Tyco Industries Inc* [1989] AC 217; *British Northrop Ltd v. Texteam Blackburn Ltd* [1974] RPC 57.
134   Bently *et al* (n 126) 119–122.
135   Ibid 122–124.
136   CDPA s 9(1).
137   CDPA s 11(1).
138   CDPA s 11(2).
139   CDPA ss 11(3), 163.
140   CDPA ss 11(3), 165.
141   CDPA ss 11(3), 168.
142   CDPA ss 9(2).

Section 9(3) of CDPA provides a special rule regarding computer-generated works:

> In the case of a literary, dramatic, musical or artistic work which is computer-generated, the author shall be taken to be the person by whom the arrangements necessary for the creation of the work are undertaken.[143]

Section 178 of CDPA defines the concept of computer-generated work. According to this definition, these works refer to subject matters that are 'generated by computer in circumstances such that there is no human author of the work.'

This provision envisages a fictional authorship. This hypothetical author is not the person who created the work but the person who made the necessary arrangements for the creation of the work. The concept of an author has been extended with this provision. In a sense, the person closest to the subject matter is accepted as the author. Juridical persons, as well as natural persons, can obtain authorship of this kind.[144] It is worth remembering that when the British legislator passed these provisions in 1988, its goal was to protect automated creations such as satellite photographs.[145]

The term of protection for computer-generated works is 50 years from the creation of the work.[146] Right holders only have economic rights on these works. Moral rights are not recognised.[147] Thus, the owner of these works cannot claim the moral rights of attribution[148] or integrity.[149] Finally, it could be recalled that this provision also applies to designs.[150]

From the enactment of CDPA up until today, the rule on the authorship of computer-generated works has only been examined[151] in the *Nova Productions* case.[152] The parties in this case are two competing computer (pool) game manufacturers. The Court of Appeal considered the graphics and frames generated by the computer program while playing Nova Productions' game, which were at

---

143 There are similar regulations in Irish, New Zealand, Indian and Hong Kong law. See; Jani McCutcheon, 'Vanishing Author in Computer-Generated Works: A Critical Analysis of Recent Australian Case Law' (2012) 36(3) *Melbourne University Law Review* 956.
144 Bonadio and McDonagh (n 17) 120.
145 Madeleine De Cock Buning, 'Autonomous Intelligent Systems as Creative Agents under the EU framework for Intellectual Property' (2016) 7(2) *European Journal of Risk Regulation* 315; Madeleine De Cock Buning, 'Artificial Intelligence and the Creative Industry: New Challenges for the EU Paradigm for Art and Technology' in Woodrow Barfield and Ugo Pagallo (eds), *Research Handbook on the Law of Artificial Intelligence* (Edward Elgar Publishing, 2018) 531.
146 CDPA s 12(7).
147 Bonadio and McDonagh (n 17) 121.
148 CDPA s 79(2).
149 CDPA s 81(2).
150 CDPA s 214.
151 *Express Newspapers plc v. Liverpool Daily Post & Echo* [1985] FSR 306.
152 *Nova Productions Ltd v. Mazooma Games Ltd* [2006] RPC 379. For a previous case with a brief reference to CDPA s 9(3), see also; *Bamgboye v. Reed* [2004] EMLR 5, 73 para 38.

issue in the proceedings, as computer-generated works within the context of section 9(3) of CDPA. In the case, it was decided that the programmer in charge of designing the game at Nova Productions was the person who made the necessary arrangements for the creation of the work. And it was pointed out that those who were playing the game did not display any artistic labour or skill and thus were not counted as authors.[153] It should be emphasised that the scope of application of the case is limited, because the issue of authorship on the subject matter in case was not disputed between the parties.

Comparing the EU, US, Australian, UK and Chinese laws, Andres Guadamuz contends that this pragmatic approach in the UK law could easily solve the problem of computer-generated works for all countries.[154] For Guadamuz, the exclusion of AI-generated subject matter from (copyright) protection could have 'serious commercial effect,' especially in the field of databases.[155] Guadamuz contends that the provision in the UK has several advantages at the following points:

> [This section] would bring certainty to an uncertain legal area; it has already been implemented internationally in various countries; it is ambiguous enough to deflect the user/programmer dichotomy question and make it analysed on a case-by-case basis; and it has been in existence for a relatively long time without much incident.[156]

The provision in UK law on the computer-generated works departs from the general principle of the authorship; that is, the author of a work is the one who creates it. With this provision, an (artificial) legal assumption is envisaged. There is no direct relation between the (hypothetical) author and the work, and the link between authorship and the element of originality is broken. An authorship isolated from the creation of the work is established.[157]

---

153 *Nova Productions Ltd v. Mazooma Games Ltd* [2006] RPC 379.
154 Andres Guadamuz, 'Do Androids Dream of Electric Copyright? Comparative Analysis of Originality in Artificial Intelligence Generated Works' (2017) 2 *Intellectual Property Quarterly* 169–186 (Hereinafter 'Guadamuz 2017'); Andres Guadamuz, 'Do Androids Dream of Electric Copyright?' in Jyh-An Lee, Reto M Hilty and Kung-Chung Liu (eds), *Artificial Intelligence and Intellectual Property* (OUP, 2021) 174. For a similar opinion see; Pratap Devarapalli, 'Machine Learning to Machine Owning: Redefining the Copyright Ownership from the Perspective of Australia, US, UK and EU Law' (2018) 40(11) *European Intellectual Property Review* 722. Cf; Ana Ramalho, 'Will Robots Rule the (Artistic) World? A Proposed Model for the Legal Status of Creations by Artificial Intelligence Systems' (2017) 21(1) *Journal of Internet Law* 17.
155 Guadamuz 2017 (n 154) 185.
156 Ibid.
157 Bram Van Wiele, 'The Human-Machine Synergy: Boundaries of Human Authorship in AI-Assisted Creations' (2021) 43(3) *European Intellectual Property Review* 169.

Many scholars have critiqued this provision.[158] The criticism can be summarised as follows: the first criticism is that this provision attributes excessive meaning to whether the subject matter is generated with the assistance of a computer or not. Another aspect of this provision that draws criticism is the uncertainty it bears on two issues. First, in the provision, it is uncertain who made the arrangements necessary for the creation of the work: is it the developer of the program, or the user of the program, or the person who feeds the system with data? Because the notion of 'arrangement' may include acts of taking initiative (investment) for the creation of the work, writing the computer program, or using the computer program. The second uncertainty is whether the originality criterion will be sought in such works or not. Another criticism put forward is that arrangement does not provide a solution for the fate of the works jointly created by humans and computers. The final criticism is that this provision is not in compliance with the EU law.

4.4.1.2 *Beyond* the binary

Daniel Gervais raises objection to this binary approach (programmer v. user) to authorship in the context of AI. Gervais maintains that 'the paradigm is a poor reflection of the technological picture painted by AI because AI machines have a degree of autonomy and make decisions.'[159] Indeed, current AI systems have gone beyond being mere tools in the hands of a human user in creating their works and have turned into technologies that can learn and to some extent make independent decisions. Bearing this in mind, Gervais thinks that the answer to the following question should be sought: 'when do they reach the threshold of autonomy that separates or delinks their productions from the humans that programmed or used them?'[160]

Daniel Gervais developed the originality causation test for AI-generated works. This test separates the creative expression of humans protected by copyright from independent AI-generated creations. AI-generated outputs (and their parts) become eligible for copyright protection only when the creative choices they reflect are caused by humans. Programmers or users may embody this originality causation. Productions reflecting choices that cannot be associated with human contribution and are not *predictable* to the humans participating in the process of

---

158 For example see; Bently *et al* (n 126) 117–118; Julia Dickenson, Alex Morgan and Birgit Clark, 'Creative Machines: Ownership of Copyright in Content Created by Artificial Intelligence Applications' (2017) 39(8) *European Intellectual Property Review* 458–459; Paul Lambert, 'Computer Generated Works and Copyright: Selfies, Traps, Robots, AI and Machine Learning' (2017) 39(1) *European Intellectual Property Review* 13–14; Jani Ihalainen, 'Computer Creativity: Artificial Intelligence and Copyright' (2018) 13(9) *Journal of Intellectual Property Law & Practice* 725; Anne Lauber-Rönsberg and Sven Hetmank, 'The Concept of Authorship and Inventorship under Pressure: Does Artificial Intelligence Shift Paradigms?' (2019) 14(7) *Journal of Intellectual Property Law & Practice* 574–575; Bonadio and McDonagh (n 17) 121–122; Dornis (n 110) 18; Wiele (n 157) 169.
159 Gervais (n 6) 2070.
160 Ibid 2098.

creation are deemed to have crossed the autonomy threshold. Therefore, productions made past that threshold do not satisfy the originality criterion required by copyright law.[161]

The test is established on the phenomenon of predictability and the establishment of human creative choices. If human creative choices encompass the AI output in a predictable manner, then the production can be associated with the human creator, and thereby the requirement of originality can be satisfied. Autonomous and ultimately unpredictable choices made by the machine are not able to lead to the type of originality required to obtain copyright protection. Therefore, elements resulting from machine-made choices must be filtered out and considered as a part of the public domain. These elements, which are deemed as public domain material, are put aside in the evaluation for originality requirement.[162] Thus, the 'originality causation' test helps separate the human contribution from machine-made choices. Under the test, machine-made creations (and their parts) that are unpredictable and autonomous are deemed as unprotectable.

Bram Van Wiele critiques Gervais's originality causation test by raising the 'black-box problem.' The black-box problem means that human beings cannot fully understand the decision-making processes of machines and cannot predict what their decisions and their outcomes will be. Particularly the ability of AI systems to make decisions on their own and to make generalisations demonstrate that the level of sophistication they have reached should be taken into consideration.

According to Wiele, the unpredictability of machine operation and its decision-making processes for humans does not pose a question on its own. When it is necessary to ascertain whether an AI-generated work is a result of human creativity, filtering out the contribution of the machine in the work bears significance. But especially when the human and machine contributions in the final work are inseparable, the AI-generated elements of a work constitute a 'black box.' Wiele claims that the existing legal concepts and institutions, as well as Gervais's originality causation test, remain insufficient in determining authorship in such cases (where human creative choices are precisely inseparable from AI-generated creative choices).[163]

Martin Senftleben and Laurens Buijtelaar state that creative human choices in AI-generated creations could be pinpointed by looking at how the AI (and robots) are used and how their algorithms are formed. As stated by Senftleben and Buijtelaar, the user of a painter robot can exhibit creativity by making arrangements and choices regarding the design parameters such as the selection of colours, shapes,

---

161 Ibid 2098–2101.
162 Ibid 2100–2101.
163 Wiele (n 157) 171. Gervais notes that 'if a work results from choices made both by human and machine, that work should be treated as any other case where someone has reused material from the public domain to create a new work: The public domain material must be filtered out.' Gervais (n 6) 2100–2101.

lines and canvas. However, pressing the button to operate the robot is not sufficient for authorship without making such creative choices.[164]

Senftleben and Buijtelaar offer a tripartite taxonomy on the programming architecture of a robot. The first type of program is built on 'step-by-step algorithms.' Robots programmed to operate in this way follow the 'if-then' decision-making model. In this model, they follow the steps based on assumptions and reach the solution by applying the instructions based on those assumptions. These algorithms function as the set of instructions that directly manage the creativity process of the robot. Senftleben and Buijtelaar argue that the author of the work created by a robot functioning as such should be the programmer.[165]

The second programming model mentioned by Senftleben and Buijtelaar is one built on 'rule-based algorithms.' In this model, the programmer does not tell the robot what to do word by word. Instead, the programmer set the limits to the operational scope of the robot. The robot acts on its own within the limits drawn and restrictions imposed.

Finally, Senftleben and Buijtelaar mention the robots based on machine learning. In this model, the programmer sets the goals, selects and uploads training data and revises the productions of the robot. Then the robot recognises data patterns and similarities and learns to create a work on its own.[166]

Senftleben and Buijtelaar argue that, for the robots having the latter two algorithm models, it is difficult to single out human creative contribution to the creation process of AI-generated works; thus, the authorship could not be granted to the programmer because the requirement of originality is not met.[167]

Bernt Hugenholtz, João Pedro Quintais and Daniel Gervais offer a broader analysis, which provides an answer to Bram Van Wiele's criticism and is contrary to the opinion of Martin Senftleben and Laurens Buijtelaar, and suggest that human authorship is possible for AI-generated works including even machine learning systems.[168] Inspired by the criteria set by the judgments of the CJEU, the authors have developed a four-step test to establish whether AI-generated (they call AI-assisted) intellectual creations qualify as a 'work.' Under this test, for such an intellectual creation to be protected, it must be: (i) a production in the literary,

---

164 Martin Senftleben and Laurens Buijtelaar, 'Robot Creativity: An Incentive-Based Neighboring Rights Approach' (2020) 42(12) *European Intellectual Property Review* 802.
165 Ibid 802.
166 Ibid 803.
167 Ibid 803–804. For a similar opinion, see; Tim W Dornis, 'Of "Authorless Works" and "Inventions without Inventor" – the Muddy Waters of "AI Autonomy" in Intellectual Property Doctrine' (2021) 43(9) *European Intellectual Property Review* 571–572.
168 Bernt Hugenholtz, João Pedro Quintais and Daniel Gervais, 'Legal Analysis' in European Commission, Directorate-General for Communications Networks, Content and Technology, C Hartmann, J Allan, P Hugenholtz et al (eds), *Trends and Developments in Artificial Intelligence: Challenges to the Intellectual Property Rights Framework: Final Report* (Publications Office, 2020) 67–96, https://data.europa.eu/doi/10.2759/683128.

scientific or artistic domain; (ii) the product of human intellectual effort; and (iii) originally and creatively (iv) 'expressed' in the output.[169]

The criterion of being 'a production in the literary, scientific or artistic domain' stems from the Berne Convention, which sets out the minimum standards for the protection of literary and artistic works at the international level. As explained earlier, works eligible for copyright protection must be in one of the literary, scientific or artistic domains pursuant to the Convention.[170] The authors think that this criterion, which has recently been applied by the CJEU in its judgments, would not preclude the classification of AI-generated outputs as works.[171] That is to say, AI may generate subject matter falling into the scope of these domains.

The second step in the test, namely being 'the product of human intellectual effort,' seems at first glance to be a significant impediment for AI-generated outputs to qualify as works, because these outputs are generated automatically. However, it is possible to see human contribution in AI-generated outputs in the following cases: development of the AI program, collection and selection of training data, identification of functional features, supervision of creative processes, editing, curation and post-production. Even in cases when the human factor has minimum creative contribution to the AI-generated output, a production without a human cannot be envisaged. Therefore, the authors accept that the criterion of the presence of human intellectual effort is satisfied in AI-generated outputs.[172]

Originality, which is the third step of the test, is undoubtedly the most controversial yet the most vital criterion. This criterion points to the free creative space in which the author can display their creativity and the person can make free creative choices. The authors explain the criterion of producing an original work by dividing the creative process into these three main stages, which were introduced the CJEU in the *Painer* case: conception, execution, redaction. They also underline that 'the creative process is usually iterative, involving multiple cycles of conception, execution and redaction.'[173]

The conception refers to 'creating and elaborating the design or plan of a work.' The creative acts done at this stage transcend mere formulation of the general idea for a work. It involves detailed design choices to be made on the part of the creator such as the selection of genre, style, technique, material, tools, format, etc. This stage also requires making conceptual choices regarding the selection of the genre (novel, painting, etc.), fiction (novel and film), idea of a melody (musical work) and functional features (computer program and database). The authors are of the opinion that AI cannot have any role in this stage, and the said creative choices are solely made by the human.[174]

---

169 Hugenholtz, Quintais and Gervais (n 168) 78.
170 Berne Convention Art 2(1).
171 Hugenholtz, Quintais and Gervais (n 168) 78.
172 Ibid.
173 Ibid 79.
174 Ibid.

The second stage of creating a work is the execution of the idea. In the execution stage, the design and plan of the work outlined in the conception stage is transformed into the draft version of the work. The acts performed in this stage for creation of a work involve writing the text, drawing the painting, composing the notes of the musical work, filming or writing the codes of the computer program. AI mostly has a dominant role at this stage. The authors suggest that while the AI is executing the idea with a high degree of autonomy in this stage, human creative choice (despite being 'mostly operational, by incrementally guiding the AI system towards the desired output') is still necessary and usual.[175]

The redaction is the third stage, where the final touches are performed before the work meets its audience. The final stage requires highly creative choices such as an intensive re-writing, editing, formatting, framing, trimming, colour setting and the filtering process, including all post-production activities that would give the work its final shape. For the time being, even the most autonomous AI systems are not capable of yielding outputs that are readily publishable or marketable. At the final stage, therefore, the AI-generated output needs human creative touches before disclosing it to the public.[176]

Hence, the design choices at the design stage, the calibration choices at the execution stage and the post-production choices at the redaction stage are made by humans.[177] Taking all these issues into consideration, the subject matter generated by AI even in a mostly autonomous process will qualify as a work under EU law, where a human being initiated and conceived the work and subsequently redacted the AI-generated output in a creative manner. The authors consider that human-made creative choices in the execution and redaction stages could suffice for European originality.[178]

The fourth step of the test is that human creativity should be expressed in the final output. This step is an important criterion for the perceptibility of the work by third persons. This requirement is one that could be easily satisfied by AI-generated outputs. Such outputs can be in forms such as music, prose, drawing, painting, etc. such as those created by humans. The requirement of expression has another implication: at the beginning of the creative process, the human actor, who operates the AI system, conceptually designs and conceives an intellectual creation before it is expressed. At this point, the human actor lays down a general idea

---

175 Ibid 80.
176 Ibid 80–81.
177 Ibid 79–81.
178 Ibid 82. Niloufer Selvadurai and Rita Matulionyte point out that the creative process of an AI-generated output is composed of: (i) selection and classification of data; (ii) the generation of the work by the AI; (iii) checking and communicating the final work. The authors argue that the originality requirement will be satisfied if the system is guided by human intellectual effort at the second stage and if editing and revisions are made by humans at the third stage. They accordingly suggest that the AI-generated works could be considered as works. See; Niloufer Selvadurai and Rita Matulionyte, 'Reconsidering Creativity: Copyright Protection for Works Generated Using Artificial Intelligence' (2020) 15(7) *Journal of Intellectual Property Law & Practice* 539.

of a work. A possibility is offered for unexpected expressional features, provided they remain within this general framework. Even though AI generates a form of expression that falls within this general framework but is not foreseeable to the human actor, this subject matter remains within the general idea of the work. In other words, unpredictable forms of expressions are deemed as part of human creative choices to the extent that they reflect the human author's initial intent in creating the work. For instance, in the *Next Rembrandt* project, the machine painted a portrait conceived by the project team but drew a face that the project team could not foresee. Therefore, creativity can be attributed to humans even in such cases when the work is created by the AI in a high degree of autonomy. Accordingly, the authors argue that when the unpredictable creative acts of AI due to its black-box nature (as mentioned by Bram Van Wiele) result in a subject matter that remains within the author's general intent to create a work, they are deemed to be caused by human creativity.[179]

In conclusion, Hugenholtz, Quintais and Gervais state that AI-generated outputs could qualify as a work and therefore enjoy protection under copyright law if they meet the four requirements listed. They maintain that authorship must be attributed to the natural person(s) who have contributed to the three stages of creative process in question. Hence, the author could be the programmer, user, owner of the AI device or a combination thereof, as is the case in *Next Rembrandt*.[180] It also seems possible that ownership of rights can be granted to other natural persons or legal entities who have not created the work (such as employer as the owner of rights).[181]

International Association for the Protection of Intellectual Property (AIPPI) adopted a resolution on AI-generated subject matter at the end of the World Congress held in September 2019 in London.[182] In the AIPPI's resolution, similar to Hugenholtz, Quintais and Gervais, it was adopted that such outputs could be eligible for copyright protection if there is a human intervention in the creation of the work and that other conditions of protection are met.[183] The protection regime to be applied to such subject matter should be identical to those applicable to

---

179 Hugenholtz, Quintais and Gervais (n 168) 82–83. Since authorship would not arise in relation to AI-generated outputs, such outputs could be protected under related rights if they meet the conditions thereof. See; Hugenholtz, Quintais and Gervais (n 168) 88–94.
180 Hugenholtz, Quintais and Gervais (n 168) 84–87.
181 Ibid 87. By implementing, Smith J's ruling in *Thaler v The Comptroller-General of Patents, Designs and Trade Marks (DABUS)* (that is 'an AI owner can possibly claim patent ownership over an AI-generated invention based on their ownership and control of the AI system,' Rita Matulionyte and Jyh-An Lee argue that 'the AI owner should be the owner of the AI-generated works' when this role is differentiated from the roles of the AI developer and AI user. See; Rita Matulionyte and Jyh-An Lee, 'Copyright in AI-generated Works: Lessons from Recent Developments in Patent Law' (2022) 19(1) *SCRIPTed: A Journal of Law, Technology & Society* 29.
182 AIPPI, Resolution: Copyright in Artificially Generated Works, adopted in 2019 AIPPI World Congress – London, 18 September 2019, https://aippi.org/wp-content/uploads/2020/05/Resolution_Copyright_in_artificially_generated_works_English.pdf.
183 Ibid 2.

other types of works.¹⁸⁴ It is also stated that AI-generated works may be eligible for protection by related rights when there is no human intervention. In this case, obviously, the conditions for protection under related rights must also be met.¹⁸⁵ As AI is still developing, the AIPPI prefers to remain neutral as to recognising a new category of copyright or related rights for works that are not protected under existing legal norms.¹⁸⁶

Bingbin Lu proposes a solution based on the 'doctrine of authorship transfer' that exists in US and UK copyright laws. In Lu's proposal, when strong AI produces a work, the authorship of that work must be transferred to from the real author (AI) to the 'controller of the creative process.'¹⁸⁷ The 'controller' here means the natural or juridical person who 'has determinative control over the creative process and has reasonably foreseen and expected the result.'¹⁸⁸

4.4.2 Work made for hire

The 'work made for hire doctrine' is a prominent example of the authorship transfer in copyright law. Under this doctrine, the authorship of a work is transferred from the employee to a legally constructed one: namely, the employer. Annemarie Bridy advocates that the 'work made for hire doctrine' in the US law can be applied to AI-generated subject matter.¹⁸⁹ Shlomit Yanisky-Ravid,¹⁹⁰ Russ Pearlman¹⁹¹ and Kalin Hristov¹⁹² make similar points in their separate articles.

Annemarie Bridy proposes that AI could be considered as the employee and the *programmer* as the employer under the 'work made for hire doctrine' codified under Articles 101 and 201 of the US copyright law.¹⁹³ The doctrine provides that 'the employer or other person for whom the work was prepared is considered the author.' Under US copyright law, authorship vests initially in the creator of the work.¹⁹⁴ The 'work for hire doctrine' is an important exemption to this fundamental rule. Since AI-generated work would not fall under the traditional definition of 'work made for hire,' Bridy suggests that the statutory definition could be amended to incorporate the definition of computer-generated work from other

---

184 Ibid 3.
185 Ibid.
186 Ibid.
187 Lu (n 12) 4.
188 Ibid 13.
189 Annemarie Bridy, 'Coding Creativity: Copyright and the Artificially Intelligent Author' (2012) 5 *Stanford Technology Law Review* 1–28; Bridy (n 26) 395–401.
190 Shlomit Yanisky-Ravid, 'Generating Rembrandt: Artificial Intelligence, Copyright, and Accountability in the 3A Era – The Human-Like Authors Are Already Here – A New Model' (2017) *Michigan State Law Review* 659–726.
191 Russ Pearlman, 'Recognising Artificial Intelligence (AI) as Authors and Inventors under U.S. Intellectual Property Law' (2018) 24(2) 2018 *Richmond Journal of Law & Technology* i–38.
192 Hristov (n 110) 452.
193 Bridy (n 189) 26–27.
194 *Copyright Law of the United States* Art 201(a)(1)(c).

jurisdictions such as, for example, Article 9(3) of the UK CDPA.[195] If such a legal provision is adopted, the *user* could also be the author as the employer in certain circumstances.[196]

Following the 'work made for hire doctrine' of the US copyright law, Shlomit Yanisky-Ravid contends that AI should be treated as a worker by the person who commissioned the work. This proposal is limited to US law and would require a legal amendment to the existing law, which provides that the hiring party is considered to have control on the manner and means by which the product is accomplished. This is not the case for independently generated AI work.[197] Yanisky-Ravid further states that a bank that is the investor of a project can be the author as the employer, as in the *Next Rembrandt* example.[198]

Russ Pearlman claims that, under this doctrine, copyright would be conferred to the programmer or the user, or joint authorship would be granted for both.[199] Kalin Hristov maintains that a programmer or owner of an AI machine could be the author.[200]

4.4.3 Alternative models of protection

The 'work for hire doctrine' does not fit AI systems, because they remain outside the traditional employer-employee relationship as envisioned by US copyright law. Other proposals to provide legal protection to AI-generated subject matter include the drafting of new alternative models through normative adjustments. Inspired by Article 4 of the EU Term Directive,[201] Ana Ramalho argues that AI-generated subject matter should be treated as public domain material, but the law should grant them a form of protection like a disseminator right.[202]

In its 'Report on Intellectual Property Rights for the Development of Artificial Intelligence Technologies,' the European Parliament distinguishes between AI-assisted human creations and AI-generated creations but opines that technical creations generated by AI technology must be protected under the intellectual property legal framework. The Parliament ultimately proposes that 'ownership of

---

195 Bridy (n 189) 27.
196 Ibid.
197 Yanisky-Ravid (n 190) 659.
198 Ibid 714.
199 Pearlman (n 191) 35–36.
200 Hristov (n 110) 452.
201 Term Directive Art 4 reads as follows: 'any person who, after the expiry of copyright protection, for the first time lawfully publishes or lawfully communicates to the public a previously unpublished work, shall benefit from a protection equivalent to the economic rights of the author. The term of protection of such rights shall be 25 years from the time when the work was first lawfully published or lawfully communicated to the public.'
202 Ramalho (n 154) 12–25.

rights, if any, should only be assigned to natural or legal persons that created the work lawfully.'[203]

Jani McCutcheon,[204] Madeleine de Cock Buning,[205] Anne Lauber-Rönsberg and Sven Hetmank,[206] Guido Noto La Diega,[207] Enrico Bonadio and Luke McDonagh,[208] Martin Senftleben and Laurens Buijtelaar,[209] Anthoula Papadopoulou[210] and Haochen Sun[211] in their separate studies express that granting a type of *sui generis* right could be a viable option.[212] La Diega, Bonadio and McDonagh, Senftleben and Buijtelaar, and Sun specify more-concrete proposals. But the others only point out that a model that is like the *sui generis* protection systems that exist in the Database and Integrated Circuit Topographies Directives could be introduced.[213]

Guido Noto La Diega believes that it could be possible to protect AI-generated outputs under the *sui generis* database right by a broader interpretation of the relevant articles of the Database Directive.[214] This argument has been criticised. The first criticism levelled against it is that such a reconstruction of the *sui generis* database right would amount to expansion of protection to any subject matter that is not original. This in turn will lead to overprotection of productions including AI-generated outputs. This could ultimately create a monopoly in favour of companies such as Google, which have a high capacity to process big data. The second criticism put forward against this argument is that overexpansion of the *sui generis* database right will also have a negative impact on (likely to undermine) the established institutions in copyright law on original works.[215]

---

203 European Parliament Resolution on Intellectual Property Rights for the Development of Artificial Intelligence Technologies (2020/2015(INI)) (European Parliament, 20 October 2020) paras 14–15.
204 McCutcheon (n 143) 965–966.
205 De Cock Buning 2018 (n 145) 511–535.
206 Lauber-Rönsberg and Hetmank (n 158) 570–579.
207 Guido Noto La Diega, 'Artificial Intelligence and Databases in the Age of Big Machine Data' (2019) 25 *AIDA 2018* 93–149.
208 Bonadio and McDonagh (n 17) 112–137.
209 Senftleben and Buijtelaar (n 164) 802.
210 Anthoula Papadopoulou suggest that the owner of the AI system should be granted a *sui generis* right for the protection of investors. Thinking that this *sui generis* right in theory should be granted to the user, Papadopoulou points out that this right will in practice be passed upon the owner of the AI through the 'work made for hire principle' in national jurisdictions. See; Anthoula Papadopoulou, 'Creativity in Crisis: Are the Creations of Artificial Intelligence Worth Protecting?' (2021) 12(3) *JIPITEC* 416–417.
211 Sun (13).
212 On this subject see also; Jane Ginsburg, 'People not Machines: Authorship and What It Means in the Berne Convention' (2018) 49(2) *International Review of Intellectual Property and Competition Law* 131–135.
213 McCutcheon (n 143) 965–966; De Cock Buning (n 145) 529; Lauber-Rönsberg and Hetmank (n 158) 577. Niloufer Selvadurai and Rita Matulionyte do not agree with the supporters of the idea of introducing new *sui generis* right. See; Selvadurai and Matulionyte (n 178) 542.
214 La Diega (n 207) 93 ff.
215 Dornis (n 167) 575.

The *sui generis* model proposed by Enrico Bonadio and Luke McDonagh envisages an economic right with a limited scope of protection. In their proposal, the protection would be provided only for literal copying of AI-generated subject matter.[216] The other economic and moral rights under conventional copyright law should be left out of the scope of protection. In Bonadio and McDonagh's model, the term of protection is three years from the date of publication of the work.[217] Bonadio and McDonagh think that AI-generated subject matter must still be original to benefit from *sui generis* protection.[218] When it comes to identifying beneficiaries of the protection, Bonadio and McDonagh refer to the actors specified by the United Kingdom Group's response to the AIPPI's survey in 2019.[219]

Bonadio and McDonagh assert that their model could yield positive results. First, it would be possible to prevent AI-generated works from being seen as public domain. This would provide an incentive, although a limited one, for those willing to invest in this field. Granting protection for a shorter period and with a narrower economic right as opposed to classical copyright protection would hinder the creation of a monopoly in favour of large, multinational corporations operating in the field. Most important, the fundamental goal of copyright law, namely the continuation of human creativity, would be achieved by preventing machine creativity from surpassing human creativity.[220]

Martin Senftleben and Laurens Buijtelaar contend that a neighbouring right with a limited content and duration should be afforded to robot (AI)-generated works. For them, the content of the neighbouring right in question must be limited to the right of an equitable remuneration afforded to phonogram producers[221] under the Related Rights Directive.[222] The term of protection for such neighbouring right in question should be two years as laid down by the Digital Single Market Directive[223] for the related right granted to press publishers.[224] Senftleben and Buijtelaar think that while the shorter term of protection and the limited economic

---

216 Bonadio and McDonagh (n 17) 134. Cf; Peter K Yu, 'The Machine Author: What Level of Copyright Protection Is Appropriate for Fully Independent Computer-Generated Works?' (2017) 165 *University of Pennsylvania Law Review* 1268–1269.
217 Bonadio and McDonagh (n 17) 134. Moreover, in a recent study it has published, WIPO has suggested that there could be shorter terms of protection as well as limited rights for AI-generated works. See; Revised Issues Paper on Intellectual Property Policy and Artificial Intelligence (World Intellectual Property Organisation, WIPO/IP/AI/2/GE/20/1 REV, 21 May 2020) para 23. Also see; Marcus Du Sautoy, *The Creativity Code: Art and Innovation in the Age of AI* (Harvard University Press, 2019) 102; Abbott 2020 (n 34) 71–91.
218 Bonadio and McDonagh (n 17) 135.
219 Ibid. The proposal by the United Kingdom Group will be elaborated in Chapter 5. De Cock Buning proposes that that in such kind of *sui generis* protection granting authorship to a legal entity such as a limited liability company, which will be established to represent the AI system, might be considered. See; De Cock Buning (n 145) 532.
220 Bonadio and McDonagh (n 17) 135–136.
221 Rental and Lending Rights Directive Art 8(2).
222 Senftleben and Buijtelaar (n 164) 808–809.
223 Digital Single Market Directive Art 15/4.
224 Senftleben and Buijtelaar (n 164) 809.

right would make it possible to avoid overprotection, such a legal arrangement would allow for obtaining the return on investments in this field.[225]

Tim W Dornis asserts that there is a gap in US and EU laws on AI-generated subject matter, which could be filled by introducing a new category of neighbouring rights.[226] In Dornis's proposal, the owner of such right should be 'the owner of the power of disposition over the AI apparatus,'[227] who is generally the owner of the AI apparatus (both the hardware and software).[228] Dornis further states that the provisions on unfair competition could be applied until this type of right is enacted.[229]

Haochen Sun's *sui generis* model relies on the protection of 'integrated circuit topographies' (mask rights) that exist in US law. Sun suggests that the respective mask-work-type *sui generis* protection should only recognise economic rights for AI-generated works, and these must include the right of reproduction, the right to prepare derivative works, the right of distribution and the right of public performance. These rights should provide protection only against one-to-one copying of AI-generated works. Protection of the new *sui generis* rights in AI-generated works should last for ten years.[230]

Gianmaria Ajani draws our attention to a different direction:

> Whenever the current law does not fit the needs of our human communities, contracts have proven to be the most adaptable, flexible and specific remedy to gaps in legislation. Agreements could determine, case by case, how to allocate privileges and rights, how to distinguish the contribution of every participant. And whenever no human involvement in the art creation is detectable, contracts will be giving legal significance to the inventiveness of the AI designers, and to the art world's openness to the disappearance of the human author.[231]

Ajani claims that 'new areas of conventional relationships have been established, mostly based on agreed commitments to share rights and allocate privileges, so as to increase information for the benefit of the parties involved and the general public.'[232] For Ajani, 'contracts and agreements among "non-authors" could provide some predictability, while waiting for the law to receive and possibly regulate the creative inputs provided by the art world.'[233]

---

225 Ibid.
226 Dornis (n 110) 45.
227 Ibid 54–56.
228 Ibid 55.
229 Ibid 17, 60.
230 Sun (n 13) 1244–1248.
231 Gianmaria Ajani, 'Contemporary Artificial Art and the Law' in *Contemporary Artificial Art and the Law* (Brill, 2020) 78.
232 Ibid 78.
233 Ibid 79.

Finally, Lionel Bently *et al* notes that AI-generated subject matter could be protected under the existing regime of related rights and the provisions on unfair competition.[234]

4.5 Conclusion

The fundamental question of this chapter has been whether a creation with a degree of *autonomy* generated by an AI system, sometimes lacking any human involvement whatsoever, can be protected by intellectual property rights (more specifically by design and copyright laws). Different arguments lead to the same conclusion: the current law is not enough. To illustrate this deficiency, several authors have elaborated on many proposals.

The views and legal systems explored in this chapter rely on the presumption that AI technologies are creative agents and offer a solution depending on whether this de facto situation is recognised by the law or not.

The romantic school follows the idea that the law recognises and extends protection to only human beings as creative agents. Thus, the advocates of this school express that the creative agency of AI is precluded from legal protection. This derives from the structure of design and copyright laws: creations without human contribution and thus protection fall into the public domain. Creations jointly made by humans and AI can still be protected. But identifying authorship in the case of creations generated by an indivisible blend of human and machine contributions might be quite problematic. This would lead to an uncertainty in the legal protection, as potential conflicts may arise in distinguishing the part of the works that can be subject to design and authorial rights of the human author from the AI-generated part that is in the public domain. As we will see in Chapter 5, the existing AI systems have distinguishable creative efforts.

The revolutionary school, in contrast, relies on the principle of non-discrimination in design and copyright laws. Here, we confront the most radical option: to recognise AI's entitlement to their designs and works. For this school, a person holding an interest in an AI-generated output would contend that a design or a work created by an AI system and not distinguishable from one made by a human should receive protection. AI should be recognised by the law as a creative agent and even be given personhood. While this would theoretically seem alluring, from a purely legal perspective such a proposal would entail not only a technical but also a 'legal and cultural revolution' within and beyond classical design and copyright laws. This might not be the time to rethink design and copyright laws, but we should recognise that granting AI systems legal personhood is a huge leap to be taken. This is something that all humanity should seriously ponder, as it implies legal changes in all areas of the law and not only in intellectual property law.

The modern school adopts a middle ground between these two opinions. Those who are not persuaded by the public domain option consider a set of different

234 Bently *et al* (n 126) 118.

solutions integrated by the method of allocating rights to individuals playing a role in the AI creative process. While some authors propose that the model in the UK should be embraced, others are in search of more apparent human codes. One suggestion of the latter is that some human actors could be granted authorship or right holdership. For instance, the programmer or user of AI, purchaser of AI device or owner of power of disposition on an AI apparatus could be the author or the right holder. As will be discussed, those solutions also suffer from serious uncertainties on the actual determination of human contributions and do not unfold the whole relevant human actors. Other legal mechanisms devised by some commentators include the extension of the 'work made for hire' doctrine or the extension of the norms on protection of 'previously unpublished works.' These solutions are all based on fragile legal presumptions, and it is not easy to adjust these models, originally intended for completely different situations, to AI-generated designs and works. Other authors dissatisfied with adjustments of current regulations express that introducing a type of *sui generis* right could be an option. Finally, others suggest that these outputs should be protected by the provisions on contracts, related rights or unfair competition.

But is AI really a creative agent as these schools accept by default? Generation of design or work cannot be detached from the technological process; it has never been so from invention of photography or other forms of art. The AI-driven creative process cannot be treated as a simple question of adopting novel technologies, as it affects the core of the relationship between process and products, authorship and originality, designership and individual character, infringement and liability. This is what should be in the agendas of legislators and policy makers. Some vague steps can be seen on the part of EU policy makers. The lack of properly addressing these issues reveals that, at least in Europe, policy makers are uncertain about the necessity to provide legal solutions for the various types designs and works generated by AI. Still, the case should be reconsidered at the EU level to prevent further divergence and ambiguity among national legal orders.

5 A post-modern approach to AI-generated fashion design

5.1 *Flow*

The American psychologist Mihaly Csikszentmihâlyi is the founding father of the 'flow theory.' *Flow* experience denotes the emotional state where a person is fully involved in an activity they are engaged in; time and space are lost, and they are deeply immersed in creativity and life.[1] Inspired by the flow theory, the composer and scientist François Pachet developed an AI called *The Flow Machine* by combining his love of music and technology. The database of *The Flow Machine* includes 13,000 songs. Most of the songs consist of jazz, Western pop music and Brazilian music, and they are based on harmonised melodies that can be translated into notes and chords. These songs are recorded as digitised notes in the database. For *The Flow Machine* to compose, music, tempo, signature, notes, style and even songs are chosen at the beginning. *The Flow Machine* then composes the melody by using the Markov model with constraints. The Markov constraints determine the musical forms. The computer calculates the probability of some chord sequences, melody sequences and rhythms, and it uses these probabilities to generate sensible new musical variations. The artist gives the final form, arranging the music produced by the machine. In September 2016, *The Flow Machine* released its cheerful and upbeat first album called *Daddy's Car*, with the lyrics composed by a human and based on a selection of Beatles' tunes.[2]

In the news, some human attributes are usually *ascribed* to AI technologies that generate designs and works, like in *The Flow Machine*, as though they had consciousness.[3] In some cases, they are even called artists.[4] What drives humans – and

---

1 Mihaly Csikszentmihalyi, *Flow: The Psychology of Optimal Experience* (1st edn, Harper Perennial Modern Classics, 2008).
2 For information about the *Flow Machine*, see; www.flow-machines.com; Arthur I Miller, *The Artist in the Machine: The World of AI-Powered Creativity* (The MIT Press, 2019) 150–153.
3 Mark Wilson, 'AI Is Inventing Languages Humans Can't Understand. Should We Stop It?' (*Fast Company*, 14 July 2017) www.fastcompany.com/90132632/ai-is-inventing-its-own-perfect-languages-should-we-let-it.
4 See for example; Simon COLTON, 'The Painting Fool: Stories from Building an Automated Painter' in Jon McCormack and Mark d'Inverno (eds), *Computers and Creativity* (Springer, 2012) 3–38.

DOI: 10.4324/9781003355922-6

perhaps AI as well – to be creative? This question goes to the very heart of the creative process. Finding an answer might require unfolding all aspects of the mystery of creativity both in humans and in machines and will be an extremely difficult task that goes beyond the extend of this chapter. So what does creativity mean (section 5.2)? How do AI technologies that generate fashion design function (section 5.3)? Are AI technologies creative agents (section 5.3)? Is it possible to find human codes within the scope of the fashion design created by AI both for authorship and liability (section 5.4)? What kind of legal norm can be adopted for the future (section 5.5)? In this chapter, we will seek to obtain the answers to each of these questions.

5.2 Creativity

5.2.1 Individualist and socio-cultural creativity

Those who have investigated AI creativity can find themselves confronted with two differing thoughts about the subject: creative AI and AI as a tool.[5] Before analysing these opinions, it would be useful to explore the interpretations on the concept of creativity itself. According to R Keith Sawyer – an American psychologist and leading expert on creativity, innovation and learning – 'creativity is part of what makes us human.'[6] Sawyer states that by following the trends in creativity research it is possible to talk about two major creativity approaches; namely, individualist and socio-cultural approaches.[7] The individualist approach maintains that 'creativity is a new mental combination that is expressed in the world.'[8] This kind of creativity has three characteristics. First, creativity means being *new*. The most basic condition of being a truly creative thought and action is to be *novel* and *original*. From the opposite perspective, saying exactly what has been said before is *not* creative. Second, creativity is a *combination*. All ideas and concepts are combinations of pre-existing ones. Creativity requires combining two or more pre-existing and separate ideas or concepts. Third, for creativity to occur, it must be *expressed*. Expressions that only exist in a person's mind and are not displayed may not accordingly be considered creative.[9] Several combinations are not new to the world. If these combinations are new to the person who created them, they are included in the scope of the individualist creativity. The individualist creativity is also called 'little c' creativity.[10]

---

5 For the artists and engineers who have different opinions on this matter, see Miller (n 2).
6 R Keith Sawyer, *Explaining Creativity: The Science of Human Innovation* (2nd edn, OUP, 2012) 3.
7 Ibid 7.
8 Ibid.
9 Ibid.
10 Ibid 8.

According to the socio-cultural approach, 'creativity is the generation of a product that is judged to be novel and also to be appropriate, useful, or valuable by a suitably knowledgeable social group.' Products that solve extremely difficult problems or significant works of ingenious are considered creative. The socio-cultural creativity is also called 'big C' creativity.[11]

Sawyer is one of those who has a negative opinion on the creativity of AI. According to Sawyer, computer programs containing AI can hold the title of world chess champion. They can easily process bulk data. They can even distinguish shapes that cannot be seen by humans. However, these programs cannot learn daily creative abilities.[12]

5.2.2 Combinational, exploratory and transformational creativity

Margaret A Boden is one of the leading researchers on creativity. She is a scientist who combines the fields of cognitive science, computers, philosophy, psychology and AI in her research. Combining these different fields of science, Boden defines creativity as 'the ability to come up with ideas or artefacts that are new, surprising and valuable.'[13] Elements of innovation, value and surprise focus more on the outcomes of creativity than the creative process. However, the creative process is as important as the product. Boden divides the creative process into three psychological mechanisms: 'combinatorial creativity,' 'exploratory creativity' and 'transformational creativity.'

Similar ideas are combined in an unfamiliar way in the *combinatorial creativity*.[14] An artist takes two ideas and combines them in a different way. This kind of creativity includes poetic imagery, collage in painting or textile art, and analogies.[15] For example, the Iraqi-born British architect Zaha Hadid combined her architectural knowledge with her interest in the pure shapes used by the Russian painter Kazimir Malevich in the suprematist art movement.[16] This combination enabled Hadid to create curved forms in a unique architectural style, giving her the title of the 'Queen of Curves.'[17]

Exploratory creativity is to explore the boundaries of science, literature, music and art. It means stretching the limits of these fields as much as possible while working within the boundaries of their rules and trying to come up with new

---

11 Ibid.
12 Ibid 3.
13 Margaret A Boden, *The Creative Mind: Myths and Mechanisms* (2nd edn, Routledge, 2004) 1; Margaret A Boden, *Artificial Intelligence: A Very Short Introduction* (OUP, 2018) 59.
14 Boden (n 13) 3; Boden 2018 (n 13) 60.
15 Ibid.
16 Zaha Hadid, 'Zaha Hadid RA on the Influence of Malevich in Her Work: Plane Sailing' (22 July 2014) www.royalacademy.org.uk/article/zaha-hadid-ra-on-the-influence-of.
17 Rowan Moore, 'Zaha Hadid: Queen of the Curve' (*Guardian*, 8 September 2013) www.theguardian.com/artanddesign/2013/sep/08/zaha-hadid-serpentine-sackler-profile.

styles, sentences, melodies or theories that no one has thought of before. The 'conceptual space' is at the centre of Boden's approach to this type of creativity. *Conceptual space* refers to an abstract route through which creative movements happen. There are countless ideas waiting to be explored here.[18] In fact, all artists, musicians, writers or scientists demonstrate this type of creativity.[19] They make new portraits. They compose new songs. They write new stories. They propose new hypotheses. They design new artefacts. These works or ideas remain within the same type of genre in which they are created, even though they are new.[20]

In Boden's taxonomy, *transformational creativity* is the highest form of creativity. In this approach, the limitations in relation to the existing styles or procedures in art and science and the 'conceptual space' are fundamentally changed. Thus, new ideas or artefacts are created. These ideas or artefacts are highly surprising because the transformation they create is perceived as impossible. Exploratory and transformational creativity are interconnected. While relatively small changes occur in exploratory creativity, great changes to the field of art or science unfold in transformational creativity. Transformational creativity can be understood upon the passage of some time,[21] because the transformational creativity is about changing the flow of art and science. For example, Orhan Veli established the Garip movement and used daily language in Turkish poetry, which up until then gave priority to extravagant and pompous literary expressions. Beethoven introduced Romanticism to classical music. Picasso created Cubism.

Boden makes a distinction between 'psychological creativity' and 'historical creativity.' This distinction is made depending on the novelty of the creative idea. *Psychological creativity* (P-creativity) means that a person creates an idea which is only new, unpredictable and valuable from their own point of view. It does not matter whether this idea has been discovered by others before. In contrast, in *historical creativity* (H-creativity), there is a new idea in terms of the entire history of humanity. Thus, under this type of creativity, saying an idea is new means that it has never been thought of before.[22]

Boden is among the philosophers who support the idea that AI can display creativity. Boden states that the three types of creativity she describes can be achieved by AI. Boden points out that, in these cases, the ownership of subject matter is often attributed to the person associated with the program. In Boden's approach, these three types of creativity are not considered separate segments, and there may be intersections among them.[23]

---

18 Boden (n 13) 4.
19 Ibid 4–5; Boden 2018 (n 13) 60.
20 Boden 2018 (n 13) 60.
21 Boden (n 13) 5–6; Boden 2018 (n 13) 60–61.
22 Boden (n 13) 4.
23 Boden 2018 (n 13) 61–62.

5.2.3 Coding creativity

The law professor Annemarie Bridy argues that if creativity means a set of 'characteristics and behaviours,' then there is a possibility that creativity can be coded.[24] Bridy relies on the definition of creativity given by Lovelace: 'showing the ability to deviate from rules and conventions to achieve the unexpected.'[25] Bridy also compares Boden's definition of 'new, surprising and valuable' with Roger Schank and Christopher Owens' definition of 'innovative response to problem solving.'[26] According to Bridy, these definitions of creativity correspond to a standard that is higher than the one required in the *Feist* case, namely the originality standard ('modicum of creativity') in the US.[27]

5.2.4 The artist in the machine

The science historian and philosopher Arthur Miller adopts a different approach to creativity. Miller's conception of creativity involves a two-step process: first, new ideas and objects are produced from already-existing ones; and second, this is accomplished by problem-solving. It considers the final product and the process of generating it.

For Miller, while Boden's psychological creativity refers to 'little creativity,' her conception of historical creativity denotes 'big creativity.' Miller states that the works of art, science and literature produced by AI, which he cites in his book *The Artist in the Machine: the World of AI-Powered Creativity*, are products of little creativity.[28] In contrast, the following seven characteristics should be demonstrated for what Miller calls 'big creativity:' (i) introspection; (ii) knowing your strengths; (iii) focusing, persevering and not being afraid to make mistakes; (iv) collaborating and competing; (v) desiring, borrowing or stealing grand ideas; (vi) thriving on uncertainty; (vii) experiencing and suffering.[29] Miller views 'problem discovery' and 'finding connections between disparate concepts' as two characteristics of creative geniuses and defines them as the 'core of creativity.'[30]

Miller believes that computers either already have these characteristics necessary for big creativity or could potentially have them with developing technologies:[31] GANs and CANs have already shown glimmers of creativity, but machines will only become truly creative when they have emotions and consciousness.

---

24 Annemarie Bridy, 'Coding Creativity: Copyright and the Artificially Intelligent Author' (2012) 5 *Stanford Technology Law Review* 1–28; Annemarie Bridy, 'The Evolution of Authorship: Work Made by Code' (2016) 39(3) *Columbia Journal of Law & the Arts* 395–401.
25 Ibid 398–399.
26 Ibid 399.
27 Ibid.
28 Miller (n 2) 273.
29 Ibid 9–19.
30 Ibid 19–22.
31 Ibid 307–309.

5.3 AI and creativity

5.3.1 Inside AI technology

5.3.1.1 Images generated by GANs

Can AI really create fashion? Can it truly be creative? Some of the designs and art that AI is currently generating are of a sort that has never been seen before or even imagined. It encompasses works that we might consider pleasing and that many artists or designers judge as acceptable. The process by which AI produces its art is also of interest because it can shed light on how it thinks. We can understand the aspects of AI creativity by looking inside AI technology. As discussed previously, the GANs[32] are popular tools for fashion designers. They typically tackle the *fashion* imagery aspects of design.[33] In addition to fashion designing, they have been employed to create art. For AI-generated artistic works, the *Portrait of Edmond de Belamy* emerges as a prominent example that attracted the attention of the art world and legal community. A group of artists called *Obvious*, three French students (Hugo Caselles-Dupré, Pierre Fautrel and Gauthier Vernier) used GANs to create the portrait. The portrait was only one of 11 portraits of the imaginary Belamy family.[34] These paintings were generated by an AI trained on 15,000 portraits from different centuries. The algorithmic code[35] used to generate this work was attached to the lower-right corner as a signature of the artist. More interesting, the work was sold at Christie's for 432,000 US dollars on 25 October 2018.

François Chollet, a senior software engineer at Google, has offered a denomination for this new art movement: GANism[36] This movement has been a source of inspiration not only for Western art but also for Far-Eastern art, which has its own unique characteristics. *Obvious* followed the footsteps of GANism in another art project called 'Electric Dreams of Ukiyo: A Series of Japanese Artworks Created by an Artificial Intelligence.'[37] The artistic works created in this project, which blends elements of classical Japanese paintings, were sold at auctions for prices such as 10.000 Euros.

---

32 Ian J Goodfellow, a researcher (now working at Google), and his friends developed these AI systems. See; Ian J Goodfellow *et al*, 'Generative Adversarial Nets' (2014) 27 *Proceedings Advances in Neural Information Processing Systems* 2672–2680.
33 Natalia Särmäkari and Annamari Vänskä, ' "Just Hit a Button!" – Fashion 4.0 Designers as Cyborgs, Experimenting and Designing with Generative Algorithms' (2021) *International Journal of Fashion Design, Technology and Education* 3.
34 For other portraits, see; https://obvious-art.com/la-famille-belamy/.
35 The code is as follows: .
36 This term was coined by François Chollet in a Twitter post. https://twitter.com/fchollet/status/885378870848901120?lang=en.
37 https://obvious-art.com/collection-electric-dreams-of-ukiyo/.

Refik Anadol is another media artist who is influenced by GANism. For Anadol, data are 'pigments'[38] and AI is a 'thinking brush.'[39] Anadol, who has been holding exhibitions using AI for some time now, has analysed NASA archives for three years in one of his latest projects. He categorised this visual dataset into two groups: concept and form. AI has been trained on these images by using the GANs technique as though they form visual memories. The result is an exciting exhibition where astronomy is interpreted through arts: *Machine Memoirs: Space.*[40]

How does this technique that has influenced many designers and artists operate? There are two deep neural networks in GANs: the discriminator (D) and the generator (G). D is fed with images of the real world, from a dataset selected by the designers. Meanwhile, G begins to generate images out of a first layer that is latent space, made up of like randomly situated dots. G is like a designer or art forger, while D operates like a fashion or art expert evaluating the images generated by G. D decides whether the image it receives from G is realistic or fake, based on the images it has been fed. The first few images G creates are meaningless, and D rejects them. G then sends them back to where they came from and tries again. By the time this new image reaches the D network, it will be better generated because the intermediary layers in G (G's hidden layers) are beginning to learn from their mistakes. Eventually, G's images look like the ones in D's training set.

The artist (designer) chooses a collection of images to feed the algorithm (pre-curation). The creative process is primarily driven by the artist (who creates the design or work by using AI) before and after the curation. The artist even makes minor adjustments to the AI algorithm. The paintings generated are surprising to the people who look at them or to the artist who manages the process. The AI algorithm generates designs or works (new images) that imitate pre-curated uploaded images with minor changes.[41]

5.3.1.2 *Images generated by AI-CANs*

'If we teach the machine about art and styles and push it to generate novel images that do not follow established styles, what would it generate?' Each artwork made by 'creative adversarial networks' (AI-CANs)[42] is an answer to this question, says Ahmed Elgammal at Rutgers University. He and his team and explore

---

38 Franziska Müller-Degenhardt, 'Refik Anadol: How he Turns Data Art into an Experience' (*L'Officiel*, 27 November 2021) www.lofficiel.at/en/art-and-culture/refik-anadol-how-he-turns-data-art-an-experience.
39 Giulia Capodieci, 'Refik Anadol: AI Is Art, Language and Hope' (10 June 2021) www.internimagazine.com/features/refik-anadol/.
40 For the project named '*Machine Memoirs: Space*' see; https://refikanadol.com/works/machine-memoirs-space/.
41 Marian Mazzone and Ahmed Elgammal, 'Art, Creativity, and the Potential of Artificial Intelligence' (2019) 8(26) *Arts* 2.
42 Ahmed Elgammal, Bingchen Liu, Mohamed Elhoseiny and Marian Mazzone, 'CAN: Creative Adversarial Networks Generating "Art" by Learning About Styles and Deviating from Style Norms' paper presented at the 8th International Conference on Computational Creativity (ICCC), Atlanta, GA, USA (19–23 June 2017); Mazzone and Elgammal (n 41) 1–9.

creative applications of deep learning in art. In 2017, they trained this AI model on 80,000 digitised images of Western paintings from the 15th century to the 20th century. These paintings cover the art movements of the period from Baroque to Impressionism. The generated images did not show typical figures, genres, styles or subject matter. They were aesthetically stunning. Does this mean AI-CANs can create?

Like GANs, there are two deep neural networks in AI-CAN: the discriminator (D) and the generator (G). D has access to a large dataset of art from WikiArt. The dataset is associated with style labels, such as *Renaissance, Baroque, Impressionism, Expressionism*, etc. D uses this set to learn to identify art and styles. G does not have access to any art. It generates art starting from a random input. G again is like an art forger. D operates like an art expert and evaluates the images produced by G. G receives two signals from D. The first signal is D's classification of 'art or not art.' The second signal is a 'style ambiguity.' G will use this signal to improve its ability to generate art that does not follow any of the established styles.

5.3.2 AI a creative agent?

We can begin with instrumentalists. Some thinkers and artists who claim AI is not creative[43] view these technologies as *tools* used in creating a design or work. For example, Aaron Hertzmann, lead scientist at Adobe Research, states that all algorithms used in the creation process of a design or work, including those based on machine learning, are tools (such as brushes and paint) for artists (designers), and they are not artists themselves.[44] Viewing art essentially as a social interaction, Hertzmann suggests that a work can only be created by social beings.[45]

Marian Mazzone and Ahmed Elgammal object to this opinion.[46] These two scientists are among the group that has developed the CANs.[47] They argue that these algorithms are more than a tool and closer to the definition of a *medium*. As Mazzone and Elgammal note, the concept of *medium* in art does not only include tools (brush, oil paint, naphtha, canvas, etc.) but also a range of 'possibilities and constraints' inherent in the conditions of creation in the artistic domain. Painting *media* includes the history of painting styles, the physical and conceptual constraints of the two-dimensional surface, the boundaries of what can be recognised as painting, the critical language developed to identify and criticise paintings, and

---

43 Damien Henry, who was interviewed by Miller and created the musical work called 'Music for 18 Musicians – Steve Reich' by using artificial intelligence, can be shown as an example for those who adopt this idea. See; Miller (n 2) 78. Miller recalls that Anna Ridler, whom he interviewed, saying, 'Would you say that my paintbrush is an artist? (Machines) cannot be creative.' See; Miller (n 2) 105. Patrick Tresset, who invented the painting robot named 'Paul,' is among those who share this opinion. See; Miller (n 2) 132.
44 Aaron Hertzmann, 'Can Computers Create Art?' (2018) 7(18) *Arts* 12–13.
45 Ibid 20.
46 Mazzone and Elgammal (n 41) 8.
47 Elgammmal and his colleagues argue that GANs are *emulative* and not creative. See; Elgammal *et al* (n 42).

so on. As a medium, AI adds new dimensions to the art of painting in this way. These are computer code, mathematics, hardware and software, printing preferences, algorithmic configuration, data collection and application, critical theory necessary to distinguish and evaluate computer creativity, and art-making intent within the scope of the computer science. Stating that 'art is a social interaction,' Mazzone and Elgammal in summary argue that AI, which is still in its infancy, is a 'creative partner.'[48]

Some other thinkers even go further and claim that the Age of AI has begun. Arthur Miller vividly highlights that:

> In the Age of AI, no one can question the effect of art on science and science on art. Instead of a swinging pendulum of influence, they have melded into one-AI art-in much the same way that two black holes merge, first circling one another, becoming closer and closer, then coming together with repercussions felt throughout the universe.[49]

When we think of GANs and AI-CAN, are these two most developed AI systems creative agents from the perspective of design and copyright laws? Stef van Gompel states that the low creativity and originality standards in copyright law have different meaning from their conception in aesthetics and creativity studies.[50] There are several variations concerning usage of these concepts across the disciplines in aesthetics and creativity studies. However, various definitions of creativity generally include the notions of 'innovation, quality and usefulness' as common aspects. Thus, for a work to be creative, it must demonstrate novelty, originality and innovation in terms of its appearance or the ideas underlying it. In addition, it must be appropriate (specific, valuable or useful) within the context in which it is created. According to these two disciplines, creativity and originality are criteria used to determine what level of creativity a person, creation or process demonstrates compared to other people, creations and processes. Consequently, creativity and originality emerge as *relative* and *comparative* concepts in these fields.[51]

In aesthetics and creativity studies, the originality and creativity of a work are measured by its 'distinctiveness.' Aesthetics employs a comparative assessment. In aesthetics, artistic evaluation is a principal objective, and it is done by looking at how much original, new and rare a work is in comparison to the other

---

48 Mazzone and Elgammal (n 41) 8. For a similar opinion that considers AI technologies as a creative collaborator, see; Sebastian Deterding *et al*, 'Mixed-Initiative Creative Interfaces' CHI EA '17: Proceedings of the 2017 CHI Conference Extended Abstracts on Human Factors in Computing Systems (6–11 May 2017) 628–635.
49 Arthur Miller, 'Can AI Be Truly Creative?' (*American Scientist*, 25 June 2020) 249.
50 Stef van Gompel, 'Creativity, Autonomy and Personal Touch. A Critical Appraisal of the CJEU's Originality Test for Copyright' in Mireille van Eechoud (ed), *The Work of Authorship* (Amsterdam University Press, 2014) 101.
51 Ibid 101–102.

pre-existing works. In addition, it is assessed by identifying how much this work contributes to the development of a specific genre or cultural domain in which it is created. In contrast, creativity studies are built on organisational, educational, functional creativity, etc. Even in these fields, creativity and innovation are 'also measured in relation to other – sometimes hypothetical – settings to which they compare.'[52]

In copyright law, the assessment of creativity and originality is constructed on a completely different ground. Courts do not determine whether a subject matter has reached the required level of creativity by comparing it with similar preceding works. Because originality essentially is a concept denoting the link between the author and the work, it is determined by only examining the subject matter itself.[53] For originality, it is not necessary for the subject matter to be new, rare or innovative. When we say that a work must be original, we mean that the author of this work makes an intellectual contribution to the creation of the work. For a work to be considered original, it is necessary that the author contributes to the final subject matter.[54] Therefore, originality is related to the way the respective work is expressed.[55] Creativity occurs through free and creative choices made in shaping the work. Thus, previous works are not taken into consideration. In fact, in determining whether a work is creative, its artistic quality or whether it is new is completely ignored.[56] Comparison with pre-existing works is only made where 'there are indications that the author has copied parts of earlier works or draws upon unprotected ideas, elements of style or materials that are in the public domain.'[57]

As Stef van Gompel reminds, copyright law's author-centred understanding of originality takes its roots from the past. In the 19th century, copyright law was established to compensate the author for expenses incurred in creating the work and to protect the labour and personality demonstrated in the work. Accordingly, the determination of originality was centred on the author who *created* the work. Manifestations of creativity of the author, namely, her *personal expression*, was regarded as the main regulatory reference for copyright protection. The requirement of originality, which focuses on the author's own intellectual and expressive effort, was seen a sufficient threshold for this purpose. No additional conditions such as novelty, quality, or superiority were sought.[58] Thus, the requirements of creativity and originality in European copyright law have been a *legal construct*,

---

52 Ibid 102–103.
53 Ibid 103.
54 Lionel Bently, Brad Sherman, Dev Gangjee and Phillip Johnson, *Intellectual Property Law* (5th edn, OUP, 2018) 93.
55 Ibid 94.
56 Van Gompel (n 50) 103.
57 Ibid.
58 Ibid.

heavily relying on authorship that signifies a lower threshold. As Josefien Vanherpe put it: 'creativity is hereby viewed as a quintessentially human faculty.'[59]

Creativity in European design law also diverges from the very definition of the concept in aesthetics and creativity studies. At a theoretical level, the point of departure can be attributed to the ideology of European design protection. Creativity in design law was prescribed with a 'market-oriented perspective.' As Annette Kur and Marianne Levin recall:

> The starting point was instead located in the manner designs become effective in the marketplace. More specifically, the situation envisaged was that of *saturated markets*, where demand is no longer driven by the urge to satisfy basic needs, and where the commodities offered are largely interchangeable in their functional aspects. It is then that the design of products becomes a key factor for enabling diversification and reaching out to particular groups of customers. This, in essence, is meant by the term "marketing approach" that was used synonymously with 'design approach' in the context of the MPI Proposal as well as in the Commission's Green Paper.[60]

From the market-oriented perspective, the requirements of *novelty* and *individual character* have been embraced as the creativity threshold for design protection. A looser novelty requirement is envisaged. A design is thought to be novel in the sense that the same or an almost-identical configuration has not been disclosed to the public before. Novelty does not in this sense mean 'previously unseen.'[61] The second aspect of creativity occurs where the design is also new in a 'qualitative sense;' that is, it creates a different overall impression from pre-existing designs. The focus is not on the designer and their skills but rather on the 'individual character' of the product appearance and the reaction it is able to evoke from the public. Based on that consideration, the assessment of 'individual character' is made from the market perspective and the target group (informed user) envisaged by the designer.[62] EU design law remains neutral concerning the 'aesthetic quality' of the design, which has been left to the public to judge out of the legal context. Design protection is also granted even in cases where the contour for creation (the freedom of the designer) is narrowly defined.[63] The distance to be kept from prior art is the main factor to qualify for protection: individual character

---

59 Josefien Vanherpe, 'AI and IP: A Tale of Two Acronyms' in Jan De Bruyne and Cedric Vanleenhove (eds), *Robots, AI and the Law in Belgium* (Intersentia, 2020) 221.
60 Annette Kur and Marianne Levin, 'The Design Approach Revisited: Background and Meaning' in Annette Kur, Marianne Levin and Jens Schovsbo (eds), *The EU Design Approach: A Global Appraisal* (Edward Elgar Publishing, 2018) 7 (Emphasis original).
61 Ibid 14.
62 Ibid 16.
63 Ibid 17.

will only be found if the design 'clearly differs' from the relevant prior art in the eye of the informed user.[64]

Although design law makes a comparative assessment between today and the past, even small variations in the appearances of the products, to the extent that they function as a marketing tool, can be regarded as novel. No eye appeal or contribution to the field is considered. Just like copyright, creativity in design law is also oriented on a legal construct that is determined by judges from the eyes of a certain fictional market actor.

How do these two levels of creativity apply to AI systems? As Daniel T Gruner and Mihaly Csikszentmihalyi note, 'While AI programs can elicit wonder, awe, and curiosity in the observer, the machines themselves cannot consciously experience the creative process.'[65] We are not witnessing AI machines self-evidently expressing themselves. They do not seem to have anything to do beyond what we are instructing them to do. They are just complicated tools serving our desires to express ourselves. We do not live like automata. Instead, we make free choices to break the routine and to suddenly create something new. Our creativity is closely related to our free will, something we cannot observe in the two processes explained.[66] Free will can be defined as 'the power to control one's choices and actions.'[67] Having this power means that an agent's choices and actions are determined by this agent. First, this includes the power to choose to do nothing or to do the otherwise. Second, it requires the agent to be the source of their actions.[68] Programming a free will that bears these characteristics is almost impossible with today's known technologies.[69] Perhaps, programming of free will would go against what it means. Today's AI machines technologically are not able to choose to express themselves by creating a subject matter on their own.[70] They do not have the capacity to decide what kind of work to create, even if they opt for creating one. AI does not have full semantical understanding of what, whether and how to create and design like human artists and designers. As Hertzmann states in his article[71] and Cohen discovered in his painting computer

---

64 Ibid 20.
65 Daniel T Gruner and Mihaly Csikszentmihalyi, 'Engineering Creativity in an Age of Artificial Intelligence' in Izabela Lebuda and Vlad Petre Glăveanu (eds), *The Palgrave Handbook of Social Creativity Research* (Palgrave Macmillan, 2019) 453.
66 Marcus Du Sautoy, *The Creativity Code: Art and Innovation in the Age of AI* (Harvard University Press, 2019) 281–282.
67 Timothy O'Connor and Christopher Franklin, 'Free Will' The Stanford Encyclopedia of Philosophy (Fall 2020 Edition), Edward N ZALTA (ed), URL https://plato.stanford.edu/archives/fall2020/entries/freewill/. For a concise study on free will, see; Thomas Pink, *Free Will: A Very Short Introduction* (OUP, 2004).
68 O'Connor and Franklin (n 67) 2020.
69 Du Sautoy (n 66) 281–282. For a discussion on whether computers can have free will, see; Jerry Kaplan, *Artificial Intelligence: What Everyone Needs to Know* (OUP, 2016) 138–141; Margaret A Boden, *Artificial Intelligence: A Very Short Introduction* (OUP, 2018) 74–81.
70 Du Sautoy (n 66) 281–282.
71 Hertzmann (n 44) 20.

program called *AARON*,[72] humans have the urge to create high-quality works and to comprehend creativity, growth and change.

AI-CAN has generated some impressive works. However, its neural networks are designed to create unpredictable combinations, and its goals are set by the artist who programmed it. Each image generated by AI-CAN is a compilation of data points from which the algorithm should deviate.[73] As David Gunkel rightly notes:

> Computer systems, no matter how automatic, independent, or seemingly autonomous they may appear to be, are not and can never be autonomous, independent agents. They will, like all other technological artifacts, always and forever be instruments of human decision-making and action. When something occurs by way of a machine, there is always someone – some human person or persons – who can respond for it and be held responsible for what it does or does not do.[74]

Therefore, AI technologies do not create designs or works in isolation and form part of a wider creative ecosystem.[75] Drawing on these roles, they do not have the ability to consciously make free and creative choices necessary for originality. They do not have a personality that they can demonstrate their creativity and reflect this creativity on the work through these choices. They cannot observe the fashion industries to design fashionable and trendy garments where novelty meets individual character. Therefore, it is the 'human code'[76] that initiates and directs the creativity we observe in AI today.[77]

So which actors does this *code* include? How should this matter be determined? Possible answers to these questions will not only shed light on the authorship or ownership of a design right but also on infringement liability.

5.4 *Human codes* around AI: a three-step test

A three-step test should be carried out to find persons to whom authorship or design ownership and infringement liability (at least potentially) can be attributed. For this, the following three questions must be answered:

---

72 Harold Cohen, 'ACM SIGGRAPH Awards – Harold Cohen, Distinguished Artist Award for Life Time Achievement' (2014) https://youtu.be/_Xbt8lzWxIQ?t=13m20s.
73 Eliza Mik, 'AI as a Legal Person?' in Jyh-An Lee, Reto Hilty and Kung-Chung Liu (eds), *Artificial Intelligence and Intellectual Property* (OUP, 2021) 430.
74 David J Gunkel, 'Computational Creativity: Algorithms, Art, and Artistry' in Eduardo Navas, Owen Gallagher and Xtine Burrough (eds), *The Routledge Handbook of Remix Studies and Digital Humanities* (Routledge, 2021) 391.
75 Mik (n 73) 433.
76 Du Sautoy (n 66) 281.
77 Some academics think that the production process of AI is still under human control. For example, see; Jane Ginsburg and Luke A Budiardjo, 'Authors and Machines' 2019 34(2) *Berkeley Technology Law Journal* 343–456; Samantha Fink Hedrick, 'I "Think," Therefore I Create: Claiming Copyright in the Outputs of Algorithms' (2019) 8(2) *NYU Journal of Intellectual Property & Entertainment Law* 324–375.

A post-modern approach to AI-generated fashion design   173

5.4.1 Is AI a fully autonomous creative agent?

Question 1: Is the AI system concerned a fully autonomous creative agent with free will and semantical understanding to make meaningful choices?

The philosophical definition of autonomy refers to 'the capacity to be one's own person, to live one's life according to reasons and motives that are taken as one's own and not the product of manipulative or distorting external forces, to be in this way independent.'[78] This definition conceives of the concept of autonomy in a broad sense. Here, *autonomy* refers to being independent in every aspect of life where human intelligence can be used. In this sense, it connotes self-governance or the ability to act independently of external directions and influences.

Eliza Mik makes a distinction between 'normative' and 'technical' aspects of autonomy. In law and philosophy (in the normative sense), the concept of autonomy is almost always associated with *personhood*. It is often assumed that the distinguishing feature of being a person is the ability to make one's own decisions depending on one's original intentions, to give explanations and to make judgements. Modern societies regard *persons* as 'autonomous agents' who can bear legal liability. Autonomy is a fundamental institution in liberal democracies as well. In liberal democracies, it is not possible to talk about rights and obligations without autonomy. Autonomy is, in this sense, postulated as an instrument to determine 'moral and causal responsibility.'[79] The normative force of the term *autonomy* regarding computers is interesting. When it is used for computers, it is somewhat absurdly presumed that the system is either like *humans* or *independent of humans.*[80]

In the technical context, autonomy does not carry any normative or philosophical connotations, and it denotes to a measurable attribute to describe the control relationship between biological or mechanical systems and their environments. The technical meaning of *autonomy* then inevitably becomes related to *automation*, and the two words are often used synonymously. Automation is 'the mechanisation of tasks and the transformation of routine actions into formal structures.'[81] Autonomy is often considered as an advanced form of automation. Automation refers to allocation or designation of power to conduct tasks between human and technology in varying degrees and forms.[82] At a minimal level of automation, it is for the human to make all decisions and perform all actions. As the level of automation increases, the decision-making opportunities for humans become limited by the actions of the computer. Thus, the more adept

---

78 Christman John, 'Autonomy in Moral and Political Philosophy' The Stanford Encyclopedia of Philosophy (Fall 2020 Edition), Edward N Zalta (ed), URL: https://plato.stanford.edu/archives/fall2020/entries/autonomy-moral/.
79 Mik (n 73) 422.
80 Ibid 423.
81 Ibid.
82 Ibid.

a system is at collecting, analysing, interpreting data and acting accordingly, the more autonomous it is considered.[83]

Regarding when an agent can be considered creative, Kyle Jennings states that a system will have 'creative autonomy' when it meets the following three criteria:

- *Autonomous Evaluation* – the system can evaluate its liking of a creation without seeking opinions from an outside source.
- *Autonomous Change* – the system initiates and guides changes to its standards without being explicitly directed when and how to do so.
- *Non-Randomness* – the system's evaluations and standard changes are not purely random.

When we apply these criteria to AI, it should be able to apply and change its standards on its own. Creative autonomy in AI is the ability to perform a task regardless of the intentions of the programmer or operator of the system; this means that it changes its preferences without being random as a reaction to the constantly collected evaluation opinions. Jennings thinks that AI can have creative autonomy.[84]

Creativity is evaluated by looking at both *what* is produced and *how* it has been produced. From this standpoint, it is possible to identify three types of AI: semi-autonomous AI, supervised autonomous AI and fully autonomous AI. *Semi-autonomous AI* controls its environment, but the human who uses the program makes the final decision. *Supervised autonomous AI* acts and decides on its own; however, a human observes the behaviour of the machine and can intervene when necessary. *Fully autonomous AI* acts and decides on its own; a human does not have any control over the machine.

It can be said that fully autonomous AI in a sense corresponds to AGI. As discussed in preceding sections and Chapter 1, existing ANI systems have limited abilities to create works or can operate in particular domains. By contrast, AGI would be able to successfully perform any intellectual task humans could. AGI would compete with human creators in every field. It would potentially be capable of doing all actions in three stages (conception, execution and redaction/curation) of the creative process and would create fashion designs for its fellow human friends. Would this require us to change the established legal institutions of design and copyright laws such as 'informed user' (whose vision sets the standard of individual character) or 'creative author' (whose intellectual choices go beyond the originality bar)?

Ryan Abbott makes two important predictions on how the use of AGI and ASI impact the 'obviousness' of an invention and the 'skilled person' test in patent law in the future. Abbott first contends that when AGI outperforms humans in

---

83 Ibid 423–424.
84 Kyle E Jennings, 'Developing Creativity: Artificial Barriers in Artificial Intelligence' (2010) 20 *Minds & Machines* 490, 499.

conjuring up new inventions in certain circumstances, it could replace the skilled person in these fields.[85] He secondly argues that when ASI is developed, everything will be obvious to it, and artificial superintelligence will be able to invent or discover just about anything.[86] This might bring the end of the patent system. Despite this, Abbott rather optimistically thinks that the financial costs of innovating will be immaterial, giving incentives will become useless and future innovation will be self-sustaining.[87]

Abbott's somewhat Fukuyaman 'end of the history' projection is debatable. One problem with Abbott's future predictions is the presumption that ASI will know everything about the universe and be able to invent anything. In Abbot's writings, ASI is treated as a divine creator. The power of AI comes from its reach to data. Where there is more data available to AI, it becomes more intelligent. We cannot clearly know whether ASI will have all available data in the world. Theoretically, ASI systems refer to technologies that can do and know things slightly (and sometimes fairly) better than humans. Outperforming humans with a slight qualitative degree does not and will not automatically put ASI systems in a position to invent everything because there will remain ample room for future inventorship. Raising the threshold for protection would be enough to maintain the patent system. Besides, the law could still set the threshold of obviousness according to the knowledge level of humans. This might be the case specifically when we presume that there would be only one ASI machine owned by just one company in the relevant innovation field. Abbott's contention is also related to the beginning of the singularity. Singularity would begin when AGI and ASI not only outperform but also outnumber human beings. Singularity also requires that ASI should quantitatively reign over our lives. When singularity begins, human beings would lose their law-making roles in democracies. AI machines would probably be the new rulers and citizens in our societies that could make decisions about our lives as well as theirs.

As discussed in Chapter 2, EU design law imagines the fictional informed user somewhere between average consumer and technical expert. AGI would grasp the fashion zeitgeist and design the outfits to surround human bodies, even though these would not fit to their wired and angular metal bodies (hardware). AGI would equally emerge as a venerable designer whose designs could meet its human admirers and fashion gurus in famous fashion shows in Paris, Milano, New York or elsewhere in the world. But AGI could only be willing to design garments for its machine bodies. Perhaps for that reason, we cannot be sure whether the taste of AGI (or ASI) would be the norm of finding individual character in fashion designs to justify design protection. Given that the taste for fashion is something socially constructed for human beings, AI machines would probably not be interested in

---

85 Ryan Abbott, *The Reasonable Robot* (CUP, 2020) 98–99.
86 Ibid 99.
87 Ibid 109.

the question of what is fashionable and how much individual character a garment has.

Foreseeing the unforeseeable inevitably would require portraying two futuristic worlds: dystopian and utopian. In the following lines, Arthur Miller elucidates how a utopian scenario for AI-*sapiens* would turn out to be a dystopian future for humanity:

> In the end, the stars will burn out and our universe will reach its lowest possible temperature. We will have long since disappeared, and there will be only computers, occupying the bodies of robots, perhaps looking exactly like us. The machines will have realized that their end is near, that their electrons will soon cease to flow and their circuits run down. With their superintelligence, they will have figured out how to enter another universe. Once there, they will inhabit a planet that need not be anything like ours. There they will replicate and pen new and very different creation myths and enjoy their own art, literature, and music.[88]

Before history ends for humanity in the way that Miller narrates, fashion, though in a more communitarian way, would still matter. In a dystopian singularity of this kind, ASI would only design Orwellian blue or black uniforms for its human subjects. In George Orwell's dystopian novel *1984*, the fashion style is bleak and depressing, mirroring the functional style and aesthetics of the oppressive and omnipresent Party-state. Adornment is looked down on, individuality is discouraged and beauty and refinement are considered politically dubious. Stylised hair or wearing makeup, silk stockings and high-heeled shoes – as well as activities, morals and even thoughts – are strictly policed, and the public sphere lacks all style, elegance and taste.

By contrast, in a more utopian world, ASI could perpetually address humanity's urge for fashion. In this positive singularity, ASI would create only one garment that could take whatever colour, shape, texture, material, etc. its wearer wishes to have. This could be called a *robe d'éternité* that could transform into one or multiple pieces whenever imagined. This way of designing could fundamentally change the fashion design landscape. Countless fashion designs would be provided for humanity in the blink of an eye. It could also solve some notorious problems of the fashion industry. New unsold garments would not simply be burned. For sustainable fashion, it would end overproduction and overconsumption. Both the dystopian and utopian future depicted here would end the design law for fashion, nonetheless only in an imaginary world. This is something that we could never certainly know now.

Predicting the future is very difficult. Many such predictions might falter, just like most of prophecies made in the film series *Back to the Future*. If we put aside these fictional portrayals of the future, there will be one clear fact when AGI

---

88 Miller (n 2) 313.

(and ASI) is developed and becomes widespread: we need to go beyond what the revolutionary school suggests and recast the concept of law itself. It will not be sufficient to grant personality and authorship to AI. Tinkering with one or two concepts of design and copyright laws (such as attribution of right holdership) would not be enough because we will have a creative and intelligent, and perhaps social, being. When technology reaches to heights of AGI, we need to bring broader rules to regulate every aspect of AI technologies, not just their creativity or infringement liability. This should include, for example, granting constitutional rights to AI systems; regulating their criminal, tort or tax liability; and establishing standards for their contractual relations. But we will not know whether AGI will like its new legal status, and perhaps in the end they will revolt.

If AI technology is semi-autonomous or supervised autonomous, we need to identify actors that participate in the designing process. In these cases, human actors still play a critical role in conception and redaction stages of creativity. Here comes the second question:

5.4.2 Are there any actors who participate in the designing process?

Question 2: Are there any actors (legal and/or natural persons) who participate in the designing process?

To identify these actors, inspiration can be taken from the UK AIPPI Group's response to the AIPPI survey.[89] The UK Group lists the actors associated with artificial intelligence as follows:

1 *AI project investor:* the person who invests resources (whether financial, human or technical)
2 *AI project arranger:* the person who takes responsibility for making the necessary arrangements
3 *AI coder:* the person who writes the codes of AI used in the creation of the subject matter
4 *AI goal selector:* the person who selects the goal to be achieved
5 *AI data selector:* the person who selects input data for AI
6 *AI trainer:* the persons who trains AI with different techniques
7 *AI output selector:* the person who make a qualitative or aesthetic selection of a work from several AI-generated works

To establish a new related right on AI-generated work, the UK Group identifies two possible approaches: the 'proximity' and the 'investment' approaches.

For the *proximity approach*, the owner of such right could be the natural or legal person who is most closely associated with the creative output. This approach is premised on the idea that creativity should be incentivised and rewarded. This

---

89 For the UK Group's answers to the AIPPI's questionnaire see; https://aippi.soutron.net/Portal/DownloadImageFile.ashx?fieldValueId=1571.

178 *A post-modern approach to AI-generated fashion design*

requires a factual enquiry to determine the right owner in each case.[90] Under this approach, considering the weight of their contributions to the creation process of the subject matter, the following persons could be entitled to the authorship of the work: (i) AI coder; (ii) AI goal selector; (iii) AI data selector; (iv) AI trainer; (v) AI output selector.

In the *investment approach*, the natural or legal person who makes the arrangements necessary for the creation of the work should be the right holder. Under this approach, investment is considered in a broader sense and not confined to financial investment; it could cover investment in human and technical resources that can be used in AI training. The UK Group suggests that AI-generated works could be protected by a new right, lasting for 25 years, which recognises the investment AI developers make in this technology.

The UK Group prefers the investment approach, as it arguably provides more certainty than the proximity approach.[91] Under this approach, the following persons may be the owner of rights: (i) AI project investor; (ii) AI project arranger.

After defining the actors who contributed to the creation of AI-generated subject matter, we should discuss the third question.

5.4.3 *Does the AI-generated design qualify for protection?*

Question 3: Does the AI-generated design satisfy the statutory criteria to qualify for protection and infringement liability?

To answer this question, it must be ascertained whether the statutory requirements sought in EU design (design, novelty and individual character) and copyright (originality and being expressed) laws are satisfied. If AI-generated subject matter meets them and is considered a protected design and work, the question of whether their creative contributions have given the final shape to the design must be examined among the five actors specified in the proximity approach to whom the authorship should be assigned. It would be appropriate to seek an answer to this question by considering the specific conditions of each case.

Under EU design law, the Design Regulation grants initial ownership of design to the person or persons who developed it. The *developer* of the design refers to a person 'who gives the final specific appearance to a product' that is new and has individual character.

Contemporary designers work in a globally connected, culturally diverse and technologically advancing world. Their work is a dynamic combination of materials, methods, concepts and subjects that continue challenging the boundaries of previous centuries. In this diverse and eclectic environment, contemporary designers frequently use expressions such as 'projects' or 'processes' to describe their works, and this has become their most prominent feature recently. This common

---
90 Ibid.
91 Ibid.

expression, denoting a discursive transformation of the concepts of 'work' or 'object' to 'project' or 'process,' has become a part of the conceptual language of the designers. This rhetorical transformation can be seen at a practical level especially in the context of AI-generated designs.

The terms *project* or *process* give rise to a leading actor or director – namely, principal designer – for the management of the respective project and process. When it comes to ascertaining the design authorship in collaborative creations of this kind, a distinction should be made between designs created under the direction or guidance of one or more leading designers and designs for which it is almost impossible to identify a leading designer in creative control. Who counts as a leading contributor to a joint design depends on various circumstances and must be determined on a case-by-case basis.

In many projects that involve using AI in fashion designing, there is almost always a principal designer who leads the entire creative process. The principal designer in many circumstances assumes the roles of all five actors specified in the proximity approach but always is the AI output selector. In this case, the ownership of design can be granted to the principal designer. This derives from the fact that the principal designer is predominantly involved in the creative process and has an initial and ultimate saying in the creative decision-making. The involvement of other actors in creation of the design would not be more than a technical assistance.

However, AI-generated designs can be created within tightly organised groups with a specified division of roles among the five actors involved. Under these circumstances, the flow of generating design with AI involves their collaborative creative contributions in different stages of the creative process. More specifically, the AI coder, AI goal selector, AI data selector and AI trainer actively take a role in the conception stage of the creative process. Then in the execution stage, the AI coder tweaks the AI algorithm to drive it to a certain direction when deemed appropriate. In the redaction stage, the AI output selector chooses the most appropriate designs among the AI outputs to exhibit or use. While the AI output selector still has the final say in the decision-making, the finished design is very much the unique result of these actors' complementary contributions. They collaboratively develop a design that could never have been created separately. In these cases, if there is no principal designer, the five actors specified in the proximity approach should be given the co-ownership of a design, as there is a correlation between their actions and the development of the final appearance of the product.

Under EU copyright law, the reflection of the personality of authors seems more difficult, if not impossible, to identify in this kind of group productions. Legal rules on co-authorship are not necessarily useful in drawing distinctions between co-creators, as the law focuses on identifying the natural creative persons who are the source of the work's original character. In traditional authorship determination, creative control appears to be an essential element. As Jane Ginsburg suggests, in dominant legal systems the author is a human being who exercises subjective judgement in producing the work and who controls its execution.[92] Just like designs, if there is a principal designer assuming all five acting roles, they should be the author of the work. This stems from the fact that the work is produced under direct creative control of the principal designer.

The question remains, however, whether the creators assisting the principal designer will necessarily also make creative choices that are expressed in the form of the final product where there is a specified division of roles. EU copyright law indeed recognises a personal stamp, not only of individual creators but also of groups of creators. The identification of creative collaborators' personal imprint on a finished work depends on the nature of the collaboration. The stronger the creative collaboration, the more the final work will reflect the joint personal imprint of the collaborators. This raises the question of whether joint subjective signatures of joint creators also count as a reflection of the 'personal stamp' necessary for establishing copyright protection.

Here, two different approaches can be adopted. In a strict approach, because only the 'personal stamp' of the AI output selector (selection of the most suitable designs amongst many others and redaction of them) is directly visible on the final product, the authorship could be granted only to that person. The contributions of the other four actors (AI coder, AI goal selector, AI data selector and AI trainer) remain unidentifiable although they have made creative contributions at the different stages (mostly in conception stage) of the process. In a broad approach, it can be presumed that the amalgam of creative contributions of all five actors leads to the creation of an original work, even though their personal stamps have merged and melded into one throughout the process and manifest themselves in the final product. The AI-generated design remains in the borders of their authorial intent. In this case, the five actors together could be deemed as the joint authors.

When it comes to evaluation of infringement liability, the aforementioned acts of the five actors should comparatively be matched with the three types of potentially infringing uses explained in Chapter 2. While the AI data selector carries out the acts (compilation and digitisation of design corpus) in Use 1, the AI coder, AI goal selector and AI trainer conduct the acts (production of intermediary copies) in Use 2. The acts of AI output selector can only lead to (partial and/or slavish copying of a previous design) Use 3. If these uses count as illegal under both EU design and copyright laws, their liability can be established according to this taxonomy. Where a principal designer takes part in the entire process of design production, they can equally be held liable.

If such a design is created under the control of the two actors specified in the investment approach as an employer, it could be accepted that the design right and copyright vest in these two actors under EU (and, where unharmonised, national) work-made-for-hire schemes. In terms of infringement, they can be held liable as

---

92 Jane C Ginsburg, 'The Concept of Authorship in Comparative Copyright Law' (2003) 52 *DePaul Law Review* 1088.

well, if national design and copyright laws provide accessory liability for these acts.

5.5 A post-modern norm for the future

In the 1990s, Sam Ricketson predicted that the authorship of some artworks soon would become difficult to determine. He was accurately pointing out that the lack of human participation in the computer's output would critically challenge the conventional notion of authorship.[93] Confirming Ricketson's prophetical foresight today, Shlomit Yanisky-Ravid argues that the traditional laws of copyright are inadequate to cope with the new technology involved in creating artworks:

> Copyright laws are simply ill-equipped to accommodate this tech revolution and are therefore unlikely to survive in their current form. In order to address the change in the way art is being created, we must either rethink these laws, give them new meaning, or be ready to replace them.[94]

The preceding sections and the proposed three-step test have demonstrated that whenever a human contribution can be detected in the creative process, the AI system remains a tool, albeit a sophisticated tool. Under the current EU design and copyright laws, even a modest human contribution or a selection of what is suitable for dissemination is sufficient to recognise that AI-generated designs are protectable.

Since the proposed three-step test is based on the broad and interpretative construction of existing intellectual property norms, it is always possible to reach different conclusions by different jurists. Where should this discussion on AI-generated designs take us? What kind of approach should be adopted to determine the authorship or ownership of AI-generated designs for certain?

On 19 October 2021, the European Commission drafted its annual work programme for 2022. Under the chapter 'A Europe fit for the Digital Age,' the Commission revealed plans to revise both the Design Directive and the Design Regulation. Since the winds of change have begun to blow for the EU design system, it would be better to craft a more specific legal norm to identify the authorship for the actors that involve in the creation of AI-generated design. Then, what kind of a norm can be created?

Since the lawyers and judges will come to different conclusions in identifying the actors around the AI technologies as right holders, it would be better to develop a hybrid approach that recognises the entrepreneurial and creative contributions

---

93 Sam Ricketson, 'People or Machines: The Berne Convention and the Changing Concept of Authorship' (1991) 16 *Colum VLA J L & Arts* 1.
94 Shlomit Yanisky-Ravid, 'Generating Rembrandt: Artificial Intelligence, Copyright, and Accountability in the 3A Era – The Human-Like Authors Are Already Here – A New Model' (2017) *Michigan State Law Review* 669.

of all actors from the *proximity* and the *investment* approaches. Here, it would be possible to refer to cinematographic works as an example of a regulatory model, which provides a blended protection for the author's creativity and the producer's investment. In modern cinema, the director is generally thought to be the creator who has the 'final cut' and thus deserves to be credited as the main *auteur* of a film, although some other creators collaborate on it. *Auteur* is a concept that has been introduced into the cinema after the Second World War and has remained valid until today. This concept was addressed as 'the director who is the creator of the film' by the critics working in a magazine called *Cahiers du Cinema*, and as 'the director using camera as pen' by Alexandre Astruc in his article 'The Birth of a New Avant Garde: La Caméra-Stylo.' Although a film is not only about directors, the signature of the director is prominent. There is a 'dominant and creative identity' that reveals the essence and character of the work, plays an important role and provides guidance. While this may be a producer or actor, it is often the director.[95] According to the *auteur* theory, it is the director who manages and directs the entire team, even though the process of film production is the result of teamwork. *Auteur* director is the person who actively takes a role in the whole process from the writing of the script to the presentation of the film to the audience. Just like Pınar Yanardağ and Emily Salvador, Yuima Nakazato, Kazuya Kawasaki, Kotaro Sano and Yusuke Fujihira, Robbie Barrat, Amber Jae Slooten, Ahmed Elgammal and others, many designers (and artists) who use AI technologies are such *auteur* directors. Empirical evidence also proves against the common perception that fashion designing is a collective process rather than an individual artistic endeavour. William van Caenegem and Violet Atkinson recently conducted semi-structured interviews with a group of fashion designers. In these interviews they found that fashion designing is not seen as 'a process of co-authoring.' Rather, as van Caenegem and Atkinson reported, a core individual dominated the process in every case, and 'the designs overwhelmingly reflected the personality, philosophy, inspiration, style, etc. of the *head-designer*.'[96]

To recognise the creativity of these *auteur designers* by following the *proximity approach* and choosing one specific actor for the sake of legal clarity, it would be possible to attribute the ownership of a design right to the *principal designer*. The 'principal designer' in this sense is like a film or art director and means the person who has creative control of the making of the AI-generated design. Like a film director, it is the steps and choices taken/made by the principal designers throughout the project that give rise to the creation of the design.

By following the *investment* approach, it would be possible to attribute the ownership of a design right to the *producer of design*. The 'producer of design' means

---

95 Linda Costanzo Cahir, *Literature into Film: Theory and Practical Approaches* (McFarland, 2014) 86–90.
96 William van Caenegem and Violet Atkinson, 'Observing Creativity in Fashion: Implications for Copyright' (2021) 16(12) *Journal of Intellectual Property Law & Practice* 1411 (Emphasis added).

the person by whom the arrangements necessary for making of the AI-generated design are undertaken. The producer of design would be either employer of the designer or the commissioner. In case of the former, the ownership of the design would naturally go to the employer, provided that the necessary statutory conditions are met. In case of the latter, just like films, the commissioner and the principal designer would be treated as joint authors.

As a policy proposal for future EU design legislation, we suggest that the following article should be adopted in the Community Regulation and the Design Directive, where appropriate:

Article X
Artificial intelligence-generated Community design

1   The right to the Community design which meets the requirements under Section 1 and is artificial intelligence-generated shall jointly vest in the person who has creative control of the making of the design and the person by whom the arrangements, through coordinating, controlling, and organising, necessary for the creation of the design are undertaken.
2   For the purposes of this paragraph, an artificial intelligence-generated design means one generated by an artificial intelligence system with a degree of autonomy under the creative control of the human designer mentioned in Paragraph 1 of this Article.

As previously mentioned, text and data mining offer new opportunities for enabling AI innovation. The European legislature has understood the importance of text and data mining and has introduced two specific exceptions in the Copyright in the Digital Single Market Directive. The main rationale behind the adoption of the text and data mining exceptions was the reduction of legal uncertainties and the diverging national implementations of existing exceptions, such as research, private copying, temporary reproduction. Several doubts have been voiced elsewhere about the potential of the newly crafted text and data mining exceptions to strike a fair balance between the promotion of innovation in research and the interests of some right holders or 'owners' of datasets.[97] Considering these legal uncertainties, a text and data mining exception should be introduced by adopting the following provision in the relevant articles the Community Regulation and the Design Directive: 'acts of text and data mining for the purpose of research, provided that mention is made of the source.'

As a last word, these two norms with an appropriate wording can be echoed and adopted within the sphere of EU copyright law as well.

---

97   Alain Strowel and Rossana Ducato, 'Artificial Intelligence and Text and Data Mining: A Copyright Carol' Eleonora Rosati (ed), *The Routledge Handbook of EU Copyright Law* (Routledge, 2021) 299–316.

Third-party materials

Some materials in this book were adapted and translated from the author's prior works with permission.

- Hasan Kadir Yılmaztekin, *Yapay Zekânın Eser Sahipliği* (*'Authorship of Artificial Intelligence'*) (Adalet Yayınevi, 2021) (published in Turkish).
- Hasan Kadir Yılmaztekin, 'Türk Fikrî Haklar Hukuku Yapay Zekâ Tarafından Meydana Getirilen Eserleri Korumak İçin Hazır Mı?' ('Is Turkish Copyright Law Ready to Protect Works Generated by Artificial Intelligence?') (2020) 2 *Galatasaray Üniversitesi Hukuk Fakültesi Dergisi* (*Journal of Galatasaray University Faculty of Law*) 1513-1586 (published in Turkish).

Index

Note: Page numbers followed by 'n' refer to a note on the corresponding page.

AARON 35
Abbott, Ryan 2n10, 132–133, 133n37, 174–175
adaptation right 113, 116, 122
aesthetics 75, 168–169, 170; art 74; 'no aesthetic considerations' test 49; and originality 102–105, 124
aggregate theory of personhood 137
Agreement on Trade-Related Aspects of Intellectual Property Rights (TRIPs Agreement) 76, 77–78, 79, 81, 84
Ajani, Gianmaria 157
Alexa 28
Algorithmic Couture project 31
algorithms 19, 148–149, 167; algorithmic fashion design 36; copyright protection for 92; machine learning 24, 26; rule-based 149; step-by-step 149
Al-Jazari, Ibn al-Razzaz 19
AlphaGo 28
Amazon 33
Anadol, Refik 166
analytical engine 19
android fallacy 140
animals, rights to 139–140
Antikainen, Mikko 60–61
appearance of products 45–46, 52, 68
application (EU design registration) 40–43
applied arts, copyright protection for 96–97, 102
Aristotle 18, 22
art 73–74, 167
artificial general intelligence (AGI) 28–29, 174–175, 176–177
artificial intelligence (AI) 1–3, 36–37, 127; Age of AI 168; AI legal neutrality 132–133; AI winters 1n1, 20, 21; autonomy of 173–177; CANs 166–167, 172; capabilities of 35–36; and copyright law 4, 6–8; creations, IP rights for 127–128; and creativity 165–172; defining 21–25; as designer 32–35, 132–135; dystopian world of 175; EU policies on 16; in fashion industry 29–35; GANs 33–34, 35, 37, 165–166; goal-driven nature of 25; history of 18–21; human codes around 172–181; impact on creative industries 4; intellectual creations of 2–3; legal personhood of 133–142; as a medium 167–168; and patents 5; photography moment impact of 4; statistical/sub-symbolic 26; strong 21, 29; as subject of contract 134; symbolic 26; types of 28–29, 174; utopian world of 175; weak 21, 28
Artificial Intelligence High Level Expert Group (AI-HLEG) 24
artificial narrow intelligence (ANI) 28, 174
artificial neural networks 27
artificial super intelligence (ASI) 29, 174, 175, 176–177
Astruc, Alexandre 182
Atkinson, Violet 182
attribution, right of 63–65
audio-visual works 84, 90, 110–112
Austrian Copyright Act 111
auteur 182
authorship 63–65, 87–88, 169–170, 179–180, 181; Berne Convention for the Protection of Literary and Artistic Works 79–81; and creative control 179–180; EU copyright law 109–113, 126; fictional/hypothetical 145, 146; joint

186 Index

66, 68, 81, 112, 154, 180; modernist school 142–158; revolutionary school 132–142; romantic school 128–132; *sui generis* protection 155–156, 155n210, 156n219, 157; transfer 153–154
automation 173
autonomy: of AI 147–148, 151, 152, 173–177; creative 174; definition of 173; and natural personhood of AI 141; normative aspect of 173; technical aspect of 173–174

Babbage, Charles 18–19
Bainbridge, David 92
Balenciaga 33
Balenciaga, Cristóbal 74–75
Ballardini, Rosa Maria 128
Barrat, Robbie 33
Barthes, Roland 8
Beethoven, Ludwig van 163
Beijing Internet Court 6–7
Benjamin, Walter 8
Bently, Lionel 113–114, 158
Berne Convention for the Protection of Literary and Artistic Works 76, 76n16, 77–81, 106, 107, 108, 150; and authorship 109, 110, 111; definition of work 84–85, 86; originality standard 88, 89
Bezpeènostní softwarová asociace – Svaz softwarové ochrany v. Ministerstvo kultury 92–93, 106, 109
'big C' creativity 162
big data 2
black-box problem 148
Blumer, Herbert 8–9
blurring (design representation) 42
Boden, Margaret 37, 162, 163, 164
Bolitho, Douglas 131n31
Bonadio, Enrico 155, 156
Borghi, Maurizio 117
Boston Dynamics 15
boundaries (design representation) 42
Bridy, Annemarie 4, 153, 164
broken lines (design representation) 42
Brompton Bicycle Ltd v. Chedech/Get2Get 96–97, 103, 105
Bryson, Joanna 139, 140
Buijtelaar, Laurens 148–149, 155, 156–157
Burgess, Andrew 36
Burrow-Giles Lithographic Co v. Sarony 130–131

Capek, Karel 19
Cassin, René 138
causative approach 49
Chanel, Coco 30
Charter of Fundamental Rights of the EU 81, 111
Chesterman, Simon 138
China 6–8
Chinese Room 26
Chollet, François 165
cinematographic works 79, 80, 81, 84, 85, 110–112, 182
citations, design 61, 63, 64, 67
close copying 10, 13
Cofemel – Sociedade de Vestuário SA v. G-Star Raw CV 75, 76, 85, 102, 103, 104, 105, 109, 115
cognition of artificial intelligence 36
Cohen, Harold 35, 142, 171–172
collaborative creations 179, 180
collective selection 8–9
colouring (design representation) 42
Colton, Simon 35
combinatorial creativity 162
commissioning 67, 134, 183
communication to the public, right of 113, 114
community design courts 57, 57n169, 71
Community Design Regulation (EC) No 6//2002 (CDR) 39, 46, 47, 54, 58, 63–64, 65, 66, 67, 178, 181, 183
community designs (CDs) 39, 41, 43
Compendium (US Copyright Office) 131
complex products 48
computer-generated works 2n10, 134, 145–146, 153–154
computer programs: authorship of 110, 112; copyright protection for 78, 83, 87, 91–96
Computer Programs Directive 47n77, 83
computers 18, 19
conception stage (creative process) 150, 179
conceptual space 163
concession theory *see* fiction theory of personhood
conditional generative adversarial networks (cGANs) 31, 31n91
connectivity exception, and design protection 50
contractarian theory *see* aggregate theory of personhood

Index   187

copying 12, 71, 156; close 10, 13; and piracy paradox 11–12; temporary 119–121
Copyright, Designs and Patents Act 1998 (CDPA) 143–147, 153–154
copyright law 4, 6–8, 128, 169, 181; and authorship 63; creativity in 168, 169–170; UK 143–147, 154; US 130–132, 153, 154, 157
copyright law, European Union 75–76, 123–124, 179–180; authorship and ownership 109–113, 126; criteria for protection 84–106; directives 82–84; exceptions 114–115; exclusive rights 113–114; expression 105–108; and formality 106; general features of 81–84; infringement 115–123; intellectual effort 109; and international legal framework 76–81; literary, scientific or artistic domain 86; originality 86–105; two-staged assessment 85; works 84–85, 86; *see also* design law, European Union
copyrights 40, 181; and author's rights 134; and customisation 32; and image-to-image translation 32; originality test 51; sensory 107
corporations, personality of 135, 137, 138, 140
counterfeits 11
Court of Appeal of England and Wales 5–6
Court of Justice of the European Union (CJEU) 38, 60–61, 67, 75–76, 84, 85, 123, 125, 150; authorship 110, 111; on creative choices 99; and definition of work 86; on design citations 64; on expression of subject matter 106, 107; on informed user 54, 71; originality standard 87–88, 91, 92–93, 94–96, 97, 98, 101, 102, 109; protection of partial design 48; rejection of aesthetics 102–103; on representation of design in application 41; on reproduction 116–117, 119; on temporary copying 120, 120n366; on use of the term 'designer' 65
crafts 73, 74
Craig, Carys 129–130
creational uses (reproduction) 117
creative adversarial networks (CANs) 166–167, 172
creative autonomy 174

creative choices 147, 148–149, 150–151, 152, 169, 180; and aesthetics 103, 104; and authorship 110; and EU copyright law 85, 94, 96–97, 126; and EU design law 67–68; and expression of creativity 106, 107, 108; and originality 91, 93, 99–101, 105, 109
creative freedom of author 99; functional and technical constraints 91–97; informational constraints 97–98; and rule-based constraints 89–91
creative process 37, 108, 151n178, 159, 162; conception stage 150, 179; controller of 153; execution stage 151, 179; redaction stage 151, 179
creativity 13, 80, 124, 168, 174, 177–178; and AI 165–172; AI as a medium 167–168; assessment of 169; coding 164; combinatorial 162; in copyright law 168, 169–170; definition of 162, 164; in design law 170–171; exploratory 162–163; expression of 98, 99, 105–108, 151–152, 161; and free will 171; historical 163, 164; individualist 161; and legal personality 141–142; market-oriented perspective 170; Miller's conception of 164; and originality 91, 93, 98, 100, 101–102, 105–106, 123; and piracy paradox 11, 12; psychological 163, 164; socio-cultural 162; transformational 163
Creativity Machine 131, 131n31
Csikszentmihályi, Mihaly 160, 171
customisation 31, 32

DABUS 5–6, 63
Database Directive 83, 86–87, 110, 112, 119, 122–123, 155
databases 146; authorship of 110; copyright protection of 78, 83, 85, 87, 113; extraction, right of 122–123; *sui generis* 83, 85, 113, 121, 122–123, 155
data mining 33, 183; EU copyright law 121–123; and trend forecasting 30
Davies, Colin R. 133–135, 141
Da Vinci, Leonardo 19
De Cock Buning, Madeleine 155, 156n219
Deep Blue 28
deep fakes 15
deep learning 21, 27–28, 33, 167
DeepVogue 32
Dennis, Caen A. 143
Descartes, Rene 22

description of design 42
design 39, 45; AI-generated, actors participating in 177–178, 181–182; AI-generated, policy proposal for future EU design legislation 183; AI-generated, protection and infringement liability 178–181; definition of 45, 65–66; development 66, 67; initial entitlement to 65–68; partial 48; rights 40, 49, 58–57, 62, 65, 66, 70–71, 127, 182
Design Directive 71/1998/EC (DD) 39, 40, 46, 65, 68n245, 70, 181, 183
designer doctrine 65, 66, 128
Design Guidelines, EUIPO 42
design law, European Union 38–40, 87, 175; appearance, features and product elements of design 45–48; assignment and licences 69–70; creativity in 170; design developer 178; designs contrary to morality/public policy 50–51, 68; duration 70, 71; functionality exception 49–50; individual character 52, 53–57; initial entitlement to and ownership of design 65–68; interconnection, designs of 50; invalidity 68–69, 71; novelty 51–53; registration process 40–44; requirements 44–57; right of attribution 63–65; scope of protection 58–62; unregistered community designs 70–71; *see also* copyright law, European Union
designs, fashion 11, 14, 38, 39, 75, 76; AI as designer 32–35; AI as designer assistant 31–32, 37; piracy paradox 11–12, 13; trend forecasting 30–31; *see also* design law, European Union
Diamantis, Mihailis E. 140
difference engine 18–19
differentiation, and fashion 12–13
digital fashion 34–35
Digital Single Market Directive 30, 114–115, 121–122, 156, 183
dimensional conversion 60–61
Directive on Copyright and Related Rights in the Digital Single Market 83–84
director (film) 182
disclosure of design 51–52, 70
distinctive signs 69
doctrine of authorship transfer 153
Dornis, Tim W. 157
Drassinower, Abraham 118
Dreamwriter 7–8
Ducato, Rossana 122
Duchamp, Marcel 74

Dunnes Stores 38
duplicates 11
duration of design protection 70, 71

economic rights 112, 113, 114, 145, 156–157
'Electric Dreams of Ukiyo: A Series of Japanese Artworks Created by an Artificial Intelligence' project 165
Electronic Commerce Directive 83
electronic personality for robots 136
Elgammal, Ahmed 166–167, 167–168
Eliza (chat bot) 20
employers: and ownership 66–67, 112, 183; work made for hire doctrine 153–154
Enforcement Directive 111–112
European Commission 16, 17, 23–24, 40, 67, 181
European Convention of Human Rights 81
European Parliament 16, 17, 136, 140, 142, 154–155
European Patent Convention 5
European Patent Office (EPO) 5
European Union (EU) 13–14, 23; copyright protection 73–126; design protection 38–72; policies on AI and IP 16
European Union Intellectual Property Office (EUIPO) 39, 40, 41, 42, 43, 44, 49, 64
Eva-Maria Painer v. Standard Verlags GmbH 99, 100, 101, 106, 109, 150–151
examination of design (EU design registration) 44
exclusive licensee 69
exclusive rights 113–114
execution stage (creative process) 151, 179
expert systems 20–21
exploratory creativity 162–163
expression(s) 118, 125; of creativity 98, 99, 105–108, 151–152, 161; idea/expression dichotomy 90, 93, 94
extraction, right of 121, 122–123

Fabricant, The 34–35
fashion 3, 8–11, 38; artificial intelligence in fashion industry 29–35; and commerce 9–10; counterfeits 11; as a cultural phenomenon 9; and differentiation 12–13; digital 34–35; duplicates 11; fast 10, 13; industry 9–10, 11–12; knockoffs 11; piracy

paradox 11–12, 13; and sustainability 13; trends 10, 12–13
Fashion Institute of Technology (FIT) 32
fast fashion 10, 13
features of products 46, 56
Federal Court of Australia 6
Feilin v. Baidu 6–7
Feist Publications Inc v. Rural Telephone Service Co 130, 164
Ferrari 48
Ferrari v. Mansory Design 48
fiction theory of personhood 137
fixation 78, 106, 108, 130
Flickr 58
flocking 13
Flos SpA v. Semeraro Casa & Famiglia SpA 75
flow 160
Flow Machine 60
Flügel, John 8
Football Association Premier League Ltd v. QC Leisure 90–91
Football Dataco Ltd v. Yahoo! UK Ltd 91, 100, 101
Fountain (Duchamp) 74
freedom of designer 56–57, 59, 71
free will, and creativity 171
Fujihira, Yusuke 31
fully autonomous artificial intelligence 174
functional constraints, and originality 91–97
functionality exception, and design protection 49–50
Funke Medien NRW GmbH v. Bundesrepublik Deutschland 97–98, 100, 101, 102, 106

GANism 165–166
Garip movement 163
Gaskin, Sam 4
generative adversarial networks (GANs) 33–34, 35, 37, 165–166
generative designs 37
Gershgorn, Dave 37
Gervais, Daniel 85, 123, 147, 149, 149n163, 152
Ginsburg, Jane 179–180
Google 34
Google Translate 21
Gordon, John-Stewart 140
Grant, Thomas D. 140
graphical user interfaces, copyright protection for 92–93, 96

Gruner, Daniel T. 171
G-Star 102
Guadamuz, Andres 146
Gunkel, David 139, 140, 172

Hadid, Zaha 162
Hague Agreement Concerning the International Registration of Industrial Designs 41, 41n11, 64n207
Handig, Christian 125
Härkönen, Heidi 13, 29, 32, 129
haute couture fashion products 103n234, 105
Hemphill, Scott 12–13
Henry, Damien 167n43
Hephaestus 18
Hertzmann, Aaron 167, 171
Hetmank, Sven 155
High Court of England and Wales 5
historical creativity 163, 164
Hobbes, Thomas 18
Homer 18
Hristov, Kalin 153, 154
Hugenholtz, Bernt 85, 123, 149, 152
human intelligence 22
human rights 138–139
Hutter, Marcus 22

IBM Watson 34
icons, copyright protection for 94
idea/expression dichotomy 90, 93, 94
'if-then' decision-making model 149
image-to-image translation 31–32
imitation game 20
incentive theory 133, 133n37
individual character 52, 53–57, 59, 60, 70–71, 170–171
individualist creativity 161
induced obsolescence 12
Infopaq International A/S v. Danske Dagblades Forening 85, 87–89, 99, 100, 101, 102, 106, 119, 120–121
informational constraints, and originality 97–98
Information Society Directive 75, 83, 89, 90–91, 93, 95, 110, 111, 113, 114, 115–116, 119, 120, 121
informed user 53, 54–56, 59–60, 61, 71, 87, 175
infringement 54, 58–62; dimensional conversion 60–61; EU copyright law 115–123; liability, and AI-generated design 180–181; partial reproduction

119; right of reproduction 115–119; temporary technology-dictated copies 119–121; text and data mining 121–123; unregistered community designs 71; *see also* copyright law, European Union; design law, European Union
initial entitlement to design 65–68
Instagram 30, 30n84, 58
instrumentality of technology, theory of 139
intellectual effort 101, 109, 124, 150, 169
intellectual property (IP): for AI-generated creations 127–128; and artificial intelligence 4–5; EU policies on 16; and fashion 10, 11, 12, 13; law 40, 59
International Association for the Protection of Intellectual Property (AIPPI) 152–153, 156, 177
International Business Machines Corporation (IBM) 32
international legal framework, copyright protection 76–77, 123; authorship and ownership 79–81; criteria for 77–79
invalidity 51, 57, 64, 68–69, 71
investment approach to design rights 178, 182–183
IP5 5

Janssens, Marie-Christine 92
Jennings, Kyle 174
joint authorship 66, 68, 112, 154, 180
Jose Manuel Baena Grupo v. OHIM 60
juridical persons 135

Kalyanaraman, Karthik 4
Karapapa, Statroula 117
Kare, Susan 94
Karen Millen v. Dunnes Stores 38, 39, 60
Katz, Andrew 139
Kawasaki, Kazuya 31
Kerr, Ian 129–130
Klein, Martin 131n31
knockoffs 11
Kur, Annette 63, 103–104, 170
Kurki, Visa 137
Kurzweil, Ray 29

La Diega, Guido Noto 155
Land Nordrhein-Westfalen v. Dirk Renckhoff 101, 109
Lauber-Rönsberg, Anne 155
Lee, Edward 117

legal personhood: definition of 135; forms of 135
legal personhood of artificial intelligence 133–137; extension of natural personality 138–142; inherent reasons 135–136; instrumental reasons 136; juridical personality 137–138
legal relations, and legal personality 141
Legg, Shane 22
lending rights 113
Levendowski, Amanda 117
Levin, Marianne 102, 104, 104n238, 170
Levola Hengelo BV v. Smilde Foods BV 86, 107, 108
licences 69–70
limited memory artificial intelligence 28
little black dress 33
'little c' creativity 161
Locarno Agreement Establishing an International Classification for Industrial Designs 43, 43n34
Lovelace, Ada 19, 164
Lu, Bingbin 129, 153
Luce, Leanne 36–37
Luksan, Martin 111

machine learning 1, 24, 26–27, 31, 149
Machine Memoirs: Space exhibition 166
Mac Síthigh, Daithí 96
Malevich, Kazimir 163
mandatory approach 49
Mansory Design 48
Marchesa 34
Margoni, Thomas 129
market economy 73
Marrakesh Directive 114
Martin Luksan v. Petrus van der Let 110–111
Matulionyte, Rita 151n178, 155n213
Mazzone, Marian 167–168
McCarthy, John 20
McCutcheon, Jani 155
McDonagh, Luke 155, 156
MENACE (Matchbox Educable Noughts and Crosses Engine) program 20
merger doctrine 93
metaverse 34
Michie, Donald 20
Microsoft 35
middle class, and art 73
Mik, Eliza 141, 173
military status reports 98, 101, 102
Millen, Karen 38

Miller, Arthur 164, 175
Minsky, Marvin Lee 20
modernist school of AI authorship 142, 158–159; alternative models of protection 154–158; autonomy of AI 147–148; black-box problem 148; creative choices 148–149; doctrine of authorship transfer 153; expression of creativity in output 151–152; intellectual effort 150; International Association for the Protection of Intellectual Property 152–153; originality 150–151; production in literary, scientific or artistic domain 150; programmer 134, 142, 143–147, 149, 153, 154; programming architecture of robots 149; users of AI 143, 147, 154; work made for hire doctrine 153–154
modular systems, and connectivity exception 50
morality, designs contrary to 50–51, 68
moral rights 113, 133, 134, 145, 156
multiplicity of forms test 49

Nakazato, Yuima 31
Naruto v Slater 132, 139
Navas, Susana 37
neighbouring rights 113, 156–157
Neue Sammlung, Die 74
Next Rembrandt 35, 152
Nilsson, Nils J. 22
Nintendo Co Ltd and others v. PC Box Srl 95–96
Nintendo v. Bigben 60–61, 64
'no aesthetic considerations' test 49
non-exclusive licensee 69
Nonhuman Rights Project 140
normal use of products 48
Nova Productions Ltd v. Mazooma Games Ltd 145–146
novelty of design 42, 51–53, 57, 70, 170

objective originality 87n105
Obvious group 165
old-fashioned artificial intelligence 26
operational uses (reproduction) 117
originality 51, 75, 79, 85, 168; and AI authorship 150–151; of AI-generated fashion designs 105; assessment of 169; author-centred understanding of 169–170; CDPA 144; objective 87n105; subjective 87n105; US copyright law 130

originality, EU copyright law 86–88, 109, 115, 123–124; aesthetic quality 102–105; functional and technical constraints 91–97; *Infopaq International A/S v. Danske Dagblades Forening* 88–89; informational constraints 97–98; level of creativity 101–102; personality and creative choices 99–101; rule-based constraints 89–91
originality causation test 147–148
ornamentation 43, 45, 56
Orphan Works Directive 114
Orwell, George 175
output uses (reproduction) 117
overall impression of design 53–54, 55–56, 57, 59, 60, 61, 71, 170
Owens, Christopher 164
ownership: Berne Convention for the Protection of Literary and Artistic Works 79–81; of design 65–68, 178, 179, 182–183; EU copyright law 109–113, 126; and investment approach 182–183; and proximity approach 182; *see also* authorship; design law, European Union

Pachet, François 160
Pagallo, Ugo 139
Painting Fool, The 35
paintings 35, 62n193, 167
Palace, Victor M. 129
Papadopoulou, Anthoula 155, 155n210
Paris Convention 43
partial design 48
partial reproduction 89, 119
patents 5–6, 49, 132, 133
pattern drafting 3
Pearlman, Russ 153, 154
peculium 139, 139n84
People for the Ethical Treatment of Animals (PETA) 132
PepsiCo v. Grupo Promer 54, 71
perceptrons 20
Perry, Mark 129
personality/personhood 179; and autonomy 173; of corporations 135, 137, 138, 140; electronic 136; legal personhood of artificial intelligence 135–142; natural persons 7, 66, 68, 80, 110, 125, 135, 138–142; and originality standard 99–101, 124; theories 137–138
photography 4, 130–131
Picasso, Pablo 163

Pila, Justine 84, 85, 95, 96, 112, 125
Pillo (robot) 28
Pinterest 30, 58
piracy paradox 11–12, 13
pix2pix 31n92
PMS International Group v. Magmatic 41
Portrait of Edmond de Belamy 165
predictability, and AI authorship 148, 152
principal designer 179, 180, 182
prior design/art 51, 52, 53, 54, 69, 87, 170–171
priority (EU design registration) 43, 51
producer of design 182–183
products 46–48; appearance of 45–46, 52, 68; complex, components of 48; definition of 46; features of 46, 56; normal use of 48; parts of 46, 48
programmer 134, 142, 143–147, 149, 153, 154
Project Muze 34
proximity approach to design rights 177–178, 182
psychological creativity 163, 164
publication of design (EU design registration) 44
public domain 128–130, 148, 154, 156
public policy, designs contrary to 50–51, 68

Quintais, João Pedro 85, 123, 149, 152

Ramalho, Ana 154
Raustiala, Kal 11–12, 13, 74
reactive artificial intelligence 28
realist theory of personhood 138
reasonable observer 49
redaction stage (creative process) 151, 179
refusal of design (EU design registration) 44
registered community designs (RCDs) 40, 57, 60; design rights and infringement 58–59; duration of design protection 70; right, transfer of 69; and right to attribution 63
registration process, design: application 40–43; and attribution of designers 64; grounds for refusal and examination 44; multiple designs 43; priority 43, 51; registration and publication 44; secret designs and deferred publication 43
Reimagine Retail project 32
reinforcement learning 27
Related Rights Directive 156

relevant date (novelty) 51
Rental and Lending Directive 84, 110, 113
representation of design in application (EU design registration) 41–42
reproduction 60–61, 64, 88–89; notion, defining 116; partial 89, 119; right of 114–119, 121–122
revolutionary school of AI authorship 158; AI as a designer 132–135; legal personality 135–142
Richards, Neil 140
Ricketson, Sam 79, 181
Ridler, Anna 167n43
robots 15, 19, 28, 136, 139, 140, 148–149
romantic school of AI authorship 158; public domain 128–130; US law 130–132
Rome Convention 81, 83
Rosati, Eleonora 86, 122
Rosen, Dan 142
Rosenbalt, Frank 20
rule-based algorithms 149
rule-based constraints, and originality 89–91
Russell, James 96

Salvador, Emily 33
Samuelson, Pamela 143
Sanchez-Bordona, Campos 101
Särmäkari, Natalia 36
SAS Institute Inc v. World Programming Ltd 94–95
Satellite and Cable Directive 110
Saudi Arabia 136
Sawyer, R. Keith 161, 162
Scafidi, Susan 12, 13
Schank, Roger 164
Schönberger, Daniel 129
scientific research purpose, text and data mining for 121, 122
scope of design protection: design rights and infringement 58–62; dimensional conversion 60–61; exceptions 62; ideas and concepts behind design 59
Searle, John 21, 26
secret designs, registration of 43
self-aware artificial intelligence 28
Selvadurai, Niloufer 151n178, 155n213
Semeraro 75
semi-autonomous artificial intelligence 174, 177
Senftleben, Martin 148–149, 155, 156–157

sensory copyright 107
Senz Technologies v. OHIM 56
Shanghai Yingxun Technology 7–8
Shelley, Mary 18
Shemtov, Noam 93, 94
Simmel, Georg 8
singularity 175, 176
Siri 28
Slater, David 132
slavery, and artificial intelligence 139
Slooten, Amber Jae 35
Smart, William 140
Smith, Bryant 141
social media 30
Society of Independent Artists 74
socio-cultural creativity 162
Software Directive 86–87, 92, 94, 95, 110, 112, 119
Solum, Lawrence 135
Sophia (robot) 136
South African Intellectual Property Office 6
spare parts 104n238
Sprigman, Christopher 11–12, 13, 74
statistical artificial intelligence 26
step-by-step algorithms 149
Stichting Brein (Filmspeller) v. Jack Frederik Wullems 120n366
Stitch Fix 34
strong artificial intelligence 21, 29
Strowel, Alain 118, 122
style constraints, and originality 89–90
styles, fashion 9, 10, 33, 47, 90, 176
subjective originality 87n105
sub-symbolic artificial intelligence 26
successor in title 66, 68
Suk, Jeannie 12–13
Sun, Haochen 129, 155, 157
supervised autonomous artificial intelligence 174, 177
supervised learning 26–27
sustainability, and fashion 13, 176
sweat of the brow doctrine 130
symbolic artificial intelligence 26
symbolist theory *see* aggregate theory of personhood
Synflux 31, 33–34
synthesised intelligence 23
Szpunar, Maciej 103n234

taste, copyright protection for 106–108
teaching purpose, text and data mining for 121

technical constraints, and originality 91–97
temporary technology-dictated copies 119–121
Tencent 7–8
Tencent v. Yinxun 7–8
Term Directive 83, 84, 86, 87, 109, 110, 111, 154, 154n201
text mining 183; EU copyright law 121–123; and trend forecasting 30
Thaler, Stephen 5, 6, 131
theory of mind artificial intelligence 28
thinking dress 34
thought couture 35
Tischner, Anna 64, 66
Tommy Hilfiger 32
Torremans, Paul 84, 85, 95, 96, 112
tort law 136, 137, 140
transformational creativity 162
Treaty on the Functioning of the European Union 81
trends, fashion 10, 12–13, 30–31
Trstenjak, Verica 109
Turing, Alan 19–20, 21
Turing test 19–20, 21
Turner, Jacob 140
Twitter 30, 58

United Kingdom, copyright law of 88, 143–147, 154
United States Constitution 133
United States, copyright law of 130–132, 153, 154, 157; *see also* US Copyright Office
Universal Declaration of Human Rights 138
unregistered community designs (UCDs) 39, 40, 48, 60, 70–71; design rights and infringement 58; relevant date 51
unsupervised learning 27
US Copyright Office 131, 131n31
users of artificial intelligence 143, 147, 154

van Caenegem, William 182
Van der Let, Petrus 110
Van Gompel, Stef 101, 168, 169
Vanherpe, Josefien 170
Vänskä, Annamari 36
Veblen, Thorstein 8
Veli, Orhan 163
video games, copyright protection for 95–96

weak artificial intelligence 21, 28
Weizenbaum, Joseph 20
Wiele, Bram Van 148, 149
Wilson, Elizabeth 8, 9
work made for hire doctrine 132, 153–154, 155n210
World Intellectual Property Organisation (WIPO) 4–5, 41, 156n217

World Intellectual Property Organization Copyright Treaty (WCT) 76, 77–78, 79, 81, 84, 111

Yanardağ, Pınar 33
Yanisky-Ravid, Shlomit 153, 154, 181

Zalando 34

Made in the USA
Middletown, DE
21 August 2024

59583083R00115